Dateline—Liberat

Dateline—Liberated Paris

The Hotel Scribe and the Invasion of the Press

Ronald Weber

ROWMAN & LITTLEFIELD
Lanham • Boulder • New York • London

Published by Rowman & Littlefield
An imprint of The Rowman & Littlefield Publishing Group, Inc.
4501 Forbes Boulevard, Suite 200, Lanham, Maryland 20706
www.rowman.com

6 Tinworth Street, London SE11 5AL, United Kingdom

Distributed by NATIONAL BOOK NETWORK

British Library Cataloguing in Publication Information Available

Library of Congress Cataloging-in-Publication Data Available

ISBN 978-1-5381-1850-4 (cloth : alk. paper)
ISBN 978-1-5381-1851-1 (pbk. : alk. paper)

∞™ The paper used in this publication meets the minimum requirements of American National Standard for Information Sciences—Permanence of Paper for Printed Library Materials, ANSI/NISO Z39.48-1992.

Printed in the United States of America

In memory of Pat Weber

We all knew that if an American communications center had been set up in Paris, it would be at the Hôtel Scribe.

—A. J. Liebling, *Normandy Revisited*

~

Contents

~

Prologue

A Hotel like No Other

In the European combat zones of World War II, press camps were an integral part of Allied operations. Accredited war correspondents attached to fighting units—outfitted in uniforms of their various countries, wearing insignia that identified them as correspondents, and treated as military captains though they bore no emblems of rank—were housed in buildings or tent encampments or whatever shelter could be found behind front lines. From here they were fed, briefed on battlefield developments, transported in jeeps with soldier drivers, and otherwise cared for and controlled by the military's public-relations officers. Censors reviewed all their outgoing material—dispatches, broadcasts, photos, films, field art, and personal letters—before transmission by cable, teletype, mobile radio unit, or by land and air in courier pouches to international media centers. As the war progressed, press camps moved with their military units to new positions behind new front lines.

The Hôtel Scribe was one of several Allied press camps on the march from Normandy to Germany. It was also one of a kind. Among other distinctive features, it was located in central Paris in a storied hotel that before the war was favored by foreign journalists and during the occupation became Nazi headquarters for information and propaganda. It had a lounge bar and dining room, an experienced French staff, chambermaids, phone service, running water, electricity, and enough coal for some heat and warm baths in limited hours. It could accommodate as many as five hundred correspondents, as against the fifty or far fewer of other press camps. And unlike press camps outpaced by rapidly advancing fighting groups—leaving stalled-in-the-rear correspondents feeling, as one newsman said, as if they were on a "vacation a white-collar worker takes in the country"[1]—the Scribe was rooted in Paris to the end of the war and beyond.

The hotel also quickly took on an aura of journalistic legend—or, as later observers put it, "the Hôtel Scribe rapidly became a subject of folklore"[2]— given that a number of correspondents and news outlets chronicled it as well as the war. In a report just after the liberation, the Reuters news service pinpointed the Scribe as the maddest place in all the mad city of freed Paris. Press jeeps and trailers packed the street outside, while inside the hotel was completely booked with Allied correspondents. The busiest spot within the hotel, Reuters added, was the dining area, where the clatter of typewriters comingled with shouts of correspondents needing hot water to brew coffee from military powder. Other reports claimed the basement-level bar as the hotel's top attraction. The war was over when in July 1945 *Life* magazine carried a striking photograph of a painting, the work of one of its combat field artists, of correspondents jammed together in the Scribe's watering hole.

In his 1947 memoir of war reporting, *Slightly Out of Focus*, the Hungarian-born photojournalist Robert Capa crisply characterized the Scribe as "the Army's grand gesture to the newspapermen."[3] Charles Collingwood, a key member of Edward R. Murrow's dashing CBS radio team, was more expansive. He gushed in a script for a shortwave broadcast from the hotel to New York in January 1945 that "before the war the Scribe was just a normal big hotel—much like any other modern hotel in a big city. Today it is like no other hotel in the world . . . the whole place has been turned upside down to serve as a base of operations for the SHAEF correspondents."

It took a staff of 250 public-relations officers (PROs) and enlisted men and women, Collingwood went on, to keep things humming in the Scribe: "There are rows of desks and typewriters in the lobby—great, clacking telegraphic machines have been installed, offices have been set up, radio studios put in. . . . Where the ballroom used to be there is the conference room with huge maps by which we follow the war. . . . And everywhere there are correspondents." The chief way correspondents followed the war was by sitting in on briefings given by PROs who had contacted forward military units for the latest information. "By the time we get it," Collingwood concluded, "the news is generally about six hours from the time it happened, which is pretty good going." And with censorship and transmission service located in the hotel, "it's only a matter of minutes from the time the correspondents rush out of the conference until the news is flashed all over the world."[4]

The Scribe's turnabout into a press camp began with the liberation of Paris on August 25, 1944, when it was—in military speak—"reserved for billets, messing, and accommodations for Allied correspondents in addition to SHAEF censorship, briefing, and information services."[5] SHAEF (Supreme Headquarters Allied Expeditionary Force) had shifted its main location from Britain to French soil and, following the liberation, to Versailles on the edge of Paris. Similarly, SHAEF's Public Relations Division (PRD), charged with managing press information coming from combat zones, moved its core activity from the Ministry of Information in London to Paris. The six-story Hôtel Scribe, stretching along Rue Scribe and around the corner to the Boulevard des Capucines in the fashionable Opéra district, became its principal site.

The PRD had come into existence in April 1944 when the Publicity and Psychological Warfare Division of SHAEF was split into two separate groups. The publicity component, now branded the Public Relations Division, was put under the direction of General Thomas J. Davis. While SHAEF was still based in Britain after D-Day, only correspondents for news agencies and major newspapers and broadcasting systems had full access to the Continent. Other newsmen worked on a rotation system that allowed them limited time in combat zones before recall to Britain.

With the shift of SHAEF to France and the PRD to Paris and the Scribe, the floodgates opened. At the time, there were over nine hundred Allied war correspondents accredited to the European theater of military operations. American and British correspondents dominated the number, but there were as well contingents from France, Canada, Australia, South Africa, and elsewhere. With Paris free after four years of German rule, as many newsmen as could scurried from press camps on the Continent or from news bureaus in London to experience the liberation and attach a coveted Paris dateline to reports. "For the first time in my life and probably the last," the *New Yorker*'s A. J. Liebling memorably said of the period of arrival, "I have lived for a week in a great city where everybody is happy. Moreover, since this city is Paris, everybody makes this euphoria manifest."[6] Robert Capa collapsed the happiness of the liberation to one part of one day: "Never were there so many who were so happy so early in the morning."[7]

The movement of all PRD personnel from London to Paris took place gradually. The Scribe was already a hastily assembled and functioning press camp when on September 11, 1944, a party of PRD officers led by British Brigadier William Turner was transported from London to the hotel. Between October 6 and 10 the remaining body of the PRD and some additional SHAEF correspondents arrived. On the 10th, Captain Harry C. Butcher noted in the wartime diary he kept at General Dwight Eisenhower's request that presently the Scribe was transmitting 150,000 words a day of military news, which he thought sufficient for the war on the Western Front at the moment. Two days later Eisenhower came from Versailles for the first of his occasional press conferences in the hotel. Within the month and a half from the liberation of Paris to the supreme commander's appearance, the hotel had been reconfigured into a self-contained living, working, and playing communications hub for war correspondents.

⁓

In an earlier book called *News of Paris: American Journalists in the City of Light between the Wars*, I told of men and women who flocked to Paris in the 1920s and 1930s to work on newspapers—at one time the city had three daily papers directed to the largest American community abroad—and magazines and in other ways scratch out a living by writing in order to continue to live in Paris. The story came to an end in 1940 with German troops closing in on the undefended city and the last remaining Paris-American newspaper, the Paris edition of the *New York Herald Tribune*, putting out its final edition.

In an epilogue, I briefly noted the return in 1944 to liberated Paris by Eric Hawkins, the longtime managing editor of the Paris *Herald Tribune*, and Robert Moora, the editor of the military newspaper *Stars and Stripes*. Riding in a jeep through streets where snipers remained active, they pressed on until they reached the imposing structure on Rue de Berri where the *Herald Tribune* had been edited and printed. Astonishingly, the Germans had left the building and its contents largely undisturbed. The book ended with Hawkins seeing the towering vertical sign on the building's facade proclaiming *Herald Tribune* and, as he wrote, choking a little on his emotions.

The present book picks up from where the other concluded—with newsmen like Hawkins and Moora appearing in freed Paris and together with a legion of war correspondents following the war to its conclusion with German surrender in the French city of Reims. The idea of telling this story through a focus on the Hôtel Scribe has its roots in a diary remark of Harry Butcher. On September 23, 1944, about a month after the hotel began operations as a communications center, he recorded a prediction: "Someday someone will write the proper history of the Scribe Hotel as the working and social center of war correspondents."[8]

Historical accounts of hotels in wartime occupy a lively niche in book publishing, though the hotels treated are commonly commercial operations where newsmen, political operatives, spies, VIPs, and thrill seekers gather in battle zones.[9] The Scribe was fundamentally different. It was a hotel wholly requisitioned by SHAEF to serve the needs of correspondents and their military handlers—and the war was far beyond Paris for much of its existence.

Harry Butcher was himself well positioned to compile a history of such a unique place. A former radio broadcaster and vice president of the Columbia Broadcasting System based in Washington, he was a navy reserve officer with ultimately the rank of captain who served from 1942 to 1945 as a personal aide and close confident of General Eisenhower, with duties mainly in the areas of communications and press relations. In correspondent speak, Harry Butcher was Ike's man Friday.

His 1946 book *My Three Years with Eisenhower*, an edited version of his war diary, became a major success. Before publication it was serialized in ten installments in the *Saturday Evening Post* beginning on December 15, 1945, with the magazine promoting it as "The World's Most Fascinating Document." The book was also a selection of the Book-of-the-Month Club and was put out in an Armed Services edition for American troops overseas. Butcher's account gives the Scribe considerable notice but in scattered glimpses. His perspective is always that of a military officer who is familiar with the work of correspondents yet is part of management through his ongoing wartime ties to the PRD. Trying to pigeonhole exactly what Butcher's function was, one correspondent decided it was "to promote good relations between the Command and the press—a sort of public relations man for Public Relations."[10]

Despite his close involvement with PRD officers and operations, Butcher points to correspondents at work and at play within the hotel as the essence of a future historical work. I follow his lead but extend it to treatment of SHAEF's Public Relations Division that maintained the hotel for the personal and professional necessities of correspondents, provided battlefield updates, and through censorship and transmission governed the news flowing from it. Correspondents needed the PRD just to be present in combat zones, and the PRD needed correspondents to convey war developments to home fronts. As essential as the press-PRD partnership was, it was also—as might be expected—highly combustible. Others drawn into my account were neither newsmen nor PRD officials but military and civilian figures who came to the Scribe for meals and its bar. I also give attention to people and events in other postliberation Parisian hotels, to SHAEF press camps other than the Scribe, to the reopening of American news bureaus in Paris, and to the resumption of Paris-American newspaper activity. As with the earlier book, I draw material from news reports, articles, letters, memoirs, biographies, scholarly histories, stories and novels, oral recollections, and archival materials that include unpublished writing.

Some correspondents and PRD figures I write about had notable careers in communications and elsewhere before and after the war, but with a few exceptions I leave such matters aside and concentrate on their experience within the Normandy-to-Germany period. I also leave aside any assessment of the journalistic quality of wartime work by newsmen. The subject has been addressed in the late Phillip Knightley's widely known history of war correspondents, *The First Casualty*, published originally in 1975. In a chapter on the European conflict in the period 1940–1945, he writes that it is "hard to reach any conclusion other than that the war could have been better reported." He adds that the main barriers to improvement were the correspondents' identification with the Allied cause and their integration into military action, rendering them at their worst into cheerleaders and propagandists for the war.[11] Subsequent writers have modestly resisted Knightley's view, though discussions of quality remain complicated by the large number of reporters who worked in the European theater and the differing needs of news outlets ranging from wire services to broadcasting networks to weekly and monthly magazines.[12]

Interested readers can make their own judgments by going to the Library of America's vast 1995 collection *Reporting World War II, Part Two: American Journalism, 1944–1946*. Or they can look into the reporting of an individual correspondent, A. J. Liebling, in the Library of America's *A. J. Liebling: World War II Writings*—a figure Knightley singled out for praise.[13] Rather than pursuing quality of work, my effort in the following pages is restricted to the settings and circumstances within which correspondents went about their war duties, with the PRD press camp at the Hôtel Scribe a central part of the story.

⌒

My account comes in three parts. In "Arriving," I tell of war correspondents gathered just outside Paris and waiting impatiently for military power to clear the way into the city. Some correspondents had worked or studied in Paris before the war and felt they knew it intimately. They had a sense of returning home. For others, Paris was a beacon of the imagination—the City of Light that had gone dark for four years under the Nazi boot. They felt the wonder of seeing it illuminated and free.

No one before the liberation could be fully certain of the city's condition. Later it became known that Hitler had ordered the commander of the German garrison to fight to the last man and leave Paris in ruins. And no one could be certain about the level of German resistance both in and outside the city. It was time for caution, though caution could hardly compete with the professional need and personal ambition of correspondents to get there, ideally first or nearly so, and transmit a story with a Paris dateline.

In this section I also give attention to the Scribe's history before and during the German occupation. And I bring into the story a competing Parisian hotel, the Ritz. It wasn't another enclave of communications but an enclave of personality since one of the war correspondents, Ernest Hemingway, chose to lodge there and appear only on occasion at the Scribe.

In "Staying," I get to the heart of the matter with the Scribe fully operational as a press camp. Here correspondents regularly interacted with an army of PROs controlling the news, with tense verbal flare-ups frequently the result. Still, many newsmen found Paris and the Scribe so seductive that they were reluctant to leave for fighting areas, which PROs thought their proper destination as war correspondents while at the same time providing the briefings, censorship, and transmission in the comfort of the hotel that allowed reporting the war from the rear. In this section I also give practical details of how the Scribe was physically rearranged for its mission as a press camp.

In "Leaving," I note the shift of General Eisenhower's headquarters from the edge of Paris to Reims, the German surrender in the city, and the messy struggle between the PRD and the press over who would cover the signing ceremony and when news of the war's end was released to the world. This contested period was preceded by a handful of correspondents reaching Berlin and sending back reports with datelines that equaled in fame those of liberated Paris. As it happened, a second surrender event, orchestrated by the Russians, was held in the shattered German capital, and the mass of correspondents never invaded it in the way they had Paris. In rapid order after the surrenders, SHAEF was dismantled, and its member countries took control of their own national interests.

The mood of this final section differs sharply from that of the freeing of Paris. The elation of total victory was mixed with the abrupt emptiness of a task finished, yet not when and where anticipation expected. In the blink of an eye, or so it seemed, there were no more pictures to shoot or prime European datelines to chase. Work on the Continent remained for newsmen, as it did for the PRD, but it was no longer *war* work. Robert Capa both captured and overstated the flattened feeling of VE Day for both groups when he wrote at the close of his war memoir, "There was absolutely no reason to get up in the mornings any more."

PART I

ARRIVING

In the jeep that morning there was talk of little else but Paris: memories of Paris, how would we find it, what had the Germans done.

—John Groth, *Studio: Europe*

CHAPTER ONE

~

The Canadian Connection

In his wartime diary Harry Butcher never addresses why the Scribe was chosen as SHAEF's Paris press camp. In a footnote to an early entry about the hotel, he reports that the wife of British Air Chief Marshal Arthur Tedder, Eisenhower's low-key, pipe-smoking deputy supreme commander, wanted it reserved for an Allied Club. Butcher was sent by Eisenhower from London to Paris to rescue the hotel for correspondents and find her another place. This turned out to be within the nearby Le Grand Hôtel, where prominent British women set up a housing and entertainment center for Allied soldiers on leave in Paris.

Following Eisenhower's first press conference at the Scribe—with Butcher among those greeting his arrival at the Allied-flagged entrance—the commander crossed the street to the Grand to greet Tedder's wife, creating a mob scene of Parisian onlookers. Butcher reported that the crowd pressed tightly on Eisenhower despite the presence of MPs, and some shop windows were broken. Charles Collingwood's treatment of the incident was more colorful: "People got pushed through plate-glass windows, the General got kissed by numerous excited women of all ages, and, in the end, it took a flying wedge of high-ranking generals running interference to get him out."[1]

Butcher may overlook questioning the Scribe's selection because the reason was apparent. Where other than a hotel of such name for wartime scribblers? In fact, the hotel was named for a writer, Eugène Scribe, a popular French literary figure who died in 1861 while the building was under construction. Certainly the military planners in Washington and London were well aware that during the occupation the Scribe had been the headquarters of the Nazi propaganda machine and the information and housing center for German, Axis, and neutral-nation correspondents. A swastika banner hung from an upper level.

Shortly after the Nazi takeover of Paris in 1940, Louis Lochner, long head of the Associated Press (AP) bureau in Berlin, was transported to the city with a group of Germans. Among them were nine correspondents, three of whom, like Lochner, were then-neutral Americans. As the band motored through its streets, Paris seemed a nearly empty ghost city largely abandoned to the occupiers. Already swastikas were flying from the Quai d'Orsay, the Arc de Triomphe, and the Eiffel Tower. German motorized loudspeakers were blaring on the streets, but few Frenchmen came to listen.

Lochner's party was searching for a hotel when a German officer met near the Opéra told them the Hôtel Scribe had been set aside by the military. But once there, the hotel's French manager, taken aback by the bedraggled appearance of the newcomers, said, "Sorry, but 160 rooms have been requisitioned by the commandery for higher German officers." The lieutenant colonel leading the group responded forcefully,[2] "I command you to make rooms available for our party." The manager acquiesced but held firm that the hotel's dining room lacked adequate fare. He suggested eating at the Ritz.

There they found another reluctant manager who said his kitchen was closed and the waiters gone. The lieutenant colonel again took charge and told chauffeurs of the party to enter the kitchen, prepare the food, and serve it. The chauffeurs produced beer and wine and, as Lochner wrote, "four French waiters in immaculate evening dress suddenly hove into sight to serve us. Delicious ham, mellow cheese, and escalloped eggs appeared as though by magic."

William L. Shirer, then the CBS radio voice in Berlin, came on a similar junket in 1940 and was booked into the Scribe, an establishment he knew well from earlier days working for Paris-American newspapers. In the hotel's lobby mobbed with Germans he found two familiar Americans, Demaree Bess of the *Saturday Evening Post* and Walter Kerr of the *New York Herald Tribune*'s Paris edition, and learned from them about the flight of the French government, French citizens, and most other American correspondents from the advancing Wehrmacht. It was from the Scribe that Shirer made his way to the Compiègne Forest to broadcast live the French acceptance of German armistice terms in the same railway car where German defeat was acknowledged in World War I. The next day Kerr came to Shirer's room in the hotel to tell him he had achieved a major scoop. For hours, Shirer's broadcast was the only news reaching America about the armistice.[3]

⌒

Allied planners surely knew, as the Axis should have earlier, that the Canadian National Railway Company, which in turn was owned by the Canadian government, owned the Scribe building.[4] It was purchased as an investment in 1923 and leased to French hotel companies, with the CNR itself capitalizing on the tourist invasion of Paris in the 1920s by opening an office along the street level. In the same decade, the Paris edition of the *Chicago Tribune* had a business office at 5 Rue Scribe where tourists who registered could see their names the next day in the paper's "Arrivals" column—and then buy added copies of the paper for folks back home.

Long before those roaring years, the Scribe had glittered for the very different crowd of the Jockey Club.[5] Founded in 1834 and modeled on London's exclusive clubs, it was an oasis for eminent gentlemen who wanted gilded lounges, servants, fine dining, gambling and turf talk, and lodging in the company of men exactly like themselves. Belonging to the Jockey Club—as Marcel Proust's Charles Swann does—meant one had reached the top drawer of Parisian society. In 1863 the club made the Scribe its new home, occupying the building's first two floors while the upper levels functioned as a small hotel. Shops on the Scribe's street level included the salesroom of the luggage maker Louis Vuitton and the celebrated Grand Café on the Boulevard des Capucines where, in its Salon Indien in December 1895, the brothers Auguste and Louis Lumière publically screened the first motion pictures.

In 1925, with the Jockey Club now removed to new quarters in Rue Rabelais, the Scribe entered a construction phase to refashion itself into an Art Deco–style luxury hotel. Albert Courtecuisse, an experienced multilingual hotel director, became the reopened Scribe's manager. He was on duty after the fall of France when a Nazi SS officer who had been a correspondent for the German news agency DNB came to commandeer the hotel for the Reich. Well before the occupation the Germans had meticulously informed themselves about the stature, capacity, and inner workings of Paris hotels, along with nearly everything else—schools, hospitals, bordellos, banks, the homes of wealthy Jewish families—about the city.[6] To Courtecuisse's initial surprise, the officer's deputy greeted him by name. He had been manager of a luxury Munich hotel with which the Scribe exchanged trainees. The personal link between the two didn't prevent the Germans from monitoring Courtecuisse during the occupation. After the liberation it was learned that microphones had been installed on his office window.

⁓

Fittingly, the first Allied contingent to enter the Scribe was nearly all made up of Canadians. In the run-up to the liberation, Colonel Richard S. Malone, a former newsman with the *Winnipeg Free Press* who had founded Canada's military newspaper the *Maple Leaf* and become head of public relations for the First Canadian Army, learned in casual conversation about the hotel's ownership and subsequently planned with British and American PROs to rendezvous at the location. With Paris outside the Canadian sector of military operations in France, getting there was wholly for his personal pleasure and that of his country's correspondents who, as Malone put it, "wanted to gamble on a Paris dateline."[7]

When it seemed certain the city would fall, Malone assembled a group of willing newsmen, and they set off in jeeps. Taking a different route himself, Malone joined with them in a tangle of American and French forces still encountering German resistance in the area of Rambouillet. In another conversation, this with a French civilian who spoke broken English (Malone would discover that he was a Canadian deserter from World War I who married a French woman, settled in the country, and had nearly forgotten his native tongue), he learned that after heavy street fighting with the Free French of the Interior (FFI) within Paris the Germans were leaving the city. Questioned about how he knew this, the Frenchman said his brother-in-law had telephoned him from Paris with the news.

It seemed improbable that phones were working. But Malone went into a shop, made a call to the sole place he could think of, the Scribe, and was immediately connected. After identifying himself, he was transferred to Louis Régamey, the French general agent for the Canadian National Railway who had remained in Paris through the occupation. After getting over his shock at hearing a Canadian voice, Régamey told Malone that battles were continuing in the area but the Germans had abandoned the hotel. He didn't, though, know of a safe route across the Seine to the right bank to reach it.

At this point one of Malone's group, Matthew Halton, the senior correspondent of the Canadian Broadcasting Company, suggested calling information, asking in French to be connected with the headquarters of the FFI, and then asking whoever answered for directions on how to travel to the Scribe. The improbable result was that the FFI told the Canadians to stay exactly where they were and a guide would lead them into Paris.

In time, a big Citroën appeared with—improbabilities mounting—an attractive young blonde wearing a white silk blouse riding the running board, a pistol in her hand and an armband bearing the Cross of Lorraine. Before darkness that evening, Malone and a group that included a signaler, a censor, and correspondents set off for Paris in jeeps following the woman, whose full name was Christianne de Sanfort, her confederates, and two other Canadian correspondents in the FFI vehicle. One of them, Matthew Halton, later described in a nearly nine-minute broadcast on the CBC the hurtling dash with the FFI to the Scribe:

> They took me in their car and we drove through the wildly cheering crowds with our arms around each other. We crossed the river to the Île de la Cité . . . and past Notre Dame, and then up the Avenue of the Opéra to the Scribe Hotel. Here the crowds were just beginning to come into the streets, mad with happiness. My friends were shouting "Il est Canadien!" [He is Canadian!] . . . And I knew what it was to feel like a king.[8]

An ebullient Louis Régamey was at the Scribe to meet them and lead the way to the lounge bar and order cases of champagne and cognac hauled from the cellars. After making his way back to the front desk in the lobby, Malone found there the hotel's manager and a smiling British press officer he knew who had taken his own route to the prearranged meeting point just ahead of the Canadians. Together with the manager, Malone signed a requisition form taking over the hotel, then wrote in the registration book, "Reserved for the Canadian Army," and dated his entry.

One of the correspondents in Malone's group, Gerald Clark of the *Montreal Standard*, was struck by the elegant look of the hotel's public area. "I manoeuvred my way through the revolving door into the lobby," he wrote. "To the left was the reception desk, and straight ahead a porter stood smiling behind a longer desk. The lounge, opening into the center of the lobby, was dark, but civilized and luxurious with its potted ferns, its settees, its armchairs."[9] Maurice Desjardins of the Canadian Press wrote his first dispatch from the hotel while seated at the bellboys' counter in the lobby as Parisians kept offering him drinks and one identified herself as the sister of the famed singer Lily Pons.[10]

When the Canadian signalman reached the rendezvous location, Malone had him place his portable wireless radio unit on the Scribe's roof and try hooking up with London. By nine o'clock that evening contact was established, and five Canadian correspondents, Matthew Halton among them, filed what Malone assumed were the first dispatches actually sent from Paris. (Rumor had reached the Canadians that American or British newsmen had also gotten into Paris before the liberation but were forced to leave the city to transmit their stories.) The hotel's dining room wasn't operating, so the Canadian group shared their rations with Christianne and other FFI members before calling it a night. "Some sporadic fighting and sniping went on in the streets most of the night," Malone noted, "but we had our first stories out, so locking my door I went to sleep that night between clean sheets and without a care in the world. We had beaten the official liberation by one day."[11]

(However satisfying, the Paris triumph was one of several other war beats Malone ascribed to Canadian public relations. He wrote that his country's group had beaten their American and British counterparts "in getting the first press copy out after the D-Day landings in Sicily, Italy and Normandy, as well as on the liberations of Paris and Brussels."[12])

～

The following day, the liberation in full glory, Americans arrived. Malone again emphasized that Canadians had already taken the Scribe and turned it into a working press camp: "By the time units of the 4th U.S. Division entered the city, our press centre at the Scribe was in full operation, with wireless transmission and proper censorship, so we were quickly inundated with American war correspondents."[13] Among the American contingent were two PROs Malone had known in Britain, Lieutenant Colonel Barney Oldfield and Lieutenant Colonel John "Jack" Redding. Before the Normandy landings, both officers had been involved with planning for press camps in France and in selecting the initial body of PROs. An agreement was struck between the Canadians and the new arrivals, who were part of a task force of what would become a full PRD detachment, that the hotel should become an Allied press center. Redding was placed in temporary control, and requisition of the hotel was handed over to him. With Paris in the American military sector, Malone knew Redding was in the best position to secure food, gasoline, and transmission equipment.

During their time in Paris, Malone and his correspondents made their way from the Scribe to Place du Canada and the building of the Canadian legation. When they banged on the door, a former French employee appeared and helped them find a Canadian flag, which was promptly hung from an upper balcony—the first Allied flag, Malone believed, to appear on a public building in the city. Thereafter Malone gathered his group, which included Louis Régamey, dapper in a double-breasted suit and bow tie, to pose for a photo in front of the legation.

The Canadians also became fully acquainted with the Scribe's bar. They were there one evening with Christianne, who spoke English, had been an actress before the war, and during it was active in helping downed Allied airmen find escape routes through France. Suddenly one of her FFI companions raced into the bar, spoke hurriedly to her, and then tore off his jacket and tie, threw them on the floor, and reached in her handbag for her pistol. After silently finishing off her cognac, the young man rushed from the bar. A puzzled Malone was asking Christianne what was going on when several shots were fired in the street outside. Only seconds passed before the man was back in the bar and replacing the gun in the handbag, putting on his coat and tie, finishing off another drink on the table, bowing theatrically, and leaving the bar. Christianne explained that the incident amounted to nothing. Her comrade had simply spotted a German in civilian clothes on the street and lacked a gun of his own.

Malone would soon depart to rejoin the Canadian army in the field, while leaving an officer at the Scribe to look after the country's interests. "The Scribe," he wrote, "had now been turned into an Allied press centre under Redding's control."[14] He had introduced Redding and Oldfield to Louis Régamey, who gave assurance that he would continue helping the Americans. There remained one last chore for the Canadian officer: Régamey had to be freed from jail.

One night Christianne and friends came to Malone's Scribe room and excitedly said that Régamey, whose son was a member of their underground cell, had been picked up by American military police as a Nazi collaborator. Some enemies or neighbors had informed intelligence figures that Régamey had been on close terms with Germans at the Scribe, had taken payments from them, and had received special ration permits. Malone arranged for Régamey's release by pointing out that any involvement with the Germans was justified by his duty to protect the Scribe's ownership and management. Régamey said he had hidden from the Germans the Canadian ownership of the building while collecting and recording rent money they paid, the sums in turn concealed by investing some of it in shares of stock in the Suez Canal, in turn sold for considerable profit. Later, with Régamey dictating the information to him, Malone informed Ottawa of its windfall, courtesy of the German army, of some seven million francs.[15]

That the occupying power bothered to pay rent money wasn't as surprising as it might seem. Intending to be in Paris for years to come, the Germans wanted a city that met their varied needs and were willing to pay for it—at substantial discounts. For elegant rooms in the Hôtel Ritz, top German figures paid on average twenty-five francs a day—a reduction of some 90 percent from standard charges.[16]

Whatever amount the Germans paid barely registered in comparison with what the French nation paid them. According to the armistice agreement of 1940, France bore all costs of the occupation. In 1940 the payment was four hundred million francs a day. When this proved more than Germany could spend, it was reduced to three hundred million in 1941, then lifted to five hundred million by 1943. Economists calculate the overall figure France paid during the four years of the occupation at over 479 billion francs, with looting adding unknown billions more.[17]

The day Colonel Malone left the Scribe to return to the war, Christianne asked about the route he was following. After he told her, she wondered if she could join him as far as a small town where she had a young son living with friends and attending school. In her work for the Resistance, she hadn't seen the child for weeks. Malone agreed to take her, in the process learning more about how she and her theater friends had coped with the occupation without collaborating with the Germans. During the remainder of the war Malone returned several times to Paris, yet he never again saw or heard about the young woman.

CHAPTER TWO

∽

Jeeping to Paris

After the Allied command chose to enter Paris rather than bypassing it for the time being while pursuing German forces in northern France, the diplomatic honor of leading the way went to the French Second Armored Division commanded by General Jacques Philippe Leclerc. An American equipped and outfitted force of some sixteen thousand men and two thousand tanks, Leclerc's division had been transported from Britain to France some two months after D-Day. While Leclerc would enter Paris from the west, supporting him from the southwest would be General Raymond Barton's American Fourth Division spearheaded by its Twelfth Infantry Regiment and a British contingent. Correspondents vying to be among the first to stamp a Paris dateline on their material had to decide whether to line up with Leclerc's or Barton's troops—or try slipping in, as some Canadians had, ahead of either group.

The bulk of correspondents and some PROs and censors were already decamped in and around the Hôtel du Grand Veneur in Rambouillet. The town was on a main Versailles-to-Paris route and some thirty miles from the city's center. To John Groth, a former art director of *Esquire* and now a field artist for *Parade* magazine and a correspondent for the *Chicago Sun* and *American Legion Magazine*, the Rambouillet newsmen comprised a vast occupying force. He wrote that "the entire correspondence corps of the army" seemed squeezed into the small town, the members forming a "brilliant assemblage." Groth ticked off some of the American "starlets"[1] among them: Ernie Pyle, Henry Gorrell, Don Whitehead, H. R. Knickerbocker, Robert Cromie, and

Larry LeSueur. Robert Capa, a star as well, added that in Rambouillet "every international typewriter was assembled" and correspondents were "wrangling and conspiring to be the first to enter Paris and file history from the great city of former lights."[2]

One of the Rambouillet correspondents, Robert Reid of Britain's BBC who was embedded with the American First Army, heard a PRO say that at the Scribe in Paris everyone would find cable facilities and censors to approve their news copy. But the officer couldn't say when they would get inside the hotel since it had first to be searched for mines and booby traps. Another officer solemnly warned that while on the road to Paris the correspondents might well come under German fire. The only really good way to enter the city, he said, was inside a tank rather than in their usual jeeps. "But if any of you are killed," he went on, "we'll give you a decent burial."[3]

The jaunty remark had a deeply serious side. Every correspondent in Rambouillet knew of the recent deaths of two colleagues. William Stringer, a former United Press (UP) reporter who had switched to Reuters for the opportunity to cover the war in Europe, was killed on August 17 by enemy fire. A PRD officer noted critically that Stringer was "jumping it a little, trying to get to Paris through Versailles ahead of everyone."[4] Thomas Treanor of the *Los Angeles Times*, who had covered the war in North Africa, Sicily, and Italy before the Normandy invasion, died on August 19 after an American tank near Chartres struck his jeep. Early in 1944 Treanor had returned home to finish a book with the breezy journalistic title *One Damn Thing after Another: The Adventures of an Innocent Man Trapped between Public Relations and the Axis.*

Correspondents had reasons of their own to ponder whether getting to Paris first or nearly so was worth the risk. "In every mind," said John Groth, "was the picture of a scale: on one side was the greatest story of the war; on the other, existence, or the things that make existence—a wife, a family—or just the instinctive desire to remain alive."[5] But Robert Capa, who had come ashore with the first wave on Omaha Beach on D-Day, probably spoke for the majority of newsmen when he proclaimed that "the road to Paris was calling."[6]

On August 24 elements of Leclerc's division (in French, the Deuxième Division Blindée or 2e DB) made a tentative incursion into the city that reached local Resistance fighters battling in the Place de l'Hôtel de Ville. German defenders exacted a heavy toll: seventy-one men of Leclerc's force were killed, with 225 wounded, and thirty-five armored vehicles were destroyed.[7] When on Friday, August 25—the feast day of Saint Louis, king, crusader, and patron saint of France—the full French 2e DB rumbled toward

Paris, correspondents wedged their way into the lines of Sherman tanks, half-tracks, armored cars, and trucks while hoping that the only enemy Tiger tanks encountered were already in flames by the side of the road.

From an Allied military standpoint, taking Paris barely registered in the full arc of the war. In *Inferno*, the formidable history of World War II by Max Hastings, it draws two sentences: "The Germans abandoned Paris without a fight. Gen. Philippe Leclerc's Free French armoured division entered the capital on 25 August to find the Resistance claiming possession, a legend that launched the resurrection of France's national self-respect."[8] *The Second World War*, Antony Beevor's equally imposing account, says that during the freeing of Paris there was "little more than a few sharp skirmishes round German-held buildings."[9]

With war correspondents unable to foresee the future, it was reasonable to expect the Germans would put up a fight, if only to preserve their honor or as a rearguard action to cover a general retreat. Later accounts by military historians would take note of German soldiers holding out in pockets of the city and a sizeable group gathered in the Bois de Boulogne. Newsmen who took the road to Paris on that late August day of splendid summer weather felt they ran a gauntlet of riotous joy, utter confusion, and sporadic fear for their lives during the skirmishes that did take place.

Unable to find shelter for their first night in Rambouillet, John Groth and his jeep mates—photographer Charles Haacker of Acme Newspictures, Gordon Gammack of the *Des Moines Register-Tribune*, and behind the wheel a French-speaking PRO of the Ninth Air Force—decided to light out ahead of the main pack of correspondents. Before reaching Rambouillet they had fortified themselves with cognac and champagne, and—as Groth wrote—with a "kind of rum courage" they "jeeped toward Paris." There was little traffic, but they could hear the firing of distant guns. In the town of Orsay they found a place to stay the night—and grasped that if they were off early in the morning they might be the first newsmen to reach Paris.

During the following day they met the French tank column and followed it into the city through Porte d'Orléans. Wildly cheering throngs reached out to touch, kiss, and pelt them with flags and flowers. The tanks grew so adorned that they seemed like floats in a Rose Bowl parade. Shooting continued between German snipers, tankers, and FFI fighters, yet in the jeep they sped on toward the city center.

They knew the press center in Paris would be the Scribe, but getting there meant crossing the Seine. Everything learned from those they passed indicated that the Germans still controlled all the river bridges. "We had reached the heart of the city," Groth recorded. "We have seen no other correspondents and no other Americans. We had come with the head of the column through the only open gate. We were the first Americans in Paris. We had a story to tell."[10]

But the only way to tell it in print and pictures was to turn about and leave Paris. Jack Redding, the top PRO in the area, had determined it was too risky to immediately bring communications facilities into the unknown situation in central Paris, so correspondents were told to get dispatches back out for filing.[11] Groth and his companions, which would soon include Frederick Graham of the New York Times, believed a First Army press camp five or six hours distant was the nearest place with censors and transmission facilities. They reasoned that other correspondents who reached Paris would need another day or more to get to the Scribe. So they turned back toward Rambouillet and Chartres, worried whether the Jeep and its gas supply would hold up. The road into Paris was now packed in both lanes with American tanks and jeeps.

The first correspondents they saw were still outside Porte d'Orléans. Near Longjumeau they were flagged down when a pair they knew noticed the press sign on their jeep and the lipsticked faces within it. To avoid the tide of traffic, they took side roads, knowing they might still be mined. When fighter planes suddenly wheeled overhead, they hit the brakes and dove into ditches.

At the First Army press camp the only newsman present was Wilfred Heinz of the New York Sun, a recent arrival from London. The camp's commander was thrilled to see the weary, ruffled correspondents and helped them get their stories out. Haacker was taken to an airfield to carry his photos to London. Gammack and Graham rapidly churned out pieces and sent them by Press Wireless, a commercial company that transmitted only print and broadcast news. With advice and editing help from Heinz, Groth wrote his account and sent it to Chicago. "As far as I knew," he noted, "my story of the liberation of Paris—the first story I had ever filed—would be the first story to reach America." Before heading again to Paris the next day, he got a wireless message from his paper's foreign editor: "First Paris story swell We bannered it front page PM [New York newspaper] also using."[12]

Don Whitehead of the Associated Press likewise entered Paris on liberation day and then left to write and send a dispatch. With a jeep driver who spoke French, Whitehead was linked with Leclerc's troops pushing to Paris when, at Porte d'Orléans, a French officer declared that noncombatants couldn't proceed to the city. Whitehead's response was to change positions with his driver and hurl the jeep forward. In his AP dispatch, he recorded that "at 9:57 a.m. my jeep rolled through the gates into Paris." The jeep then followed French tanks, but heavy gunfire caused Whitehead and the driver to get out and take cover. On streets around them men and women of the FFI were going from house to house to eliminate snipers. An FFI member cried out to them in English, "Give us arms and ammunition. That's all we ask. We'll clean out these bastards."[13]

Whitehead stayed in Paris about an hour before heading back to Rambouillet, where a pressroom had been hastily set up in a lounge of the Hôtel du Grand Veneur. In forty-five minutes the correspondent, popularly named "Beachhead Don" for his competitive zeal,[14] typed a 1,600-word report with a Paris dateline. The *New York Times* later credited the lanky, war-tested correspondent who had covered fighting in North Africa, Sicily, and Italy with being the first American reporter to file a dispatch out of liberated Paris. *Liberated* was the operative word. The *Baltimore Sun* boasted that one of its correspondents, Lee McCardell, entered the capital while it was still under German control and filed a dispatch with a Paris dateline. Clinging to the roof of a civilian car, he had ridden in with five FFI fighters in summer sports outfits. "It wasn't the easiest method of travel," said McCardell of his perch on the car, "but the driver was in a hurry to get home."[15]

Don Whitehead also claimed another liberation first. In a story datelined Paris, August 25, he wrote, "Yesterday, even before I entered Paris, I learned by a telephone call that Mme. Blanchard, who has been housekeeper for the American Embassy in Paris for sixteen years, was excitedly awaiting the arrival of the Americans so she could raise the Stars and Stripes over the embassy again." Like the Canadians motoring to Paris, Whitehead and his driver had discovered to their surprise that phones in the city were working. From Longjumeau the driver placed a call to the embassy, speaking in French. Mme. Blanchard answered him in English. Speaking then with Whitehead, she disclosed that the Swiss government cared for the embassy after it closed in 1941. She had returned to it along with her mother because of street fighting within Paris. "I hope the Americans move in tomorrow," she told Whitehead. In readiness, she carried an American flag wherever she went. Whitehead ended the story with the first-of-a-kind scoop, however marginal, that correspondents eagerly sought: "And that concluded the first telephone call to the American Embassy from outside Paris since it was closed three years ago."[16]

～

Robert Reid was among the newsmen who did cross the Seine to the Scribe on liberation day. With Robert Dunnett, a fellow BBC correspondent, and Stanley Gardinar of Britain's Exchange Telegraph wire service, he rode in a big Humber station wagon rather than a jeep. The three traveled with a tank convoy from Rambouillet to Longjumeau, where they were advised to leave the convoy and rush for Paris in small groups of two or three vehicles in hopes of staying free of snipers. Reid found the journey a "mad, gay race, cars driving sometimes two and three abreast and bumper to bumper until we swung round a bend in the road, and saw to our left the Eiffel Tower beckoning to us in the shimmering distance."[17]

The enormous cheering crowds they passed in the suburbs of Paris abruptly vanished when they entered areas where Germans or German sympathizers were firing from rooftops. Cars ahead of them began veering off the road, leaving the station wagon in the lead. A French policeman near a building frantically signaled them to run for it. The driver, wrote Reid, "set his jaw very grimly, put his foot down on the accelerator, and the car leapt forward, running the gauntlet, and bringing us out onto the banks of the River Seine, and across one of the bridges, and to the Hotel Scribe, our press headquarters."[18]

Charles Wertenbaker, the head of *Time-Life*'s team in France, joined up with Robert Capa in Rambouillet for the thrust into Paris. With their jeep driver they were on the road on August 25 when they encountered a barrier of felled trees and a squad of Spanish volunteers preventing anyone from passing ahead. Leclerc's 2e DB had some four hundred Spanish Republican fighters now enrolled against fascist Germany.[19] After Capa convinced them in Spanish that he had also been with the Republicans in Spain, they let the jeep proceed.[20] (A running gag among correspondents was that the photographer spoke seven languages, all of them badly.) They caught up with the French column, worked their way around the full length, and finally pulled in line until they were only a jeep behind Leclerc's armored vehicle. Nothing slowed the French advance approaching Porte d'Orléans other than ecstatic crowds falling back just enough to let the column slide through. As Wertenbaker timed it, he and Capa entered Paris proper behind Leclerc at 9:40 a.m.

In a dispatch published in *Time* a week after the liberation, Wertenbaker—billed by the magazine as "the first U.S. newsman to enter Paris"—told of civilians along the road becoming walled crowds crying out "Merci! Merci! Merci!" Capa labeled liberation day the most joyous one of his life, while Wertenbaker exclaimed that "Bob Capa and I rode into Paris with eyes that would not stay dry. We were no more ashamed of it than were the people who wept as they embraced us."

After Leclerc established his temporary Paris headquarters at the Gare Montparnasse railway station, Wertenbaker and Capa drove ahead into the Boulevard des Invalides. They had left the jeep and were walking when at the Chamber of Deputies and the Ministry of Foreign Affairs they saw French tanks firing into burning buildings, the blasts drowning out the sound of machine guns and rifles.

Back at the jeep, Wertenbaker set his typewriter on the hood and began writing while Capa went off to shoot photos. Among the jubilant figures who swarmed about Wertenbaker was a woman who brought him a sandwich while another provided a bottle of champagne. When the woman who carried the sandwich returned to offer a bath, he readily accepted.

After Capa and Wertenbaker were again together they found the apartment of Olivia Chambers, who had worked for *Life* before the war and remained in Paris through the occupation. In his *Time* report, Wertenbaker summarized Chambers's notes of several days of heavy battling in the city between the Germans and FFI fighters. He ended his piece with the German surrender of the city and prisoners paraded through the streets while snipers were still at work and the Chamber of Deputies remained in flames.[21] By later consensus, Wertenbaker and Capa had won by a nose the race of American correspondents into freed Paris.

A dozen women correspondents were confined in a hotel in Rennes by the PRD until Paris was considered safe for their entry, with the result that most of them missed the day of liberation. Lee Carson of the International Press Service avoided the precautions only because, as a PRO put it, she had jumped ship while on a press visit to Normandy. A SHAEF directive called for her apprehension and return to Britain, but Carson couldn't be found. She came in from the cold in time to ride a jeep into Paris with Robert Reuben of Reuters, G. K. Hodenfield of *Stars and Stripes*, and the American Fourth Division.

At the Scribe, Carson worried with good reason about the reception awaiting her. But one of the early PROs to reach the hotel, Major Frank Mayborn, ignored her rule breaking. "How nice to see you," he remarked. "It's good to see that you got here safely."[22] It may have helped Carson's cause that, according to the officer who told of her jumping ship, Carson was an attractive "charmer of the first order." Another correspondent characterized her as "an attractive, knockabout reporter" who took credit for being the first woman correspondent to reach liberated Paris.[23]

Helen Kirkpatrick was also spared confinement in Rennes. Tall and French speaking, she had worked in France as a journalist before the war, and in London in 1940 she became a correspondent for the *Chicago Daily News*. While London was under blitz attacks, Edward R. Murrow tried to hire her for his CBS group.[24] When the New York office balked at adding another woman, he went with Charles Collingwood, a United Press reporter with little experience. Kirkpatrick's London colleagues with the *Daily News*, William Stoneman and Robert Casey, reported on the D-Day landings, but Kirkpatrick remained office bound. It was nearly a month after the invasion before SHAEF allowed women reporters to cross to France, where they were largely limited to covering field hospitals.

With her wide experience, Kirkpatrick had more freedom of movement on the Continent than most women journalists. Soon after the breakthrough from Normandy she linked up with the French armored division because she guessed they would have priority in liberating Paris. While with them she learned their manner of eating when in the field. They dispensed with dutiful British and American-style mess kitchens and ate in small groups with their own mess and fires. "There were the Germans just over the next hill," she recorded, "and here are the fires and the French merrily cooking."[25]

Kirkpatrick eventually moved on to Rambouillet with the French while riding in a captured German jeep lacking doors or a top with John Reinhart, an American naval officer who was a liaison official with Leclerc's force. During a toilet stop behind roadside bushes, she injured a toe while climbing from the jeep. At a hospital in Rambouillet a doctor said the toe was broken, but he didn't bother with minor matters like that. After a shot of novocaine, she managed to get a shoe on.

When they learned that the 2e DB would set up roadblocks preventing unauthorized figures from entering Paris, Kirkpatrick and Reinhart scouted the countryside and found a bistro where they could stay overnight. The next morning they took a route that avoided the roadblocks and joined the French force for the run to Paris. "I shall never forget," she wrote, "coming over the hill and there below is Paris—white and shining in the sun."

The travelers were unable that day to cross the Seine because of massive crowds and enemy shooting from rooftops, with return fire coming from FFI and Resistance fighters. For the night they found rooms in the Hôtel des États-Unis and joined French police who were rounding up captured Germans. After each return trip to the station with prisoners there would be champagne amid cries of "*Vive la France* and *Vive les États-Unis*," and—as Kirkpatrick added—"Johnny Reinhart, who spoke German, would interrogate these poor terrified Germans."[26]

Photo 2.1.   Helen Kirkpatrick in field gear posing for army photo.
Source: From the Helen Paull Kirkpatrick Papers, Sophia Smith Collection, Smith College
  (Northampton, Massachusetts)

~

Irwin Shaw and a cameraman, Philip Drell, reached the Scribe on liberation day in a jeep with girls clinging to the side. After dropping off their store of film, they—as Shaw logged—"grandly registered for two large rooms, knowing that the day of the Pfc in Paris would be short and determined to make the most of it."[27] They then took long baths while hearing joyous noise lifting from the street below. "Paris was liberated in just the right way," Shaw later observed, explaining why in a single flowing sentence:

> It hadn't been bombed, except on the outskirts, and all the bridges were still standing, and the inhabitants themselves had spent the last five days firing off small arms and feeling heroic, and the weather was sunny and warm and all the girls wore their best dresses, and there were enough Germans left to put up a show of war and give the local boys an opportunity to behave martially in front of good audiences before the final surrender.[28]

In the hotel's lounge bar that evening, Shaw and Drell learned from other correspondents about the filming of the liberation by the leader of their film and photo unit, the Hollywood director Lieutenant Colonel George Stevens. The following day Shaw, known at the time more as a short-story writer rather than the popular novelist he became, moved into the large suite Stevens took in the Scribe.

Like such other established moviemakers as Frank Capra and John Huston, George Stevens had volunteered for military service and been given an open-ended charge of making a documentary record of Allied military activity in North Africa and Europe. During an organizing phase in the United States, Shaw, a drafted private, was among the writers he added to his film group. When the team reached Egypt, Stevens went off hunting for more action to film, and Shaw stayed in Cairo and became an accredited correspondent for *Stars and Stripes* and the military magazine *Yank*.[29]

In 1943 Stevens relocated to Britain with orders from General Eisenhower to put together in London a forty-five-member Special Coverage Unit to film the invasion of Europe. The group, linked directly to SHAEF and with abundant supplies and near-total freedom to move on the Continent, again had Shaw as one of its writers. Another drafted private, William Saroyan, was picked by Stevens to join the unit in London. Like Shaw, Saroyan had enjoyed early literary acclaim—in 1939 three of his plays were on Broadway, with one, *The Time of Your Life*, winning a Pulitzer Prize—and like Shaw, he was acquainted with Stevens from his own Hollywood days. His role with the film unit, however, both in London and later in Paris, would amount to little more than keeping Stevens company and joining in poker sessions.[30]

On D-Day the Stevens unit was held in transport off the beaches until some hours after the first wave of troops had landed. Later they were attached to General George Patton's Third Army, with their footage from Normandy sent to America for newsreel and documentary use. During the advance into Paris, Stevens aligned his group with Leclerc's troops. They reached the city's Gare Montparnasse in time to film the arranged meeting between the head of the German garrison in Paris, General Dietrich von Choltitz, who had previously surrendered to Leclerc and the commander of the Paris FFI in the Prefecture of Police, and French general Charles de Gaulle. Stevens would ultimately transfer his entire group from the Scribe to a loft near the Arc de Triomphe and make film excursions to nearby fighting areas while remaining based in Paris into 1945.

With Stevens's recommendation, Shaw became a warrant officer in the fall of 1944, which stirred mocking delight among companions in the Scribe bar. Drew Middleton of the *New York Times* said, "We used to call Irwin 'Marshal' after that; we'd say, 'Marshal, it's your turn to buy the drinks.'"[31] Shaw stayed a member of the Stevens unit as it filmed in France and Germany through the end of the war. Its footage from the Dachau concentration camp was later used at the Nuremberg trials.

When the Stevens unit left Britain for France, William Saroyan stayed behind, working now on a special writing project that he hoped might rescue him from a military life he despised. It didn't, and it was late January 1945 when he flew to cold and snowy Paris to reconnect with the unit. With Stevens away, Saroyan reported to a PRO and was billeted with enlisted men in the Hôtel Louis La Grand. He resumed poker games with London acquaintances, managing one evening to drop $3,000 to Robert Capa.

After his PRO came up with a scheme of creating a picture book about American soldiers, with Saroyan doing the captions, the writer prepared to do some work. With the officer and a photographer he embarked on a jeep tour of nearby camps, which was cut short by chronic back pain, attributed to an old fall in a San Francisco bar. After admission to a hospital and examination, Saroyan was sent back to the United States for more evaluation, the beginning of a long struggle to disentangle himself from the military.

~

Handsome, wavy-haired Charles Collingwood rode into Paris with *Time*'s William Walton. At the moment, Walton was a rising star among correspondents since he was one of a handpicked group that, portable typewriter strapped to his body, parachuted into Normandy on D-Day. Collingwood, on the other hand, had reason to believe his journalistic career was in jeopardy.

Just earlier he had written a broadcast that infuriated SHAEF's PRD and deeply embarrassed CBS.

Two days before the liberation, the radio network carried Collingwood's detailed and dramatic story of ecstatic Parisians welcoming Leclerc's force. "The French Second Armored Division," the report began, "entered Paris today after the Parisians had risen as one man to beat down the German troops who had garrisoned the city." After writing the premature script, Collingwood recorded it and placed the recording and the script in a press pouch to London, from where it reached the CBS office. A backup copy was sent to censors who, apparently, assumed the story had been passed by censors in France and approved it for transmission.

When Richard C. Hottelet, on duty in the CBS London office, read the report, he excitedly phoned the network in New York with the sensational news. While the recording was played repeatedly in New York and London—CBS proclaiming Collingwood as the first American newsman to enter Paris— newspapers put out extra editions. The *New York Times* prefaced its page-one story with a statement repeating the network's claim: "The following dispatch, by a representative of the Columbia Broadcasting System, the first American correspondent to enter the city, was cabled to London and broadcast from there."[32]

For correspondents still stalled with the French force in Rambouillet there was stunned surprise. Collingwood's colleague and competitor, Larry LeSueur, sought to correct the report with another broadcast. "Paris has not yet been entered by Allied troops," he announced. "The French Second Armored Division is still outside the city, held up by diehard bands of German anti-tank and mine fields and small groups of German tanks."[33]

Edward R. Murrow stoutly defended Collingwood's story, but some believed his own credibility and that of his radio team had been badly tarnished. Collingwood's explanation, as quoted by CBS's news director Paul White, pointed to failure on the part of censors. "Everything was sent through regular channels," said Collingwood. "I had no more than the normal desire to get my copy out first, and naturally assumed my story would receive the same censorship wherever it went, correcting my errors on the basis of the information I then had available."[34]

Collingwood faced no lasting harm from the PRD. In his diary, Harry Butcher warmly praised him for his CBS broadcast about the Scribe, and later Collingwood would be one of the select group of correspondents chosen by the PRD to witness the German surrender that ended the war. But on the day of liberation he may have thought it prudent to avoid immediate contact with colleagues at the Scribe. While he and Walton were inside Paris, the welcoming crowds were so immense that they decided to seek refuge in a hotel. When they asked an FFI gunman to help lead them, he got in their jeep and took them to a hotel in Montmartre. Outside the building, women streamed from everywhere—a population, as Walton later portrayed them, made up of the district's entire population of whores.

In a short piece written for *Life* about liberating Montmartre—leaving Collingwood noted but unnamed—Walton said it took them a half hour just to get from the jeep to the hotel through the mass of passionate ladies. He and Collingwood then stood on their room's balcony waving to the crowd below and making V signs until the light faded. "For one night," Walton ended the article, "every American was a Lindbergh."[35] In a postwar recollection of the experience, he added that the following morning he went to Collingwood's room and found him on the balcony in a scarlet dressing gown drawn from his knapsack and chatting and laughing with women still massed below.[36]

Alan Moorehead rode into Paris from Rambouillet in a Volkswagen rather than a jeep. It had belonged to a dead German officer who seemingly was deserting while wearing a civilian suit. A well-traveled Australian journalist covering the war for London's *Daily Express*, Moorehead realized it wasn't a wise car to be seen in amid the hoopla of the day, but with little mileage on it and otherwise in good condition, he was determined to keep possession.

He and British and American correspondents with him could glimpse the Eiffel Tower in the distance when they were stopped near the Porte d'Orléans by a French officer in the middle of the road insisting in perfect English that only the French could enter Paris. They were challenging him when an American colonel appeared in a jeep. He identified himself as a liaison officer with Leclerc's 2e DB, but the Frenchman insisted he needed a special pass to go forward. When he added that his orders were to shoot, the American said, "Then shoot," and bolted ahead.

Emboldened to a degree, Moorehead and his companions slipped off on a side road that led to a highway to Paris. In central Paris a sea of celebrators passed them bottles of wine and held out babies to be kissed but took cover when snipers fired and Resistance fighters answered. Moorehead was hunting for someone to lead them toward the Seine when a young man with an FFI armband said to him in English, "Come on. I'll take you to our headquarters." He turned out to be an Australian with Britain's Royal Air Force who had been shot down over the Channel and had been in hiding for three years. He was now a member of a multinational FFI cell.

At the group's sprawling garage headquarters, they held some twenty prisoners, many of them French snipers of the Vichy regime, whom they would execute after a cursory trial. "To the FFI youths who had captured them," Moorehead wrote of the prisoners, "they were merely abstract evil." One was said to be a dentist who had turned over his patients to the Gestapo. After toasting the correspondents with seized liquor, the FFI fighters guided the Volkswagen to the river.[37]

The only Allied troops Moorehead saw in Paris on liberation day were elements of Leclerc's division. Yet a hundred or so cars were already jammed outside the Scribe, and twice as many men—correspondents, censors, and PRD officers—filled the lobby, all clamoring for rooms. Moorehead found the Scribe's French staff, who had witnessed Germans leaving the hotel not long before, "utterly baffled by this invasion" and "crying out in despair" that they had no more rooms and to try somewhere else. From their side, the new arrivals kept insisting that they had to stay in the hotel. Possibly someone like the New Yorker's James Thurber, Moorehead imagined, could have captured the comic crosscurrents of dialogue.

"All over Paris," Moorehead noted about the muddled situation, "there were huge hotels, luxury hotels, simply dying to take in the first Allied troops. But all the vehicles headed straight by them for the Scribe. You could almost feel the managers of the Ritz and the Vendôme and the other hotels saying to themselves: 'Now what has the Scribe got that we haven't got?'"

Given the bedlam there, Moorehead decided to scrap orders to check into the Scribe and "head for somewhere comfortable like the Ritz." While he drove to the Place Vendôme it seemed likely his group would be the first to liberate the hotel. With what he described as "precision and great aplomb," the Ritz staff welcomed the visitors before asking, "Will you go up to your rooms now or have dinner at once?" As it happened, the new guests found Ernest Hemingway already installed in the dining room with a bottle of champagne. "He had," Moorehead ruefully accepted, "liberated the Ritz just an hour before."[38]

CHAPTER THREE

~

Mon Général

In occupied Paris the Germans commandeered some five hundred hotels. Such landmarks as the Majestic in Avenue Kléber, the Lutetia on the Boulevard Raspail, and the Meurice on the Rue de Rivoli became headquarters for major Nazi ministries. Other elegant hotels were set aside as living quarters for high-ranking German officers. The crown jewel among them, the Hôtel Ritz on Place Vendôme, remained open as a fully functioning luxury hotel, though partitioned between leading Nazis and those well-heeled civilians willing to lodge and dine in close proximity.

The Swiss-owned hotel comprised two buildings linked by an interior corridor. The main entrance on Place Vendôme led during the occupation to armed sentries, a kiosk for leaving weapons, and a grand stairway to an exclusively Nazi preserve. A second entrance on a side street on Rue Cambon led to bars, a restaurant, and hotel accommodations open to the public. Leading Nazis came and went as they pleased on the Cambon side but were under orders to appear in civilian dress.

When Hermann Göring, the rotund Luftwaffe commander and Hitler's second in command, came to Paris, he stayed in the Place Vendôme side in an imperial suite spread across an entire floor and took lavish meals in the public restaurant. Joseph Goebbels, Hitler's propaganda chief, spent a night in the hotel before he was summoned back to Berlin. Attired in a stylish business suit, the diminutive Goebbels was proudly photographed stepping from its front door. He had time enough to see some of Paris and was impressed. "A marvelous city,"[1] he remarked. "What a lot we've still got to do to Berlin!"[1]

As the Wehrmacht marched into Paris in 1940, among the last American guests fleeing the Ritz was Clare Boothe Luce, then a journalist writing for her husband's *Life* magazine. With the liberation, among the first Americans checking in was Ernest Hemingway, a forty-five-year-old celebrity war correspondent for *Collier's* magazine. Hemingway came to the war late, left before it was over, and produced just six wartime articles during his months—July 1944 to March 1945—in the European theater. He nonetheless managed to cram into his "Papa Hemingway" life a romance with the correspondent who would become his fourth wife, immersion in military action that led to an official investigation, the self-proclaimed liberation of the Ritz, and up-front presence during some of the bloody fighting on the way from France to the Belgian-German border.

⌣

Hemingway had published no major work since the vast success of his 1940 novel of the Spanish civil war, *For Whom the Bell Tolls*, when he left his home in Cuba for Britain in May 1944. A week after arriving, a nighttime car crash in London left him hospitalized with a serious head injury. In London he later palled about with other correspondents, some of whom, like Robert Capa, he had known while covering the war in Spain for the North American Newspaper Alliance. For *Collier's*, which billed him as their "famed war correspondent," he worked while staying in the Dorchester Hotel in Mayfair at his assigned task of reporting on the dazzling pilots of Britain's RAF. In a letter written afterward, he said that any terrific material he turned up wouldn't be wasted on *Collier's*, though in another letter he at least had the passing thought that his wartime magazine "pieces—with censored parts put back—could make a book if we were broke."[2]

On D-Day, Hemingway secured a place in the cross-channel armada. A transport ship lowered him into a landing craft that brought him close to Omaha Beach before emptying its troops and supplies and returning to the ship. After D-Day he accompanied the RAF on flights over France and harrowing attempts to destroy in-flight German V-1 missiles aimed at British sites.

On July 18 a light plane that ferried correspondents back and forth across the channel brought him to France. As a magazine rather than newspaper man, he had the freedom to follow any military group he chose. He was first attached as a correspondent to General Patton's Third Army, then switched from grinding tank warfare to the American Twenty-Second Infantry Regiment commanded by Colonel Charles "Buck" Lanham. A close bond developed between the two, due in part to Hemingway's admiration for Lanham as a hard-charging military leader and Lanham's own ambition as a writer.

In the hedgerow country beyond the Normandy beaches, Hemingway roamed about largely on his own terms in a jeep driven by Private Archie Pelkey and loaded with rifles, hand grenades, and liberated German maps. Reuters reported on August 3 that Hemingway and his driver had taken six prisoners after first tossing grenades into a house in which the Germans were hunkered down.[3]

Soon thereafter Hemingway went in search of Saint-Pois, a village that was under attack by Lanham's regiment. He was riding in the sidecar of a captured motorcycle with Pelkey driving and followed by a captured Mercedes carrying a public-relations officer and Robert Capa when, rounding a corner, they saw a German tank down the road. Pelkey slammed the brakes, and Hemingway flew from the sidecar into a shallow ditch along the roadside. The others were protected by the curve of the road, but Hemingway was pinned down in his position for two hours until the Germans withdrew. Afterward he turned angrily on Capa, whom he claimed had stood around waiting to photograph the dead body of a famous writer rather than leaving to get help.[4] In a subsequent letter Hemingway said of the incident that he had needed to "pretend to be dead until quite a while later and could hear Germans talking on other side of hedge at about 10 feet."[5]

Due to injuries incurred in the incident, Hemingway left the war for rest and relaxation at Mont-Saint-Michel with a group of correspondents, Capa among them. The ancient monastery rising from sand flats—"this old hang out of Henry Adams," as Hemingway identified it in a letter—had been freed by American forces but was off-limits to all but high officers and correspondents. The correspondents settled into rooms within the Mont in the Hôtel de la Mère Poulard and savored its fine wines and famed omelets. Other newsmen on the outing were Charles Wertenbaker, Charles Collingwood, A. J. Liebling, John Carlisle, Matthew Halton, William Walton, and Ira Wolfert, who had won a Pulitzer Prize for his war coverage in the Pacific. "He had a good time," Liebling said of Hemingway's time at the Mont, "and wrote and recruited his strength for his dash on Paris."[6] Helen Kirkpatrick, the lone woman present, remembered Hemingway as "good company, amusing, dogmatic and holding forth always on strategy and interpreting the next moves."[7]

In his own next moves, Hemingway shed what lingered of his role as a mere war correspondent writing for a weekly magazine. Just after the liberation of Paris he wrote in a letter that he had "not been operateing [sic] by the book and I threw the book away somewhere the other side of Chartres."[8] The book said correspondents could not bear arms. But in Chartres and especially Rambouillet, Hemingway was closely allied with local FFI fighters and operatives of the American Office of Strategic Services (OSS). He bore with him at the time a scrap of paper that announced in block lettering: "This is authority from the CG Dynamite to provide Mr. Ernest Hemingway with small arms, grenades or other captured articles he desires." Major R. L. Norling, an army intelligence officer, signed the message.[9]

In the Hôtel du Grand Veneur in Rambouillet, Hemingway ran a self-designated command center. With the town thought vulnerable to German counterattack, he and a band of fighters—variously identified as guerrillas, a Maquis outfit, and irregulars—conducted patrols in the heavily wooded territory, gathered intelligence about land mines and German gun positions, and interrogated prisoners. Hemingway was in country he knew well from his time in France in the 1920s; he could communicate in English, French, and broken German; and his irregulars took his orders as if coming from an officer. They addressed him over time as *Capitaine, le Colonel,* and *Mon Général.*[10] He in turn found them, as he declared in a letter, "Very fine peoples . . . but temperamental."[11]

When Colonel David Bruce, the chief of the London branch of the OSS and charged with gathering intelligence in the Rambouillet area, came on the scene with other OSS men on August 20, he noted in his war diary that they were "enchanted" to see Hemingway. But the hotel in Rambouillet "was like being in Bedlam. . . . Agents were nipping in and out and everyone . . . was buttonholing me, asking questions and giving the answers at the same time. Newspaper correspondents had sprouted out of the ground, and the world and his wife were eating and uncorking champagne."[12]

Hemingway's room in the hotel was equally chaotic. "Army gear littered the floor," Bruce later recalled. "Carbines stood in each corner, revolvers of every nationality were heaped carelessly on the bed, the bathtub was filled with hand grenades, and the basin with brandy bottles, while under the bed was a cache of Army rations and whisky."[13] In another room Hemingway's irregulars—Bruce put their number at about ten—rushed in and out with reports.

Bruce, who had met Hemingway in Cuba before the war (and in 1949 became the American ambassador to France), joined him on patrols and intelligence gathering and in grilling prisoners. When General Leclerc and his Second Armored appeared in Rambouillet on August 23, what had been learned was passed on to him for use in the drive on Paris. Bruce, who found the French officer "handsome, stern-visaged, and a striking figure," recorded only that Leclerc asked him to give all his information to one of his commanders. Bruce said he did so with the assistance of Hemingway, an FFI leader, and another OSS officer.[14] When Leclerc's force eventually started for Paris, Hemingway carried a note from Bruce telling him to arrange transportation for his irregulars into the city, with Bruce seeing to their reasonable expenses. "I feel that it is important," Bruce stated, "to keep them together to be used for certain future purposes that I have in mind."[15]

Fellow correspondents gathered with Hemingway in Rambouillet had varied views of him. Some were awed by his stature as a fiction writer, his knowledge of military tactics, and his risk taking under fire that at times seemed bordering on madness. Others grumbled that the military allowed him to play professional soldier, appear without his correspondent's insignia, and brazenly go about as a combatant. Anyone else, they contended, would have lost accreditation and been shipped home. And there was concern that Hemingway, given his ties to the military, might have inside access to information sources.

Bruce Grant, a newsman from Chicago, had a personal gripe. When he couldn't get a place in the Rambouillet hotel while Hemingway and his band tied up rooms, he loudly challenged the writer in the dining room. Hemingway responded with raised fists. Another newsman managed to defuse the schoolboy clash, and Hemingway left the room—only to return and demand that Grant come outside and fight. One witness of the scene thought Grant would have been slaughtered by the more physically imposing Hemingway if the fight hadn't been averted again.[16] There were also complaints among correspondents about Hemingway acting as mayor of Rambouillet and that anyone wanting a room in the hotel had to check with him first.[17]

In "How We Came to Paris," the second of two articles about the city written for *Collier's*, Hemingway puts in his jeep driver's words his own clipped assessment of the guerrillas with him on the day of entry. Archie Pelkey says,

> They're a good outfit. Best outfit I ever been with. No discipline. Got to admit that. Drinking all the time. Got to admit that. But plenty fighting outfit. Nobody gives a damn if they get killed or not. Compris?

To which Hemingway answers simply, "Yeah." He can add nothing more because of a welling of emotion that comes at the sight of Paris just ahead: "There now, below us, gray and always beautiful, was spread the city I love best in all the world."[18]

In letters to Buck Lanham and others, Hemingway gave scattered details of the fighting he and the guerillas encountered within Paris and their eventual arrival at the Ritz. Later historians and writers have added more, and varied, information to the legend of Hemingway taking the hotel. David Bruce, presumably the most reliable witness, recorded in his diary that after meeting up in Paris with Hemingway, Pelkey, and some of the irregulars, they jeeped together at high speed down the empty Champs-Élysées to the door of the Travellers Club, a private men's club. All its rooms were closed save for the bar, where the club president and some members toasted with champagne the first Americans to arrive. This was followed by a stop at the Café de la Paix for more drinks before weaving through massive crowds to get to the Ritz.

They found the hotel undamaged and, save for the manager, Claude Auzello, seemingly deserted. So the newcomers, Bruce noted in his diary, "arranged to quarter there as well as take lodging for the Private Army" of Hemingway. When the manager asked what else was needed, he was asked to provide fifty martini cocktails. According to Bruce, the drinks turned out to be poor, since the bartender was missing, but an excellent dinner followed. During the night nearly constant shooting was heard in nearby streets. "The French Forces of the Interior," wrote Bruce, "are well out of hand, and draw on anybody whom they consider suspicious."[19]

Among those at the Ritz dinner mentioned by Bruce was Colonel S. L. A. "Sam" Marshall. A military historian who before the war had been a newsman with the *Detroit Free Press*, Marshall and his driver-escort, Lieutenant John Westover, had been with Hemingway and Pelkey through much of the battling within Paris. In a letter written at the Ritz on August 27, Hemingway said it was fortunate that he had an "official war historian" with him, since otherwise what he said of the fighting on the Rambouillet-to-Paris trek would be dismissed as a "damned lie."[20] Marshall was the historian.

In "When Papa Took Paris," an *American Heritage* magazine article published twenty years after the liberation and later reprinted with slight changes as a chapter with the same title in a memoir called *Bringing Up the Rear*, Marshall gave a freewheeling and no doubt embellished account of how he and Hemingway reached Paris.[21] Near a town in the area of Versailles, the French armor had engaged some German tanks. Hemingway and Pelkey took shelter inside a bombed-out café, where they found Marshall, Westover, and a young Spanish girl named Elena who was searching for her lover among the FFI fighters. Marshall and Hemingway had met years before in Florida, so Hemingway immediately called out, "Marshall, for God's sake, have you got a drink?" Marshall didn't, but Westover remembered a bottle of Scotch stowed in their jeep. For the rest of the way into Paris, Elena jeeped with Marshall and Westover.

With Leclerc's force moving again, Hemingway's jeep was followed, in Marshall's account, by a "long line of Renault sedans, taxis, jalopies, and trucks, all of them crammed with Task Force Hemingway's fighters, now numbering more than 200."[22] Leclerc would find more pockets of resistance from Germans left behind and, along with the jeep riders, pass perilously close to a burning enemy ammunition dump with exploding shells and flying metal within the intense heat.

"Where the dump ended," Marshall recorded, "the metropolitan city began. We were soon among houses and stores and banking both sides of that broad, lovely avenue were the people—and what a people!"[23] With ecstatic crowds pressing on them all manner of drink, progress for tanks and vehicles was slow and at times impossible. Hemingway, Marshall, and others had to spend the night of the 24th in a building still short of the Seine at Pont de Sèvres. They wouldn't cross the river until noon the next day.

They hadn't ventured far into the carnival frenzy of liberation day when the French column came to a halt in Place St. Cloud. Rifle fire from a building and an artillery shell from some unknown location took down a large tree on the parkway. Hemingway leaped from his jeep and ran toward the building. Westover left Marshall and with his carbine took a firing position behind the downed tree. French tanks and half-tracks sent rounds of machine-gun bullets into the building, then backed off, and in the silence a man's voice was heard. He was shouting in French from a crouched position on the third-floor balcony of a building across the Place. It was Hemingway, as Marshall and Westover recognized, yelling to all below that there were Germans in the building behind them and that everyone had to get away because the French were calling in artillery to topple the building. While people fled, Hemingway covered their escape with his carbine.

Near the Arc de Triomphe and Avenue Foch, Marshall and Westover stopped an angry crowd from cutting the hair of a woman considered overly friendly with the Germans. Then they had a tussle with a French major, who after spotting Elena in the jeep cried out, "Get these ___ women out of the vehicles." After Marshall told the major off loudly and profanely, Hemingway roared, "You tell 'em, Marshall. Since when hasn't a soldier the right to company in his sleeping bag?" Elena took the exchange as a suitable moment to take her leave. "Without a word," said Marshall, "she slipped away to seek her lover, and we never saw her again."[24]

~

At the Ritz that night, Hemingway held sway at a dinner with a group of military officers, Marshall, Bruce, and Westover among them. During the meal Marshall and Westover told of being denied rooms earlier at the Claridge. "What could you expect?" responded Charles Ritz, the scion of the hotel family. "Hotel men have no country. They're the only true internationalists." Recalling the remark led Marshall to add that on liberation day Charles Ritz "was waiting there with Dunhill pipes as souvenirs for each of us when we made the Ritz lobby, slightly ahead of Papa [Hemingway]."[25] Marshall was already having a drink in the Ritz when Westover came and told him, "Ernest is here, just came in. Imagine, this morning I was just a lieutenant of artillery and tonight I introduce Hemingway to Ritz of the Ritz."[26]

CHAPTER FOUR

~

PROs Move In

Joined with correspondents heading to Paris were SHAEF PROs operating on military orders. Lieutenant Colonel Jack Redding and Major James Quirk were told to organize a convoy of communications equipment as part of a task force destined for Paris. Their assembly point was a grand chateau in Normandy, some sixty miles distant, where they were quietly enjoying themselves until news came that the German garrison in the city was about to surrender. The two officers immediately set off in a jeep ahead of their slow-moving convoy of vans with radio equipment and trucks holding army rations and gasoline. Their mission was to proceed as rapidly as possible to the Hôtel Scribe.

Redding, a former newspaperman in Chicago and then an officer in the Air Corps, had been sent from North Africa to the United States in 1943 to create a public-relations group to work in Britain before D-Day. The preferred choices were men with experience in areas of communications who also had military training. Once assembled in the UK, Redding put the original group of some twenty-five through a boot camp to harden them for working with correspondents in whatever awaited on the Continent.[1] Barney Oldfield, one of the group members, said Redding's manner was that of a "long-term top sergeant suddenly commissioned as an officer." He added that Redding "had a ferocious scowl, which he wore in various styles for various occasions. The one for mornings could curdle cream."[2]

Redding was also an active author. In 1943 he cowrote with Captain Harold Leyshon, a fellow PRO, *Skyways to Berlin*, a factual account of American bomber pilots stationed in Britain. An action novel, *Wake of Glory*, cowritten with his PRO colleague Lieutenant Colonel Thor Smith—like Redding an air force PRO before joining SHAEF—and once again featuring American bomber crews in the UK, appeared in the United States late in 1944.

James Quirk had risen in the ranks of radio broadcasting to become a program director in his native Philadelphia when, shortly after Pearl Harbor, he joined the army. He was a captain based in Washington when he was posted to North Africa in 1943 as a staff officer. At the start of 1944 he was in Britain and was now attached to SHAEF's PRD. Shortly after D-Day he reached France and, a newly minted major, began work as a public-relations officer.[3]

Tall, slender, and bespectacled, Quirk was obviously adept at weathering whatever professional storms came his way. He would eventually hold lead PRO positions with General Omar Bradley's First Army and General George Patton's Third Army. Barney Oldfield classified public relations as hazardous duty given that its officers were positioned between military superiors and the war correspondents. He noted that when PROs were sacked, it was typically due to grievances by newsmen rather than superiors. Yet from whatever direction protests came, Oldfield wrote that all PROs knew they "were there to be sacrificed if the going gets rough." So there was "nothing too disgraceful about being pulled off a public-relations job." Quirk illustrated Oldfield's point. "Major Quirk, in fact, was given several public-relations lives," he wrote, "and made good on all the others."[4]

In the area of Chartres, Redding and Quirk caught up with the French armored division and jeeped on to Rambouillet. An inveterate writer of long, literate letters home to his wife (which he hoped might later form a booklet for their son), Quirk told her that "every press vehicle in the American armies" was already crammed into the town. This made him realize that there was public-relations work to perform there before Paris. Redding and Quirk got rooms in the local hotel, set up a writing area in its bar and restaurant, and found couriers and light planes to carry press material back to transmission points. The correspondents, Quirk remarked, occupied their time turning out feature stories while complaining that, the hotel's liquor supply extinguished, they were left with nothing but *vin ordinaire*.[5]

While quick to record heavy drinking by newsmen, Quirk didn't spare himself. "The day began very peacefully," he wrote his wife from Rambouillet. "I got up with the usual hangover. . . . All of us drink too much because wine is plentiful and cheap." In another letter he said, "We have all been drinking much too much and I am going to take a day or two off to dealcoholize myself. After wines and champagne I have lost my taste for whiskey and just don't like it any more."

When on August 25 the French force began motoring to Paris, Redding and Quirk learned through intelligence that they probably that day would get only as far as Longjumeau, some eleven miles from central Paris. They decided to split up, and Quirk and William Drake, a PRO with the Third Army, went ahead with their jeep drivers to get billets for themselves and correspondents in the town. They took a route they thought free of Germans and drove rapidly, believing they were on the same path as the French troops until they came upon American MPs directing traffic and realized they were following the American Fourth Division.

In Longjumeau, Quirk and Drake found a regiment of the Fourth preparing to enter Paris. Out front of a blacksmith shop on the town's main street, the PROs placed a press bag on a chair as an improvised copy room so correspondents could drop off dispatches they were turning out on the hoods of jeeps. They also learned that some of the regiment was heading into Paris immediately and would rendezvous at Notre Dame on the Île de la Cité. Quirk chose to leave Drake with the copy bag and join a colleague, the PRO of the Fourth Army, on the move into Paris.

Quirk was concerned about the whereabouts of the convoy he and Redding had formed, but he made a pact with his current jeep mate to deliver him to Paris and then go back to Longjumeau to direct the convoy when it arrived. As the regiment rolled on toward Porte d'Italie, they passed shuttered shops and littered German vehicles but few people. Suddenly, as Quirk wrote, "we could see a great section of the city of Paris lying in the saucer of the Seine below us. The Eiffel Tower stood out above everything and we seemed to be about on a level with it looking down on the city." At about this point Quirk's jeep was joined by two others carrying correspondents: Mark Watson of the *Baltimore Sun*, H. R. Knickerbocker of the *Chicago Sun*, Ivan H. Peterman of the *Philadelphia Inquirer*, and Thomas Wolfe of the Newspaper Enterprise Association.

At nearly the same time, a car with three FFI members appeared, and after conversation in French with Watson as interpreter, the fighters said they would lead the way to Notre Dame. Germans were all around, but fighters were confident about driving straight ahead through Porte d'Italie. Soon the new grouping came upon the first Resistance barricades they had seen— paving stones, iron bedsteads, radiators, and felled trees thrown across the road meant to cripple German movement. Similar barriers would block nearly every street the rest of the way into the city. As troops tore apart the first obstacle, people began to emerge and celebrate the presence of the

American army. The hugs, kisses, and thrusts of flowers, bread, and wine into the jeeps and cars began. When the stalled procession could move again, they could hear shooting, but nothing that seemed dangerous enough to hold them back.

The military mission halted at Notre Dame, but Quirk's party went ahead on the island before stopping. An old gentleman appeared with a bottle of champagne he had saved for four years, and they savored it in the street. But firing in the area was now heavy, and most of the cheering crowd had scattered. Since Quirk's goal was to get to the Scribe, he wanted to keep moving, but FFI members told him it wasn't possible because the Germans were still active in the area. Quirk and the Fourth Army PRO decided to try anyway.

As Quirk framed it in a letter, they "picked up an FFI joe as a guide" and pushed ahead in their jeep. After trying two routes and encountering repeated rifle and machine-gun fire, they changed their minds. The other PRO had to go back to his military group, so Quirk rejoined the correspondents, now reduced to Watson, Peterman, and Knickerbocker. Accepting that he had no choice but to wait for troops or the FFI to clear away Germans from the Scribe, Quirk and the others parked in the shadow of the Tour Saint-Jacques and, as Quick wrote, "just stood around letting the French admire us."

Meanwhile, Knickerbocker went searching for an apartment he had abandoned in 1940. When he returned he said the apartment was untouched and suggested they gather there. On the way two other correspondents, Robert Casey and Ira Wolfert, joined the band. The apartment, ideally located on the Seine on Île Saint-Louis, was in perfect condition. When the concierge and remaining tenants of the building appeared and champagne was popped, a story emerged that Knickerbocker's Danish housekeeper had been on close terms with the Gestapo, which explained the flat's fine appearance. The housekeeper was now held somewhere by the FFI.

While the correspondents wrote stories that Quirk promised to get to transmission somewhere, he visited Knickerbocker's upstairs neighbor, Donald Liddell, a widely known collector of chessmen and author of a book on the subject. While shots rang out and fires burned, Quirk was calmly shown the collection, Liddell inscribed for him a copy of his book, and they sipped champagne. "It seems fantastic now," Quirk told his wife, "but it's true." Back in Knickerbocker's flat, Quirk picked up the correspondents' copy and decided to make a last try to reach the Scribe. He found two FFI members who believed they could get him there, and with his jeep driver and the fighters they set off, speeding as fast as possible while the FFI wildly signaled directions and bullets flew around them. "Quite suddenly," Quirk said, "we arrived at the Hotel Scribe."

He rushed inside and informed the manager that he was requisitioning the hotel, that he wanted two of its best suites held for himself and Jack Redding, and that correspondents and PROs would soon fill its other 250 rooms. The manager told him that Germans had breakfasted in the hotel before leaving. If the manager said anything about the prior presence of Canadians or about their turning over the Scribe to Redding and the Americans after the first wave of correspondents arrived, Quirk failed to record it. His reticence is part of the general silence among SHAEF's PRD officials and correspondents, with the exception of Canadian newsmen, about any Allied presence other than Americans in the hotel after the Germans fled.

Some two hours after Quirk arrived, correspondents and PROs began straggling into the Scribe. Quirk saw to billeting them, set up a temporary copy room in the bar where newsmen simultaneously wrote dispatches and drank, and tried to get a courier service underway. He worried about the whereabouts of his convoy of supplies—it wouldn't arrive until the following morning—but had to get on with what was at hand. When he briefly stepped from the hotel to see what was happening in the street, he couldn't get back inside for thirty minutes. People kissed and clutched him. After he fought his way in, he ordered the FFI men still with him to stay outside and allow only military figures and correspondents to enter.

By Quirk's count, during that day and night two hundred correspondents entered the hotel. New PROs were put to work the moment they appeared. It seemed to Quirk that all the whores in Paris had also arrived and were actively practicing their trade. By midnight he believed all copy had been cleared by censors and moved by couriers. Exhausted, he climbed to his suite but slept badly due to continuous shooting in the streets. Sometime during the night he was awakened by Redding's appearance. After Quirk told him everything was under control, he too took to bed. The nighttime mention of Redding marks his initial appearance in Quirk's account of taking over the Scribe during the liberation.

Throughout the next day, August 26, Quirk found the Scribe an ongoing madhouse:

> Correspondents were dashing in and out, everyone with a hair raising story, the bar was running like a Klondike saloon, and the place was overrun with women. The Colonel [presumably Redding] ordered the hotel cleared of

women and the FFI did the job for us. In the evening we made a check of the identity cards in the bar amid the bitter protests of the correspondents. They all insisted that the little girl was either a very old Parisian friend or a former fiancée. Of the first ten girls checked, seven had yellow tickets with the overprint of the German army on them. They were prostitutes from Wehrmacht bordellos. That news tended to slow the men down a little.

Quirk was too occupied in the Scribe to witness General de Gaulle's parade to Notre Dame on day two of the liberation but became involved in firing near the hotel. He was in the lobby in mid-afternoon when the action began. Outside he found American troops crouched behind jeeps and firing toward roofs across from the hotel. He instructed a sergeant and six men to get to the roofs and investigate while the French still crowding the area huddled in doorways.

When a machine gun opened up on the Boulevard des Capucines, he went with two men to investigate and found four FFI gunmen firing down the length of the street at Germans they thought they spotted on roofs. A rifle then discharged right beside him, and he found four more FFIs shooting in the opposite direction down the boulevard. It was all good French opéra bouffe, Quirk decided, and went back with American troops until the firing subsided. The battle toll for the day was some wounded French civilians and several Scribe windows struck with bullets.

⌒

Quirk had left the Scribe and was following the war in France as a PRO when he told his wife he had been approved for a Bronze Star for "the Paris action." He had mentioned the possibility of the medal earlier but questioned whether it would actually come about. Now he asked his wife not to mention the award because nothing could still come of it.

General Bradley awarded him the medal in late October 1944—Quirk at the time was Bradley's temporary lead PRO—in a small ceremony in his office at his field headquarters in northern France. Bradley read out the award's citation, pinned the medal on Quirk's field jacket, and said, "That was a very fine job. Very fine. Congratulations." As later forwarded to his wife, the citation read in part,

While the City of Paris was still under control of German forces, Major Quirk personally proceeded in advance of the main party of the "T" Force, Twelfth Army Group, in an effort to reconnoiter a convenient route and to establish a press headquarters in the City of Paris. On several occasions he was compelled to turn back by intense enemy fire. However, on the afternoon of August 25, 1944, he succeeded in enlisting the services of members of the French Forces of the Interior and was able to reach the Hotel Scribe and establish headquarters there while there was fighting still going on in the streets.

⌒

"Every individual you talk with has a fascinating story to tell," Lieutenant Colonel Thor Smith remarked,[6] "of his personal experiences in getting into Paris." His own story differed substantially from James Quirk's, though like Quirk he regularly chronicled it in letters home to his wife, an Associated Press bureau chief in Reno, Nevada. Before joining the army in 1942, Smith worked as an advertising and promotion manager for newspapers in several cities, with the *San Francisco Call-Bulletin* the most recent. Following D-Day, he moved from a posting in Britain to France as a SHAEF PRO attached to General Eisenhower's advance headquarters.

His entry into Paris began on the day after the liberation when he and a group of four pool correspondents—among them Merrill Mueller of NBC and Howard Cowan of the AP—accompanied the supreme commander on a tour of what was known as the Falaise Pocket, a decisive Allied battleground in Normandy. Later that day they stopped at General Bradley's advanced headquarters and, Bradley absent, there was talk of Eisenhower going into Paris. Thor Smith believed he was looking for an excuse to do so despite the fighting in the streets. "And so it was decided," Smith wrote, "that we (four correspondents, two photographers, and myself) would go in, check in with the HQ there for message from the General if it was decided that he was coming in."[7]

The group examined maps, loaded pistols and carbines in a command car, and set off for Paris, weaving around troops moving up. At one point, Air Chief Marshal Tedder, Eisenhower's deputy commander, passed them. He was going to the city to see it for himself. They followed Tedder's car, proceeding by way of Versailles and through areas dense with applauding crowds. "We had the feeling," wrote Smith, "that we personally had captured Paris single-handed."

It was getting dark when they reached the city center, and, needing a place to stay, they picked the Ritz. They took three rooms, and Smith logged the miniscule cost: "The three rooms cost us the grand sum of 235 francs . . . $4.70." Dinner with champagne, on the other hand, was "frightfully expensive." Smith noted that "German officers had been living there and eating there 48 hours earlier." He shared a room with Merrill Mueller, who had once worked with the International News Service bureau in Paris and spoke French, which was helpful since Smith didn't. But the PRO wasn't enamored of the correspondent, whom he described as "the type that thinks that the whole PR set-up stinks, and tells everyone in no uncertain terms." But Smith acknowledged that his having to deal daily with Mueller and the three other correspondents in the pool was nothing compared with other PROs "with some 200 of them on their necks."

That night Smith went to press headquarters at the Scribe. He took note of Jack Redding's presence but made no mention of James Quirk. As for newsmen in the hotel, he believed that "90% of the correspondents in France were there, most of them drunk and on the loose." Smith's overall account of the hotel mirrored Quirk's chaos-laced portrait, minus only the heavy presence of Parisian ladies of the night:

> PR was just unable to cope with the mob [of correspondents and others] that went in on one pretext or another. Everyone wanted transportation, of which there was little. The messing was catch-as-catch-can. The copy had to be taken by courier for great distances before it could even be filed. Nerves were rubbed raw . . . everyone fighting with each other, shouting at each other, doing everything possible to chisel and cut corners on one of the terrific stories of this war, or any war. And the combination of trying to play and get drunk and still work was too much for most of them. . . . The censors were ragged-eyed . . . most of them having had about four hours sleep in three days.

The following day, after a breakfast of rations at the Ritz, Smith and Mueller went to a tentative headquarters in Paris to see if there were messages from Eisenhower and found the general himself there. He had been in Paris for a half hour but hadn't yet gone about. So what Smith called a procession of ten vehicles was formed, with Eisenhower in a sedan, and including French generals Leclerc and Pierre Koenig, American generals Bradley and Leonard Gerow, and Britain's Tedder. They toured celebrated areas of the city and, among milling crowds at the Arc de Triomphe, stopped for picture taking before driving down the Champs-Élysées to the Place de la Concorde. At this point the procession ended, and Smith informed Eisenhower that, for security reasons, he would put a two-hour embargo on news of the commander's day of seeing Paris.

For the time being, the day was also Smith's last in Paris. When he returned to Eisenhower's headquarters he spent the evening with him talking over reactions to the city and feelings about France. He informed his wife, "It was a fascinating evening. . . . It was all 'off the record,' but talk about history in the making! What a privilege!" Soon thereafter Smith would accompany Eisenhower to the UK for a major news conference. A short time later he went home for a family visit before returning to Paris and beginning a long period of service as a top-level PRO at the Scribe.

PART II

STAYING

The first ones in the city to stay were such nonfighters as the psycho-logical-warfare and civil-affairs people, public-relations men and cor-respondents.

—Ernie Pyle, Scripps-Howard newspapers

CHAPTER FIVE

~

Liberation Revels

Don Whitehead thought day two of the liberation at least matched day one. "And this day is just as fantastic," he claimed for August 26 in an AP dispatch, "as those hours of last evening, when the millions of Paris swarmed through the streets in a carnival of celebration of their long-awaited liberation." Adding to his personal pleasure was the fact that in the Scribe that evening the "electric lights still were on and there was running water."[1]

Edward Beattie of the UP, who had worked for the wire service in Berlin before the war, strained for imagery to describe a second day that seemed even better than the first. "Describing Paris today," he wrote in his story's lead, "is like trying to paint a desert sunset in black and white." "Yesterday's celebration," he went on, "was quite frankly nothing compared with today's, when the whole city was in the streets, mobbing every Allied soldier, French, British or American, who dared show his face outside his hotel." The still-festive city contrasted vividly with the "dark blotch" of German prisoners held in the Hôtel Majestic. Some of them, Beattie noted, had been put to work cleaning the officers' mess in the dining room, where German black bread remained on tables.[2] (After returning to combat reporting, Beattie was one of three American newsmen captured and held in Germany until shortly before the war ended. When he suddenly reappeared at the Scribe, thin but in good health, a spirited reunion broke out among the correspondent corps.[3])

For Ralph Allen, a correspondent with Toronto's *Globe and Mail*, portraying day two required clashing images. "Paris today is Betty Grable on a bicycle and Billy the Kid on a bender. Paris is the Mona Lisa in a jeep and Francois Villon behind a Sten gun. . . . Paris today was partly itself at its best, partly Deadwood Gulch at its worst and partly Strauss' Vienna at its most improbable." On liberation night Allen had found a room in a small hotel in Montparnasse, then the following day shifted to what he felt was "a sinfully luxurious suite" at the Ritz. While he typed his dispatch, bullets were splattering the walls of the courtyard. There was nothing to do about the gunfire in the city, he decided, but ignore it. The last "incipient movie actress" who had kissed him in the streets had said, "Why let a little shooting spoil a day like this?"[4]

For Andy Rooney, liberation revels lasted three days. "I had never been to Paris," he wrote, "and I was unaware that I was about to experience three of the most eventful days of an eventful life. It's better if you don't know you're going to be in on history."[5] The drafted army sergeant covering the war for *Stars and Stripes* had joined Leclerc's force heading to Paris, wedged between two Sherman tanks, and proudly documented that correspondents with the French entered it more than an hour before those following American troops.

Rooney's notes on the early hours of liberation day had the same festive details as those of other reporters, as well as grim scenes of revenge. He saw a Frenchman smash a wine bottle over the head of a captured German with hands clasped above his head. French troops dragged the bloody and possibly dead man to a truck and threw him inside. He also saw French women who had consorted with the Germans forced into the street and their hair chopped off while crowds jeered crudely. The action struck Rooney as amounting to a lynching.

With his notebook entries worked into a news story, Rooney's next step was getting it to a *Stars and Stripes* printing facility in Rennes. He had visions of the story played across the front page of the newspaper the next morning, if he transmitted it in time. He left a copy at a French information center in Paris that would try to get it to wireless facilities in Rambouillet. While at the center he met an American pilot who was ferrying documents from various fronts to rear headquarters. The pilot said he was going to Rennes within an hour and would try to deliver the story. So Rooney entrusted a copy to him as well.

Later he learned that the story left with the French had vanished and the pilot had gone down with engine trouble shortly after leaving Paris. The page-one account *Stars and Stripes* carried was by a reporter who had reached Paris with the Fourth Infantry well behind Rooney. His own liberation story that never saw print, he maintained for long thereafter, was the most disappointing event in his three years as a war correspondent.

Before entering the Scribe on liberation day, Rooney encountered Larry LeSueur and was asked to do a short eyewitness account for CBS radio of what he had seen that morning. Rooney readily agreed. The three-minute radio report faintly foreshadowed his long postwar career with the network.

At the Scribe, the PRO in charge, Jack Redding, denied Rooney a room on the grounds he was a soldier reporter rather than a civilian newsman. The refusal became another Paris disappointment that clung to him. The inconvenience of getting to the hotel in subsequent days for its press facilities—and its bar where he was allowed to mix with colleagues—made the loss all the more annoying.

Rooney found lodging with other *Stars and Stripes* men in the Hôtel Haussmann, and after about ten days in Paris he left to follow the war. "The next press camp after the Scribe Hotel in Paris," he recalled, "from which I had been excluded, was in Spa, Belgium, where I was finally just one of the guys again."[6]

The centerpiece of day two of the liberation was Charles de Gaulle's hastily organized parade from one Parisian shrine to another. A small number of American and British officers observed the festivities, but American troops were kept elsewhere. The US commander in Paris, General Gerow, had opposed the parade out of concern that German or pro-German fighters might fire on the French troops.[7] But the French were insistent. "The parade was very much a French event," a historian would write, "and deliberately so. De Gaulle wanted to use the parade to demonstrate and cement his importance and to show that French unity and power had been restored."[8]

In mid-afternoon de Gaulle appeared at the Arc de Triomphe and relit the flame over the Tomb of the Unknown Soldier, shut off during German rule. He then set off in ideal weather to Notre Dame Cathedral. Preceded by police cars and four tanks of Leclerc's armored division, and accompanied by other French generals and civilian leaders along with the remainder of the tank force and FFI members, he strode down the Champs-Élysées, a towering stiff-backed figure amid a jubilant crowd said to have numbered more than a million people, nearly all arriving on foot or by bicycle.

Just after the French leader entered an open car in the Place de la Concorde for the rest of the short distance to the cathedral, shooting broke out from what seemed to be either the Hôtel Crillon or the American embassy beside it. Onlookers scattered to find cover, and nearby French tanks began blasting away at the hotel. De Gaulle acted as if he hadn't heard the shooting—which resulted in the deaths of a half dozen or more people—and went on by car to Notre Dame.[9]

As he entered the cathedral, more shooting erupted. Police and FFI men responded with fire directed at the upper recesses of the building. Chunks of masonry fell, causing people in the congregation to flatten themselves behind pillars or under chairs. Alan Moorehead, who was within the cathedral, wrote that when some officers tried to drag de Gaulle behind the pillars, he shrugged them off and walked rigidly to the altar where a religious service of thanksgiving was to take place.

Robert Reid of the BBC was in position in the cathedral with his equipment to capture the event. His recording of shots and screams and his running commentary drew wide interest when, after a delay during which censors at the Scribe were reluctant to pass a story that might indicate an attempt was made on de Gaulle's life, it was broadcast in London on the BBC and rebroadcast in the United States on NBC and CBS.

Helen Kirkpatrick intended to cover de Gaulle's procession at the Arc de Triomphe starting point. But when blocked from seeing anything by the crowds, she moved to Notre Dame and joined Reid in the cathedral. Together they witnessed the shooting, the falling masonry, and the shortened service. Kirkpatrick wrote that when the service concluded the French officers departed as if nothing out of the ordinary had occurred. General Koenig, de Gaulle's pick for military governor of Paris, passed near her on an aisle and, "smiling, leaned across and shook my hand. I fell in behind them and watched them walk deliberately out to their cars. A machine gun was still blazing from a nearby roof. Once outside, one could hear shooting all along the Seine."[10]

Assault of another sort ended the day. Sometime after 11 p.m., air-raid sirens wailed as the Luftwaffe bombed Paris in a random revenge attack. David Bruce, who had gone to bed early in the Ritz since it lacked electricity, noted in his diary that "people were shooting at the airplanes with pistols, rifles, and machine guns." He added that "at five o'clock another small flight of bombers came over and the performance was repeated."[11]

James Quirk was asleep in his Scribe suite when the attack began. He admitted that it frightened him more than the blitz in London or being strafed in France. He assumed the Germans believed, as it seemed to him all Parisians did, that the Scribe at the moment was the American headquarters in Paris. When he and other PROs went into the street to disperse their vehicles, the planes seemed to be coming in at rooftop levels, bombing and strafing at will. Back in the hotel, the PROs found men in pajamas and thinly dressed women huddling together in the upper corridors. "I felt sorry," Quick remarked, "for a guy caught like that in an air raid."[12]

The following morning revealed heavy damage to a hospital and ware-houses. Later reports said that as many as two hundred people were killed in the attack and some nine hundred injured.[13]

⌐

Ernie Pyle thought the second day of liberation was unlike the first because "it was a deliberate holiday. It was a festival prepared for and gone into on purpose. You could tell that the women had prettied up especially. The old men had on their old medals, and the children were scrubbed and Sunday-dressed until they hurt. And then everybody came downtown."[14]

Pyle had crossed into Paris on liberation day, but it took him another day to reach the Scribe. Of all American correspondents, the small, wiry, self-effacing newsman was the best known to readers back in the United States. With their down-home manner—or as A. J. Liebling called it, their "highly emphasized simplicity"[15]—and their focus on GIs and himself more than generals, his six-day-a-week columns were circulated to hundreds of news-papers throughout the country by the Scripps-Howard chain. Prior to the Normandy invasion, Pyle had won a Pulitzer Prize for war correspondence. A month before the liberation of Paris he was on the cover of *Time* magazine.

In the eyes of fellow correspondents he was equally popular. Andy Rooney said that in press camps set up in France before the Scribe, the tent near-est the local château always held the same eminent correspondents: Hal Boyle of the AP, Henry Gorrell of the UP, John Thompson of the *Chicago Tribune*, William Stoneman of the *Chicago Daily News*, and Bert Brandt of Acme Newspictures, with Pyle holding sway as the den mother.[16] It no doubt helped that, as a feature writer, Pyle wasn't competing with his tent mates for insider positions or news scoops.

In Rambouillet, Pyle was holed up for days with other newsmen before the trek into Paris. "The streets were lined as by Fourth of July parade crowds at home," he wrote of the scene, "only this crowd was almost hysterical." He and three companions were swamped by the human traffic and "hugged and kissed and torn at. Everybody, even beautiful girls, insisted on kissing you on both cheeks."

Machine-gun fire and the whine of shells overhead gave Pyle and his jeep mates second thoughts about continuing on, but they told themselves they were safe as long as the crowds remained. They had been in Paris an hour and were near the Seine when they encountered firing from unseen sources. Their response was to find a hotel room and, in Pyle's words, decide "to write while the others fought."[17]

At the Scribe the next day, Pyle was billeted across the street at the Grand. In the Scribe's bar he became, as Walter Cronkite wrote, the "magnet of the moment" among admiring newsmen.[18] But it was the view from his room's balcony of women embracing every American soldier in sight that caused Pyle to utter to companions his oft-quoted liberation remark that "Any GI who doesn't get laid tonight is a sissy."[19]

Walter Cronkite missed the liberation. As a young United Press correspondent stationed in Britain, he was scheduled to make a parachute drop during an airborne mission to land troops in the Rambouillet Forest and then make a surprise entry into Paris before French and American forces arrived. Men were already aboard planes, faces darkened, when it was learned that rapid-moving ground forces were already nearing the French capital. The mission was finally scrubbed on August 19. Had it gone forward, Cronkite and a fellow correspondent, William Boni of the AP, might have been the first American newsmen entering Paris while it was still in German hands.[20]

It was the end of September before Cronkite got to Paris for a weekend, staying at the Hôtel Edouard VII in the Opéra area and drinking and dining at the Scribe. The hotel's food, he observed in a letter home, was the usual army rations, yet it wasn't "too bad and you don't quite starve to death if you eat there regularly."[21] As for the Scribe's bar, he later passed along an Ernie Pyle–Ernest Hemingway story. One evening Hemingway found a sizeable group surrounding Pyle at one end of the bar, while he was left unattended at the far end. Finally he banged on the bar to summon the bartender. "Let's have a drink here," he commanded. "I'm Ernest Hemorrhoid, the rich man's Ernie Pyle."[22]

John Groth got to the Scribe on the evening of day two and, like Pyle, was housed with the overflow of correspondents in the Grand. In the morning, swarms surrounded everyone leaving the hotel, giving Groth a sense of what it was like being a Broadway or Hollywood star. Crossing the street to the Scribe took minutes. Exiting the building's front door was the same crushing experience. "If you put your hand into your pocket," Groth wrote, "people thrust francs upon you; if you opened your lips, someone kissed you. It took courage just to go into the street. We drew deep breaths every time we stepped out of our happiness-proof shelter, the Hôtel Scribe."[23]

Groth established a routine of eating lunch each day with correspondents in the Scribe's mess but otherwise toured about Paris with a renewed enthusiasm for art. In Montparnasse he was acclaimed as the first American artist to reappear in the quarter. When he told French artists that he stayed at the

Photo 5.1.   Massed onlookers among VIP sedans outside the Scribe.
Source: National Archives

Grand, they insisted he move to the left bank with them. They flocked to find him a studio and soon located a large and ornate one that had belonged to a Dutch businessman who fled with the occupation. Eventually Groth had studios in the Grand, Montparnasse, and a hotel in Versailles where the Ninth Air Force, with which he was attached, had its headquarters. When sketching outdoors, people wanting to touch an American immediately pawed him. A better way to work was to stand on the seat of a jeep with his sketchpad.

A high point of his Paris art period was a day spent with Pablo Picasso. Groth believed he was the first American artist to visit the painter's studios in a former monastery in Rue des Grands-Augustins. Picasso told him he had spent the occupation painting, and the walls of his studio were stacked with canvases six or seven deep. Tacked to walls were drawings done just the day before. He showed Groth another studio where he worked on sculptures and a print room.

In yet another room Groth watched Picasso make a drawing that would appear in a book artists meant to present to de Gaulle. While he worked on his contribution, the Spaniard moved around as if he were a bullfighter, viewing it from various angles, including standing on a chair to see it from above. At times a phone in the studio rang, and while talking on it in lively fashion the artist kept studying his drawing. While Picasso worked, Groth sketched him, dating his work August 29, 1944.[24] In turn, Picasso turned out a small sketch of Groth in profile. An exchange of sketches wasn't part of the visit, though Groth naturally wished it had been.

~

When Iris Carpenter, a British journalist reporting for the *Boston Globe*, was released from confinement in Rennes, she followed trucks with British drivers bringing sacks of white flour to hungry Paris. The roads were thronged with exuberant masses. In the area of Versailles one of the sacks fell off and burst open. At once onlookers were knocked down by a stamped of people scooping up the flour with any means at hand.

At the Scribe, Carpenter found still in full force what she called "the greatest party of all time. Champagne corks popped with the monotony of a machine-gun barrage and there was a flow of newcomers arriving from various fronts." One of the new men, Paul Bewsher of London's *Daily Mail*, had just come from Rome. He regaled the bar with tales of his patched-together travel by plane and jeep—and of finding a lost overcoat. He had stayed at the Scribe in 1940 and left the coat behind when the Germans entered. In the lobby the hotel's manager had just informed him that he had the coat. Bewsher said to all in the bar who would listen, "I call that jolly good management, don't you?"[25]

In her reporting in Paris, Carpenter joined an FFI group for a different sort of party, one she called nocturnal "Hun hunting." Resistance fighters were searching for Germans who spoke French, dressed as civilians, and continued rooftop combat well after the liberation. Carpenter's group had ten men, but the commander insisted on two more to guard her. The manhunt began in the Montmartre area with a good meal in a small café followed by hurtling car rides and then rushes into houses and up stairways and across roofs.

While on lofty levels, one of Carpenter's guides told her to look only straight ahead, never down, and she would be OK. As it turned out, the worst moment of the night of climbing was her embarrassment while traversing a bedroom when a Frenchman exclaimed, "By God, is there no sanctuary?"

The raid snared no Germans but arrested two youths who were wearing FFI armbands in order to loot and intimidate. The commander said that controlling possession of the armbands was more difficult than the earlier need to stay beyond the reach of the Gestapo. Everyone on the raid got back to FFI headquarters unharmed, though Carpenter discovered that after censorship at the Scribe her report of the night wasn't as fortunate.[26]

She also felt that censorship made it difficult to fully report on the impressive victory march on August 27 of American troops through central Paris. The men, spruced up with fresh uniforms but in full battle gear, were both a parade passing before an applauding populace and a military force moving to a front just beyond Paris. "The head of the parade," wrote Carpenter, "was entering the battle area almost before the tail had passed the reviewing stand, with the Arc de Triomphe in the background in the scene which is now so familiar on the special issue of the three-cent stamps."

Blue pencils at the Scribe, she discovered, would allow no indication that the parade depended on the tactical need of the troops passing through the city to carry on the war while also making the point to Parisians that, rather than Resistance fighters, Allied arms had freed the city.[27] Later, Irwin Shaw, recalling the absence of music during the parade, noted that the troops "were all going to fight that night at Saint-Denis and they had no time for bands."[28]

〜

For some correspondents the liberation of Paris effectively meant the war was over. John Groth proclaimed, "After Paris, home!" And added, "Each correspondent's breast was bursting with the excitement of thoughts like 'I'll get to Paris first, I'll file my story, I'll go home.'"[29] Yet after some time in Paris, Groth followed the war. His next press camp after the Scribe was a Ninth Air Force facility in a school in Verdun. Thereafter he crossed the Elbe, met Russian troops, and saw ruined Berlin.

Some newsmen—burned out by the war, feeling they had covered it enough, wanting to write books rather than dispatches—did go home after the liberation. Ernie Pyle was a notable leaver. While still in Paris he wrote in letter, "I can't take any more war—at least not now. . . . I'd give a fortune right now never to have to write another column. . . . I'm so indifferent to everything I don't even give a damn that I'm in Paris."[30] After a short period in the city, he left for Britain and then the United States. (Pyle eventually returned to war reporting in the Pacific and was killed by enemy fire on an island near Okinawa in April 1945.)

Though he was never indifferent to Paris and stayed longer after the liberation, A. J. Liebling joined Pyle in heading home. He first knew Paris in the 1920s as a student, and when the war began he returned as the *New Yorker*'s replacement for Janet Flanner. One of the last American newsmen to leave Paris before the Germans marched in, he came home via neutral Portugal.

Liebling was back in Britain for D-Day and in a landing craft that delivered infantry to Omaha Beach. As chance would have it, the skipper of the craft was Henry "Bunny" Rigg, a lieutenant in the Coast Guard Reserve who before the war wrote about yachting for the *New Yorker* and whom Liebling knew slightly. When they connected again it would be in liberated Paris.

On D-Day plus three Liebling came ashore in France briefly, then after more time in Britain he reached France again on June 24 and joined the pack of correspondents in Normandy and Brittany. When the movement to Paris got underway, he was already preparing for the war's conclusion. "In my mind," he wrote of the period, "the war would pretty well end with the road back to Paris. The rest would be epilogue."

He rode into the city with Leclerc's 2e DB in a prewar Chevrolet touring car that had once belonged to Germans. With him were Allan Morrison, a soldier reporting for *Stars and Stripes*, and Lieutenant Jack Roach, a PRO ordered to report for duty at the Scribe. At the Gare Montparnasse station the group stumbled upon the encounter between de Gaulle and von Choltitz, whom Liebling dismissed as "a worried, fat little soldier."

Also present in a jeep with a soldier driver were two other American correspondents, Paul Gallico of *Cosmopolitan* magazine and Harold Denny of the *New York Times*. On his portable typewriter, Denny at once punched out a story that, given he was the sole reporter present working for a daily newspaper, would be a significant scoop. A day earlier the *Times* had carried a Denny story with the lackluster dateline "Near Paris."

As Liebling profiled Denny at work, he "lit a cigarette, ran a hand through his hair, filled a sheet of paper, and instinctively yelled 'Boy!'"[31] With no copy boy available, the next task was to deliver the story to a censor and then transmission at the Scribe. The sensible thing was to entrust it to Lieutenant Roach in the Chevrolet. Morrison then went into the streets to find stories for *Stars and Stripes*, while Liebling joined Gallico and Denny in their jeep. Later it was revealed that Roach got the story to the Scribe, yet there, as Liebling phrased it, "he found a press center installed and functioning normally—so normally that it managed to lose poor Denny's exclusive eyewitness story of the surrender."[32] At any event, the *Times* never got the story, leaving it reduced to a page-one AP account of the de Gaulle–von Choltitz meeting.

Denny's bitterness about the lost scoop rose in volume when, days after the liberation, the missing story was returned to him for retransmission to New York. Iris Carpenter recalled that for the rest of the war the mishap illustrated what Denny called "the bumbling criminal incompetence of SHAEF Public Relations officialdom."[33] There were, of course, various culprits when dispatches failed to reach their destinations. Gerald Clark of the *Montreal Standard* found out, long after the fact, that a choice report he had written about first entering a German city and entrusted to a British dispatch rider got to a division headquarters, where it was mistaken for an intelligence report and filed away as such.[34]

When A. J. Liebling got to the Scribe the day after the liberation, he dropped his gear in a room but stayed in the Hôtel Louvois. He had been housed there more than four years earlier yet now was greeted as casually by the owner as if he was just returning from an afternoon stroll. After several weeks spent in Paris and elsewhere, reporting mostly about French political matters, he went back to New York in late December 1944. Before leaving, he wrote in a letter home to a close friend on the *New Yorker* about "feeling that I will never learn anything more from the experience of war."[35] "I never came back to the war," he later said in the magazine. "Before I could feel sufficiently ashamed for that, it was over."[36]

⌒

Paul Gallico's explanation for turning heels after the liberation was the need to get home and write while the war was still fresh in his mind. After witnessing the frantic shooting at Notre Dame, he jeeped directly back to a press camp in Rennes. Over a dinner that night, Iris Carpenter—one of the women correspondents still holed up in Rennes—heard him say that it was "the practicality of the French in contrast with everything else about them that gets me." Gallico's example was an old woman with white hair standing next to him in the cathedral who had flattened herself during the shooting quicker than he did. "An old lady in my country would have passed out from the shock," he said. "Not this one." The moment the shooting stopped, she got up, shook dirt from her dress, and helped take the wounded into a house used as a dressing station.

"I never dreamed," Gallico went on, "people could react the way I've seen them react today. Do you know what I'm going to do? I'm going back to the States now to write about it, for if I stay out here another day after this I won't be able to feel any more. I shall go home tomorrow."[37] And, Iris Carpenter reported, he did.

CHAPTER SIX

∼

Good Quarters

Once established in the Ritz, Ernest Hemingway wasn't in the mood to resume work as a *Collier's* correspondent. In a letter written the day after the liberation he told of loaning his typewriter to Joseph Driscoll of the *New York Herald Tribune* so he could write a liberation story. And he made clear in the same letter that he had "taken no advantage as correspondent over other correspondents on acct of participating in action."[1]

On day two of the liberation he hosted a luncheon in the Ritz that included Helen Kirkpatrick, John Reinhart, Charles Wertenbaker, Ira Wolfert, and Irwin Shaw. When Kirkpatrick mentioned that she wanted to see de Gaulle striding to Notre Dame, Hemingway tried to change her mind. "Daughter, sit still and drink this good brandy," he said. "You can always watch parades but you'll never again celebrate the liberation of Paris at the Ritz."[2] Markedly absent at the lunch was another American woman correspondent whom Hemingway first met in London while she was a member of Wertenbaker's *Time-Life* team.

On D-Day, Mary Welsh went on a prearranged tour of American air bases in Britain that had more photo than news value. Later she found better reporting material after she crossed the channel to report on medical activity behind front lines. When it seemed likely Paris would be freed, she lobbied *Time's* London bureau chief, Walter Graebner, to join in the coverage since she was the only member of the magazine's London staff who knew the city before the German occupation.

After early newspaper years in Chicago for the *Daily News*, Welsh had shifted to London early in the war and caught on with the city's *Daily Express*. For a time she lived in Paris and reported for the paper on British forces and French affairs. With the collapse of France, she escaped from Bordeaux on an overcrowded ferry with a host of other fleeing journalists.[3]

When Graebner posted her to Paris, Welsh flew to France on August 24, and after a long jeep ride with an American major reporting for duty she reached the Scribe at dusk on liberation day. Lugging a typewriter, bedroll, and knapsack, she found that "chaos reigned supreme"[4] in the hotel. Censors were present, but correspondents milled about with cables they weren't able to transmit. She learned that Wertenbaker had a room in the hotel but was unable to locate him. Many London friends were among those she saw in the building, though her husband wasn't among them. She believed that Noel Monks, a veteran Australian journalist now working for London's *Daily Mail*, was following British troops somewhere north of Paris.

With the Scribe fully booked, Welsh was billeted in a nearby hotel. Back at the Scribe the following morning she found Wertenbaker and her *Time-Life* colleagues at work in a temporary office. "Go get us a piece on Paris fashion," Wertenbaker instructed her. As she left the hotel it struck her as "noisy, badly ventilated and crowded," so rather than try again for a room she chose to walk to the Ritz.[5]

At the entrance on the Place Vendôme, she asked the concierge if Hemingway was registered in the hotel. A uniformed elevator operator in white gloves took her to room 31, knocked, and asked the soldier who answered if Hemingway was in. Archie Pelkey yelled over his shoulder, "Papa, there's a dame here." Hemingway greeted her with a whirling bear hug around the room while two French fighters sitting on the floor cleaned weapons and sipped champagne.[6]

As she left the Ritz on her work assignment, Welsh asked the concierge if she could have a room in the hotel. She was placed above Hemingway in room 86, a setting in richly ornate contrast to the place she had slept the previous night. She exited the Ritz from the Rue Cambon side, which took her along the passageway between the hotel's two parts that she called a "lane of enchantment" with "stylish showcases along the walls." She then toured the dress houses that were open and afterward rushed back to the Scribe and typed out a story in Wertenbaker's room. She followed this by covering the march of Leclerc's troops and de Gaulle along the Champs-Élysées to Notre Dame and the thanksgiving service, a total amount of journalistic work of fifteen to sixteen hours of racing about Paris.

After a late dinner that night with Hemingway on the left bank, she collapsed in sleep in his room, whose other bed held rifles and hand grenades. She awoke the next morning to the sound of Hemingway opening a bottle of champagne. She joined him for a drink and at the same time rang for coffee. She hadn't noticed Archie Pelkey making some on a GI stove set up in an empty fireplace.

⌒

While active in London writing for both *Time* and *Life*, Mary Welsh—as a Hemingway biographer delicately put it—"did not lack for male attention."[7] The thirty-six-year-old Welsh was having lunch with one of her closest male friends, Irwin Shaw, when Hemingway asked to be introduced to the petite and shapely blonde with him. While Hemingway was hospitalized as a result of the car crash, Welsh paid him a visit. After he was released from treatment and was back in the Dorchester, Welsh and a woman friend moved under the same roof for better shelter during nightly German bombing raids.

One evening Hemingway came to the women's room and launched into an account of his early life in Oak Park, Illinois, before abruptly switching course and informing Welsh he wanted to marry her. "This war may keep us apart for a while," he said. "But we must begin on our Combined Operations." Welsh replied, "You are very premature." Hemingway carried on, "Just please remember I want to marry you. Now and tomorrow and next month and next year." Later that evening Welsh's roommate told her she might be sorry for casually dismissing someone of Hemingway's importance. "He's too big," Welsh countered, meaning both his size and status.[8] Left unmentioned was that Welsh at the time was loosely married to Noel Monks, her second husband, while Hemingway was loosely married to Martha Gellhorn, his third wife and an accomplished journalist and fiction writer who was also in the UK covering the war for *Collier's*.

⌒

After Hemingway reached France well after D-Day, he and Welsh exchanged letters. From the Ritz just after the liberation he asked if he should nudge Wertenbaker to shift her *Time-Life* duties from London to Paris. He added that he couldn't leave Paris himself "but can give you good quarters whenever and wherever you come."[9]

Unknown to Hemingway, Welsh had made her own arrangements with her employer and was already in Paris. Unknown to Welsh, Noel Monks also reached Paris on liberation day and took a room in the Hôtel de Vendôme in Place Vendôme, just steps from the Ritz. It was a hotel where he had often stayed before, and the management greeted his return with hugs and champagne. He remained in partying Paris less than a week before pursuing the war with British troops and later the American Ninth Army.

On D-Day Monks had come ashore in France in water up to his chin, a typewriter raised over his head, and among soldiers below the water line desperate to free themselves from heavy packs. Fire pinned him down on Red Queen Beach for an hour before he reached a shattered house behind the beach and began tapping out a story that he hoped would be carried across the channel that day by a Royal Navy launch. After that he set off with other correspondents toward an area in Caen where they were to assemble. The distance was six miles by direct line, but due to intense fighting it was six weeks before the reporters were able to enter the city.[10]

Monks had returned to London for a spell when a phone call from the War Office gave him the latest news: "If you want to be in on the liberation of Paris, you'd better get back right away. The Americans are all around it, and the Free French tanks are about to move in." That same day he was again in Normandy and with correspondents gathered in the Hôtel Lion d'Or in Bayeaux, a press camp where many correspondents were billeted before Rambouillet and Paris. "Piles of kit were stacked besides jeeps and command cars," as he described the scene, "and correspondents were milling about loading up. Some were shedding gear, others were acquiring it. Everyone was pulling out—for Paris."[11] His companions in a command car, Ronald Monson and William Forrest of London's *News Chronicle*, made an ideal unit since they had been among the last leaving Paris in 1940. Now they were counting on being among the first back.

While still in Bayeaux, Monks saw a launch deposit General de Gaulle on a nearby beach. As he stepped ashore, a jeep bearing an American and a British officer appeared; the men saluted the lone figure and said they would take him to Britain's Field Marshal Bernard Montgomery. In Bayeaux a dazed crowd emerged from all directions to tightly surround the Free French leader. When Monks glimpsed him again it was in Notre Dame in Paris. "In the sombre cathedral I knelt behind him," he wrote, "saw him quivering as with bowed head he gave thanks to God. . . . Shots rang out in the galleries high above him, but de Gaulle never even raised his head."[12]

Mary Welsh was also in the cathedral during the shooting and wrote about it as well. But in a later autobiography she made no mention of seeing her husband that day, nor in a later war memoir did Monks mention seeing her. In her autobiography, Welsh recorded that in early 1945 she wrote to her parents in the United States about her crumbling marriage: "I finally must tell you that I have left Noel. We grew apart." She added within parentheses for the benefit of her book's readers: "When we were both in Paris, just after the reoccupation, I had finally got around to telling him." The letter to her parents then went on: "There is a man to whom I am devoted, for all the things he is and some of the things he isn't."[13] She didn't mention Hemingway by name.

～

The story Mary Welsh wrote about Paris fashion was bracketed with pieces by Charles Wertenbaker and William Walton and prominently displayed in *Life* in September 1944 under the heading "Life Correspondents See the New Paris." When a copy of the magazine finally reached Paris, the heavy editing of their work in New York infuriated the writing trio. "We were embittered," Welsh declared, "but not for long. Too much work demanded our attention."[14]

But in subsequent days she took what she called French leave from work and with Hemingway revisited places and people they both knew in Paris. Hemingway had an emotional reunion with Sylvia Beach, one of his closest friends from the 1920s. After being interned by the Germans for six months, she stayed in the city through the occupation but shuttered her famed bookstore, Shakespeare and Company. Another old friend from the past, Picasso, had worked steadily through the period. "Les boches left me alone," he told his guests. "They disliked my work, but they did not punish me for it."[15] Welsh turned the visit with the artist into an item for *Time*'s art section.

When Welsh resumed her reporting duties, she and Hemingway developed a routine of meeting for drinks and lunch at the Ritz bar. Evening meals were usually in the dining room of the hotel, though in the immediate postliberation days they knew the food supply was better at the Scribe. Their sleeping arrangements openly shifted back and forth between their rooms, a breach of the hotel's traditional decorum that caused the mother of the hotel's owner, Mme César Ritz, to wholly ignore Welsh's existence while she stayed in the Ritz.

One day Welsh found a notice at the concierge's desk that the Ritz by Allied military order now accommodated only very important persons. As a war correspondent she doubted she qualified, but she learned that as an original inhabitant dating from the liberation she could stay. She kept her good quarters in the Ritz for seven months.

When *Time-Life* shifted its office operations to the *Herald Tribune* building on Rue de Berri, Welsh found the space there as crowded and boisterous as the Scribe. She got Wertenbaker's permission to work in her Ritz room and only sat in on weekly story conferences at the office. When she had

doubts about a cable, she lunched with her boss at the Scribe and got sug-
gestions about revising her work or heard him tell her to "just bung it off" to
filing and transmission.

～

Martha Gellhorn was following an Allied group fighting on the Adriatic
coast of Italy when Paris was liberated. Keen to see the city she knew well
and learn the fate of friends during the occupation, she hurriedly managed
to get to France on a military flight and then hitched a jeep ride with intelligence officers on their way to Paris. Rather than the Ritz with her husband
or the Scribe with correspondents, she chose to stay in the Hôtel Lancaster.[16]

On D-Day she had set foot in France by stowing away on a hospital ship
anchored off Omaha Beach and then wading ashore with ambulance teams
before the ship returned the wounded to Britain. Her unauthorized crossing
onto French soil resulted in arrest by military police and banishment to a
nurse's training camp outside London. Determined to get back to the war,
she fled the nursing preserve and talked her way aboard an RAF flight to
Italy. Her accreditation gone and considered an outcast by PROs, she used
her blonde glamour and war-reporting experience to follow Allied fighting
regiments in Italy and file stories. She later wrote that it was only toward
the conclusion of the European war "that I dared attach myself to American fighting units. The war may have softened the PROs, or they no longer
cared what anyone did, with the end so near."[17] At the Scribe, she was still
officially at odds with the military but nonetheless dined there, visited the
bar, and filed pieces to Collier's. Her censor at the hotel, the British writer,
scholar, and self-identified aesthete Harold Acton, remembered her work as
"the best written and most vivid of the articles submitted to me."[18]

Gellhorn tried to avoid Hemingway in Paris while at the same time wanting his agreement to a divorce. When he surprisingly asked her to a dinner
one evening, he turned up with his irregulars and insulted her repeatedly.
Or so Gellhorn told Robert Capa, who said he found her weeping in the
Lancaster early the next morning. He informed her about Hemingway's affair with Mary Welsh and as evidence of it suggested she telephone Welsh's
room at the Ritz. When Hemingway answered rather than Welsh, Capa
told Gellhorn to tell him she knew what was going on with Welsh and to
demand a divorce. After a stream of profanity, Hemingway agreed to end the
marriage.[19]

Another story attributed to Capa has it that one day Gellhorn was dining
in the Scribe when Mary Welsh appeared. Also dining there was Virginia
Cowles, a correspondent for the North American Newspaper Alliance and

a close friend of Gellhorn. They had come to know one another when both, and Hemingway, were covering the Spanish war. As she walked through the room, Welsh passed Gellhorn on one side and Cowles on the other. According to Capa, both women sent visual daggers in Welsh's direction.[20]

While in Paris, Gellhorn went on a press tour of secret German locales used for beating, torture, and killing during the occupation. The final lines of the report she produced became the title when "The Wounds of Paris" appeared in *Collier's*. She set off the "intact and beautiful" atmosphere of freed Paris and the reality that "in a way Paris never had a war as we know it and it has no war now," with evidence of the systematic brutality of the occupation. She told of the dank, cold tunnel system beneath the city that became a prison where French men and women were locked away to die. She described a cemetery where German trucks dumped caskets of the dead and it was forbidden to mark the graves with names. She believed that possibly the worst place she saw was a windowless brick building where originally the Germans kept a large fire going to disinfect clothing and blankets—and then turned it into a blazing torture chamber. "It is necessary," she ended her detailed account, "to know all this, and to try to imagine these places because these are the wounds of Paris."[21]

Gellhorn left Paris at the beginning of September to track the war into Belgium—and to continue pushing the boundaries women faced as correspondents. At this stage of the war, SHAEF still tried to hold to the rule that women could go no closer to the front lines than field hospitals. "Liberal interpretation was always given this edict," admitted Barney Oldfield, by three women he chose to name: Lee Carson, Iris Carpenter, and Martha Gellhorn. For these correspondents, he said, "this meant as far forward as surgical teams would be called and often included battalion headquarters. Nobody in his right mind wanted to get any closer than that."[22]

About the same September time that Gellhorn left Paris, Hemingway rejoined the war for the first of several perilous back-and-forth trips between Buck Lanham's infantry in combat and reunions with Mary Welsh at the Ritz. In a letter to her from Belgium, he mentioned cryptically that he hoped he was "not in any bad trouble."[23] In October, bad trouble arrived in the form of a directive from SHAEF headquarters that Hemingway report to Nancy in France to answer charges brought against his actions as a correspondent in and about Rambouillet from August 18 to 25. The source of the formal charges was not fellow correspondents but military figures, and the point of the investigation was to determine if the charges had merit.

Interviewed during the investigation, David Bruce firmly defended Hemingway. He hadn't, said the OSS officer, acted in an overt military fashion and deserved praise for getting French irregulars to abide by Bruce's intention that they avoid combat with the Germans and act only as intelligence gatherers. Bruce held as well that General Leclerc's advance on Paris had been planned according to information about German positions gained by Hemingway's band.

In his testimony, Hemingway said that he had only advised Bruce and had not commanded troops. He explained being addressed as an officer by Resistance fighters as nothing more than citizens in the state of Kentucky bearing the title of colonel without any implication of military rank. If he was sometimes without his correspondent's insignia it was only because he was in his shirtsleeves due to warm weather. Ultimately, the military found no grounds to pursue charges against him.[24]

Hemingway was back with the Twenty-Second Infantry in November 1944 for the battle of Hürtgen Forest. When Lanham's regiment was finally pulled back from the horrendous fighting on December 3, it had gained six thousand yards of forest territory, freed a small village, and lost 2,700 men.[25] While in the area also known as the "Valley of Death," Hemingway remembered in a letter to *Collier's* that he hadn't chosen a beneficiary for the insurance the magazine carried on him. He named Mary Welsh his sole payee.[26]

~

VIPs were now much in evidence at the Ritz. Marlene Dietrich, whom Hemingway had known earlier and called "the Kraut," soon became Welsh's friend as well. Others filling the hotel were businessmen, diplomats, and well-heeled tourists eager to see Paris again. Clare Boothe Luce, now a member of the US House of Representatives, reappeared in the hotel as a member of a congressional investigating group. A Russian delegation in the hotel struck Welsh as "the most circuitous and mealy-mouthed of all government representatives," though their presence happily coincided with a brief spurt of hot water in the hotel.[27]

Nearly as troublesome as the Russians for Welsh to deal with on her Paris reporting rounds were lower-level secretaries of the French foreign office who offered only streams of noninformation. From the press gallery of the Ministry of Justice she covered the trials of traitors, collaborators, and—as she called them—"small, gray malefactors." She believed the court sentences they received were overly harsh—and as such were a reflection on the part of judges and lawyers of their own failings during the occupation.

In November 1944 Welsh left Paris for the Vosges Mountains near the French border with Germany. Hemingway had learned that his oldest son, John "Jack" Hemingway, had been wounded, captured, and then hospitalized by the Germans while on an OSS mission. He had parachuted into enemy territory to train French partisans to penetrate German positions when he came under fire. Desperate for more information but believing his presence in the area might do his son more harm, he persuaded Welsh that as a *Time-Life* correspondent she could go and talk to members of his son's group and his commanding general.

With Wertenbaker's agreement and SHAEF authorization, she jeeped with a driver into the mountains and toured about with officers and soldiers, learning only a little more than was already known. Jack had been wounded in the shoulder and treated properly in a prison camp in Germany. When Welsh returned to Paris, she wrote Hemingway a report to read when he was back from the combat zone. For *Time* she produced a couple of cabled dispatches that she called local-color-plus-information pieces.[28] Jack Hemingway remained a prisoner until the war's end.

Welsh got her first hint of what became the Battle of the Bulge while a dinner guest of the commander of Allied bombing in Europe, General Carl "Tooey" Spaatz, in mid-December 1944. When aides whispered in Spaatz's ear, she realized something was in the wind and left as promptly as she could. At briefings in the Scribe, PROs claimed that the Nazi winter counteroffensive was contained and Allied forward progress would resume. Correspondents in the bar were doubtful. There was talk of the Nazis marching toward Antwerp, with retaking Paris possibly next on their list. The censors in the hotel, Welsh later wrote, "turned heavy-handed. They did not want us to tell the enemy how far off guard they had caught us."[29]

Hemingway at the time was back at the Ritz, feverish and exhausted after the misery of the Hürtgen Forest. When he learned of the Bulge attack, he managed to contact General Barton's Fourth Army headquarters in Luxembourg and ask him if the situation was such that it required his presence at the division. For security reasons Barton could tell him little more than that it was a hot show and to come up.[30]

Hemingway considered his reporting for *Collier's* finished, yet in mid-December he set out with a jeep and driver in wintry weather for what would be his final foray into a combat zone. The worst of the fighting was over when he felt well enough to be out and about and making notes. It so happened that Martha Gellhorn was in the same combat area at the same time.

In the company of Buck Lanham, Gellhorn and Hemingway one day toured his battalion command posts together and saw in the sky the vapor trail of a German V-2 rocket flashing to a target. After Gellhorn made a note of the time and place, she said to Hemingway, "Remember this, Ernest. That V-2 is my story, not yours."[31]

Early in January 1945 Hemingway was back at the Ritz, now interacting with men of the Fourth Division and other groups on leave in Paris and thinking more about a future that didn't include seeing the war to the end. Later that month, Welsh returned to London to help out in the shorthanded *Time* bureau. While in the city she stopped at a bank to get money from her joint account with Noel Monks—and discovered he had withdrawn as much as five hundred pounds of her earnings. From his editor at the *Daily Mail* she learned she couldn't confront her husband since he was now covering the war in the Pacific.

Earlier she had asked Charles Wertenbaker to contact *Time* in New York about a leave of absence so that she and Hemingway could make what she labeled "a trial run of living together in Cuba." She had deep reservations about giving up her career as a journalist—"my lifetime companion," she called it—and turning over her life "to such a complicated and contradictory piece of machinery as Ernest."[32] Her career at the time was at a strong point. In March, *Life* carried her detailed report on "GI Crime in France," which opened with a dramatic shootout between three AWOL soldiers who were part of a gang selling looted gasoline in Paris and men of the army's Criminal Investigation Division.[33] Yet when her leave came through, she at once sailed from Scotland for the United States. Hemingway had already gone home on a military flight. In her Ritz mail, Welsh found a scrawled farewell note professing his undying love.

CHAPTER SEVEN

~

An American Crossroads

Leon Edel was told to report to the Scribe on liberation day, but it was the morning of the second day before he got there. After being propelled through the revolving front door into the startling disarray of the lobby, the hotel seemed hardly an upgrade from a previous night of sleeping on straw in a Paris police station. He found himself "amid a scattering of café tables, some overturned, and a stale heavy smell of tobacco and whiskey."

> Facing me, in deep sleep in a chair, was a U.S. major in full uniform, his head cradled in his arms. Beside him, a young second lieutenant . . . seemed in a state between sleeping and waking. . . . A few bleary-eye celebrants sat at tables, drinking what looked like the national coffee. Broken and spilled glasses, and the detritus of the Army PX littered the carpet—bits of food, candy wrappers, peanuts, empty beer and champagne bottles, and occasional pools of vomit. A small swastika flag had been placed in a bottle, doubtless in derision; there were candle ends in some others. Army gear lay between the tables. A few trim-looking officers sat to the rear at a cleared table, deep in talk. Clean-shaven, they looked as if they were waiting for a commuter train. Two or three young hotel employees were sweeping up the debris. A solitary clerk sat at the desk—his eyes fixed, as if in a stupor.[1]

The French clerk managed to tell Edel that after German officers left the hotel the previous morning, Americans had poured in the remainder of the day. The present disorder, he assured him, would soon be cleared up. A room check was already underway to determine who was already inside the hotel.

Gunfire in the streets had delivered some unexpected guests. In the meantime he politely offered coffee, which meant supplying heated water and a cup and saucer for use with Edel's powdered coffee.

Edel had made his coffee and was nearly asleep in the lobby when a hand gripped his shoulder. Looming over him was Alexander Uhl, the foreign editor of *PM*, the New York newspaper Edel had been working for when, at age thirty-five, he was drafted into the army. Uhl, now bearing a war correspondent's badge, expected to lodge in the Scribe. After the two spoke for a while and the lobby filled with new arrivals, Edel took his leave for the more refreshing street outside.

American born but raised in Canada, Leon Edel worked for newspapers in Montreal after returning from Paris, where he came for the first time in 1928 at age twenty-one. With two degrees from McGill University, he was on a three-year scholarship to the University of Paris. His thesis subject for the doctorate he earned from the Sorbonne was Henry James, the distant start of what became his honored five-volume biography of the American master. In the mid-1930s Edel returned to Paris to work for the French news service Havas. Now, as trained and promoted by the American military, he was a technical sergeant in the Psychological Warfare Division of SHAEF. As he termed it, his work was that of a "media soldier" who joined with other language specialists in employing print and broadcast means to convey the Allied spin on the war.

Four weeks after D-Day, Edel reached Normandy, his psychwar unit, as he condensed the name, commanded by a French-speaking captain and attached to General Patton's Third Army. During a pleasant month in the country the unit waited for Patton's force to become fully operational before launching its strike toward Germany. While Edel's team lived in pup tents in an orchard, nearby was an orchard press camp occupied by some fifty correspondents embedded with Patton.

At the time, Edel considered journalism his own profession. Yet his view of the nearby "assemblage of well-known byliners"—whose camp was off-limits to noncorrespondents—lacked any touch of glamour. The newsmen were "handsomely accommodated" in their orchard, and for this he envied them, yet without rubbing shoulders he knew well their behavior: "They drank, they swore, they swaggered. They were vocal in their criticism of the delay [by Patton], almost as if the war was being fought for their benefit. . . . To me, the big tent seemed like the usual alcoholic press club one might find in many cities, now transferred across the Atlantic, and set up among the apple trees of Normandy."[2]

Later, Edel was sent to Rambouillet to serve on a task force heading to Paris—presumably the task force organized by James Quirk and Jack Redding. After an agreeable time in the town where, he noted, "only the correspondents were unhappy" because editors back home were chewing them out by cable for lack of liberation stories, his psychwar unit began moving. Edel was placed in charge of a five-man command car with a convertible top, a driver, and three German linguists crammed in the rear seats. He was told to keep in bumper-to-bumper formation with French military vehicles and tanks, with the Scribe in Paris the final arrival point. The column went forward in long stops and starts because, as Edel learned, de Gaulle was in a head vehicle and making an unannounced entry to Paris. Eventually the crowds along the way were so enormous that the military lineup broke into disorder.

That night, uncertain about how to reach the Scribe, Edel's group stayed at the Prefecture of Police within view of Notre Dame Cathedral. Edel explained to the police captain that he and the other men were linguists with the US Army; their only weapons were radios, microphones, and printing presses; and they needed to get to the Scribe. "The Scribe!" exclaimed the captain. "That's where Goebbels's propagandists were billeted!" Edel replied, "We're propagandists too." The captain then suggested phoning the hotel. When Edel did and asked to speak to American officers, he was told, "No one is reachable. No one knows anything. Please call tomorrow."[3]

After waking in the morning from a bedding area shared with policemen and the linguists, Edel went to check on the whereabouts of his driver. He was peacefully sleeping in the front seat of the car, his weapon beside him. No French guards were in sight. The square fronting Notre Dame was deserted. That morning, a dozen or so hours later than expected, Edel's group drove to the Scribe without difficulty.

After leaving Alexander Uhl and the Scribe and finding the Café de la Paix open but with little food or drink, Edel noticed that a nearby kiosk was in business. Instead of newspapers, the vendor offered one-page sheets on letter-sized paper that announced current news. "There you have it," the vendor explained, "the press of the underground—now above ground, quite legal." Edel brought some sheets back to his table and began reading them. They would prove useful for his future work in Paris.

Later that day, the captain of Edel's psychwar team met with the members in his room in the Scribe—a room, Edel noted, that was comfortable and commandeered by a captain as smart looking as if he had just left his tailor.

The captain announced that de Gaulle would make his first formal appearance at the Arc de Triomphe that afternoon. The group was to take a jeep and a driver and record the ceremony, with the recording flown to London for broadcast on the BBC.

Burdened with young people clinging to it, the jeep carrying the group moved slowly down the Champs-Élysées through surging crowds until, in the Place de la Concorde, shooting began. The jeep's driver turned into a side street, and everyone took cover. It seemed to Edel that the shooting was fitful and meant to spread general fear rather than pick off particular figures. Yet when someone indicated a possible sighting on top of a building, he fired shots in that direction—his first use of his weapon in anger. After some minutes of hiding in the street, the group decided to make a run back to the Scribe. They expected a hail of gunfire, but nothing more happened. Back at the hotel they went without delay to the bar, where the captain ordered champagne for everyone.

That night, Edel, housed for the time being in a tourist hotel, was awakened by the German bombing of Paris. With the sky lit with burning buildings, he left his room for the street and joined other GIs who preferred being outside during air raids. John Pudney, a British poet and Royal Air Force intelligence officer, saw Parisians react in similar fashion to the indiscriminate bombing. "This is the first time we have ever left our beds," they told him. "When the British [bombers] came over we knew it was never necessary to get up unless one had gone to sleep on a war target."[4]

The day after the attack Edel again reported to the Scribe. While the group's captain continued living in what Edel now thought of as luxury, he and other specialists were moved to rooms in the Hôtel Perey, a shabby commercial hotel. The psychwar group began operating from offices earlier used by the Germans on Rue d'Aguesseau, a short walk from the Perey. With little required work to do, Edel wandered about the Opéra area. A habitual route took him from the Perey to the Café Weber to the Scribe to the Rainbow Corner, a Red Cross haven for troops on leave that had been a lounge for Nazi troops visiting Paris.

Added work came when Edel suggested writing daily intelligence reports on contents of the French press as viewed in the little sheets he had been reading. In them he learned of French courts punishing collaborators, of firing-squad executions, and of suicides of leading figures. There were also accounts of American courts-martial of GIs who sold stolen military goods on the black market—the sort of story that SHAEF's PROs preferred to sweep under the rug. His summaries became an unexpected success with intelligence figures who couldn't read French but wanted to stay current with the papers. Soon the reports were mimeographed each day and delivered to readers on a regular schedule.

Edel's other psychwar duties in Paris brought him into contact with Americans who would have imposing postwar careers. He came to know Morris Janowitz, at the time a corporal in military intelligence, who also stayed in the Perey but moved back and forth between the hotel and the front lines. After the war Janowitz had a distinguished academic career as a sociologist at the University of Chicago. In the Paris offices of the OSS, Edel met Arthur Schlesinger Jr., at the time also a corporal and later a Harvard professor and author of numerous historical works. Another Harvard academic and OSS member, Captain Perry Miller, sought out Edel as a French interpreter, and they strolled together in the Opéra area, never getting around to discussing any need for an interpreter. After the war Miller became a renowned authority on American Puritanism.

Parisian life ended abruptly for Edel in January 1945 when, a member now of a new psychwar unit, he was sent to Strasbourg, the French city on the Rhine that had been liberated in November but now feared a Nazi counterattack. Nearly a month later he returned to Paris and again worked in Rue d'Aguesseau. But he was housed now in a vast warehouse-like building in the Avenue Rapp that he thought had been used as a German barracks.

He learned later that American troops had been removed from the Perey and the building returned to civilian use, apparently a consequence of an article in *Life* magazine on December 4, 1944. In a sweeping survey of the US Army in Western Europe, Hanson W. Baldwin, the military editor of the *New York Times*, mentioned in passing that the "American Army and SHAEF's command and headquarters personnel are occupying more than 150 hotels in Paris." This was evidence of Baldwin's belief that the army was bloated with rearguard and staff officers. "It is probable," he wrote, "that if the Army sloughed off its excess 'fat,' five to six more combat divisions might be formed out of this personnel." Edel and his drafted colleagues believed that Baldwin's remark about hotels prompted the army brass to empty hotels like the Perey while, as Edel caustically observed, "officers remained in their luxurious quarters, sleeping on mattresses between laundered sheets, and dining nearby."[5]

The war was nearly over when in April 1945 Edel was elevated from a media soldier to a war correspondent, if only briefly. He was chosen to cover a press conference at the Scribe by General Walter Bedell Smith, Eisenhower's chief of staff, and write a summary of his remarks for the psychwar office in London. He was ushered into the wall-mapped information room at the hotel after, as he wrote, he was "promptly accredited as a war correspondent" and listened as fellow newsmen pressed Smith about how long the war would last. He would only guess it might extend another three or four months.[6] As it turned out, the end came much sooner.

⌒

The earliest figures passing through the Scribe in the autumn of 1944, making it what Leon Edel labeled an American crossroads as well as a correspondents' press camp, were civilian and military figures attached to the US Office of War Information, the OSS, and Allied intelligence, counterespionage, and psychological warfare specialists like Edel. Thereafter came American politicians, entertainers, businessmen, and media moguls, all transported across the Atlantic courtesy of the military to see freed Paris for themselves.[7] With rooms at the Scribe reserved for correspondents, the dining room and bar became a compelling gathering spots for visitors.

Forrest Pogue, a French-speaking sergeant and army combat historian, was notably drawn to the bar. Shortly after the liberation, he was there one evening with a friend who was hunting for newspaper comrades with *Stars and Stripes*. The bar was among the few in Paris with electricity and open at night, and it let enlisted men drink in a private room. "It was amazing," Pogue wrote in a diary, "to be sitting in this rather swank bar, only a few steps from the opera and the Café de la Paix, being served champagne in fragile glasses by white-coated waiters," this despite his own garb of a stained field jacket and carrying a helmet and sidearm.

In a sardonic aside, Pogue remarked that "by the next evening, the war had progressed far enough for the private dining room to be reserved for colonels, wine and champagne had doubled in cost, a woman correspondent turned up in evening clothes, and some of the male correspondents turned up in pinks [the light-colored trousers worn by army officers]. Ernie Pyle . . . turned up in his usual battered battle togs."[8]

The prolific British writer Malcolm Muggeridge, an officer working for his country's intelligence service and wandering Paris in the liberation period with no work yet to do and in self-acknowledged states of intoxication, ventured into the Scribe and found it in a chaotic state. It was, though, a clutter he enjoyed since it involved old newspaper comrades. "How familiar a scene!" he exclaimed in his memoirs. "The fingers questing over a typewriter keyboard, the faces momentarily pulled together to concentrate wavering attention, the cigarette pulled at for inspiration, the glass to hand to fuel the motor when it faltered." The fueled motors led to bursts of journalistic prose that Muggeridge gleefully parodied in cable style: "TONIGHT TRICOLORE BRAVELY OVERFLYING PARISES FAMOUS ARCDETRIOMPHE FIRST TIME SINCE GER-

MAN UNDERGOOSE-STEPPED." Around him newsmen shouted out to others for details: "Hey! can anyone tell me, is there a flag over the Arc de Triomphe? Not! Well, what about the Effel [*sic*] Tower?"[9]

⌒

The Scribe was equally a crossroads for its correspondents in that new ones kept appearing while veterans left for tours of the front and then reappeared during down periods. Michael Moynihan, a young pipe-smoking British journalist writing for London's *News Chronicle*, was among the returnees. He had stayed in the hotel for the first four days of the liberation, caught up in the emotional swirl and living, as he later wrote, "mostly on champagne and spam" among the hotel's convergence of "correspondents from all over the free world" who seemed "variously elated or dazed by it all."

"Invitations were also thick on the ground at the Hotel Scribe," he added about those early entente cordiale days.[10] While one of the random Luftwaffe raids on Paris was underway, Moynihan and two fellow newsmen were guests of a French fashion designer for an elegant candlelight dinner that included four of the host's most gorgeous models. The guests paid no heed to the racket of bombs and fire engines in the streets.

Coming back seven weeks after the liberation and with a new assignment to follow the American Ninth Army, Paris seemed to Moynihan wholly changed. "The new Occupation—of the Allied troops—has passed the stage of novelty," he recorded. "People go about their business as in any city, with private preoccupations, no longer turning to stare after a khaki uniform, no longer a community in rejoicing."[11] Still, in the diary he kept, most of Moynihan's entries were about the beauty of Paris that still took his breath away and life within the Scribe.

On the way to his room in the hotel on the day of his Paris return, together with Ned Roberts of the United Press who would also trail the Ninth Army, they met an American friend of Roberts who had two women with him and a bottle of Armagnac. The conversation upstairs was, as Moynihan told his diary, "pidgin sex," and he left after a time to see who was in the bar. It was even more filled with correspondents than during the liberation, though "organized now, efficient and tame." Over the course of an evening's drinking, he met two other American newsmen bound for the Ninth and "ended up with cognac in Iris Carpenter's room."[12]

Moynihan devoted the rest of his Paris time to solo sightseeing, while in his diary he turned back to the changed atmosphere in the city. It seemed that Paris had experienced what had earlier taken place in London when American troops largely took over the city's West End. He wondered how far the American occupation of Paris—as against what he previously called the Allied occupation—"will oust the terrific pro-British enthusiasm we encountered seven week ago. British correspondents I have met see it happening already—the loud-mouthed Yanks throwing their weight around, taking all the kudos. Not that they are all like that. How different I will now be finding out."[13]

During time in his next press camp in the Netherlands, Moynihan also learned about German war correspondents in that he made the unsurprising discovery that they existed. A woman in a ravaged town told him that just earlier correspondents had occupied a room in her house, working very busily and then angered at having to leave. "It had somehow never occurred to me," wrote Moynihan, "that we would have opposite numbers, driving around on their side of the front, typing dispatches just as eulogistic of their troops, just as slanted."[14]

～

James Quirk of the PRD wasn't a returning newsman but, as he said in a letter home, a "prisoner of the hotel Scribe and haven't had my nose outside the door for three days while I talk to Frenchmen on a hundred little missions." Those internal missions were enough to cause him to believe, with Moynihan, that postliberation Paris had changed dramatically. But while the British newsman pointed to the presence of annoying Yanks, Quirk found the French citizenry hard to bear.

They obsessively told of their suffering under the occupation yet struck him as the best-dressed people in the world with shops that were filled with merchandise. They considered the war over, and they had won it singlehandedly. They seemed never to have heard of the Allies. They expected a prominent seat in any future peace conference. "The French are very charming," Quirk allowed, "and that's about it."[15]

John Preston, a soldier writing for *Yank* magazine, felt at least passing sympathy for French citizens who still gathered around the entrance to the Scribe, seekers now rather than celebrants. "Almost all Frenchmen who can speak English," he wrote, "can be found in the crowd that concentrates around the Hotel Scribe trying to get a job as an interpreter. All of them are angling hopefully, steadily, pitifully for new jobs and a new life, trying to identify themselves in every way with the Allies."[16]

～

Like James Quirk, Thor Smith's life in Paris as a PRO revolved around a three-block orbit from the hotel where he was billeted to the building where he had an office to the Scribe where the correspondents were. He had been ordered to Paris after the group of four pool men covering Eisenhower for the world press was reduced to a single reporter, drawn in rotation from American, Canadian, and British military publications. ("I imagine," Harry Butcher remarked about the change, "it is one of the few times in history that a leading general has asked for a diminution of news coverage about himself."[17])

His present work, as Smith obliquely informed his wife, was with one of the main branches of SHAEF's PRD, and he was accountable only to the general heading the division. Another way of conveying the lofty level of his job was to tell her he was a three-telephone man, though none of them on his desk fully worked. The French phone for Paris exchanges had operators who thought they spoke English, and "after a few wrestling matches with the telephone, one is almost ready to go out and start cutting paper dolls."[18]

Smith's assistant, Captain Frank Mayborn, had a strong newspaper background, and the two functioned well together. The rest of Smith's public-relations group included ten officers, over a dozen enlisted men, and some Women's Army Corps (WACs). They worked in close proximity with a similar British unit that had about a dozen people. Smith found time within his desk duties for sporadic work with Jack Redding on the novel they were writing together. Redding was currently a PRO with General Bradley's Twelfth Army, so they mostly dealt with one another on the phone. Presumably they turned out alternating chapters of the story and passed them through censorship as they were finished.

In a letter in mid-November 1944, Smith announced that the "ms is finished . . . got it away [to the publisher] several days ago, after a fancy interchange with Jack." The interchange had apparently produced flashes of anger on both sides. "After I 'took umbrage' at his red-hot note," Smith wrote of Redding, "he's been too, too nice over the telephone. I know him . . . and am tolerant of his spells of high dudgeon."[19] In a later letter, Smith told of Redding coming to Paris and the two of them dressing in field clothes and going to the Bois de Boulogne to have photos taken for promoting the book. The process made them feel like actors wearing costumes, despite the fact that they had lived in just such gear for months on end.

Smith added in the same letter that he was writing it while back being "a big desk staff officer" waiting to have a Paris breakfast with the PRD's commanding general. His desk work, though, was frequently and happily broken up with visits back and forth to armies at the American, British, and Canadian fronts. He alternated the trips with Frank Mayborn, the two of them staying away for days and becoming, in Smith's words, mud sloggers rather than desk sitters.

∽

There was movement of a civilian sort within Paris as American correspondents with bureaus in the pre-occupation city reopened offices while still tied to the censorship and transmissions services of the Scribe. For PRO brass in the hotel, activating the bureaus was a sensitive matter since SHAEF considered that such decisions—as well as verdicts about restarting Paris editions of American and British newspapers—also involved the French government. SHAEF had charge of all communications in Paris yet wished to appear at least aware of French sensitivities.

In early September a *New York Times* story had said discussions were ongoing between SHAEF and the French government about whether news bureaus already opened could continue operating. The story also indicated that the French had asked the Allied command to limit for the time being the number of newsmen in Paris because there were already "too many mouths to feed"[20] in the city. It was late October when Thor Smith reported in a letter that the French government wanted the three hundred or so correspondents presently in Paris reduced in number, and he was charged with the unwanted task of being the policeman doing the job. It meant, he wrote, getting the correspondents out into the field and reporting on the army, or else "get their own billets and feed themselves and transport themselves."[21]

Soon after the liberation, Helen Kirkpatrick found the bureau of the *Chicago Daily News*—prominently located across from the Café de la Paix and with a private entrance on the Boulevard des Capucines leading to its second-floor space—bypassed by the Germans. The concierge had told them, "Oh, it's a storage space." Edgar Mowrer of the paper had left the office in June 1940 as the Germans entered Paris, a copy of his last report still on the dust-thick desk. While she remained in Paris, Kirkpatrick acted as the bureau chief, with aid from an Egyptian who had worked for years with the paper and a former secretary, an English woman married to a French man, who also turned up to get the bureau functioning.[22]

In the United Press bureau at 2 Rue des Italiens, Henry Gorrell and Richard McMillan found the mahogany desks gone but learned that an office worker had hidden the well-worn typewriters in his home.[23] The *New York Times* reported in a story by Harold Denny that its bureau at 37 Rue de Caumartin had reopened. Denny and two colleagues, Frederick Graham and Gene Currivan, hunted up all they could find of the old French staff. The offices were in better shape than expected. Some furniture was missing, but typewriters were still there, newspaper files were intact, and some telephone transmission equipment had been safely hidden. A French association of some sort was occupying the premises, but the *Times* agreed to wedge into two rooms while the French group looked for new quarters. The *Times'* sign had remained out front of the offices through the occupation and was now decorated with Allied flags.[24]

Edward Kennedy and a group of Associated Press colleagues arrived at the Scribe a fortnight after the liberation. Kennedy had come to Paris originally in 1927 to study and returned for a time in 1931 to work on the Paris edition of the *Chicago Tribune*. Back in the United States, he went to work for the AP and quickly rose to the Washington bureau and, in 1935, to the Paris bureau. After reporting on World War II in Italy, Kennedy's present task was to restore and lead the wire service's headquarters in Paris, combining all staff members in France into a single entity covering seven armies and three air forces in the field, SHAEF headquarters, and French political and civic affairs.

This required a sizeable number of correspondents—among them, established figures like Wes Gallagher, Hal Boyle, and Don Whitehead, not to mention Kennedy himself—as well as photojournalists, clerical workers, and former part-time French stringers in the countryside. The AP rented a floor in the nine-story Paris *Herald Tribune* building, a site that provided adequate space for employees, yet with briefings, censors, and transmission links in the Scribe, a room on the fourth floor of the hotel was kept as an office.[25]

The most startling discovery in a former Paris bureau came when Charles Wertenbaker went to the *Time-Life* office on liberation day. Tucked away in a hidden safe he found $100,000 in American currency. "Dispose of as you will—insurance company already paid off," he was told when he cabled New York about the find. So he began passing out bills to correspondent friends— and to at least one noncorrespondent.

The skipper of the landing craft that had carried A. J. Liebling close to Omaha Beach on D-Day, Bunny Rigg, was at the time in Paris on a two-day leave. At the Scribe he joined with Liebling. With Rigg short of money for dining and other Parisian pleasures, Liebling got him together with Wertenbaker who, according to Rigg, handed him $1,000 of the safe money. When Ernest Hemingway soon thereafter came for a handout, Wertenbaker denied finding the windfall because, again according to Rigg, he wasn't giving anything to someone who "had been trying to scoop everybody and get credit for liberating the city singlehandedly."[26]

⌇

The Haussmann where Andy Rooney spent his Paris days was near the building on Rue de Berri where the Paris *Herald Tribune* was produced before the occupation. During the following four years a caretaker had rented out some of its space to French agencies, and a former electrical worker for the newspaper periodically returned to keep the presses in order.[27] With the liberation, *Stars and Stripes* took over the building and, on September 5, began publishing a five-column tabloid Paris edition. Newsprint and ink were in short supply and controlled by the military. With civilian manpower equally scarce, privately owned English-language papers like the Paris *Herald Tribune*, London's *Continental Daily Mail*, and the Paris edition of the *New York Post*—a new venture going up against the other two—had to wait their turn to start operations.

When the *Herald Tribune* was first to roll the presses on December 22, 1944, it leaned heavily on manpower from *Stars and Stripes* desk men who moved over within the same editorial area to work for added pay. Aid also came from *New York Herald Tribune* correspondents based at the Scribe. "The *Herald Tribune* had full accommodations in this press headquarters," Eric Hawkins, the British-born managing editor of the Paris edition of the paper, said of the Scribe, "and from time to time we could snag a correspondent for a short turn of duty on the Paris *Herald*." At times, the snagging might have been more like strong-arming them. "Some nights," Hawkins said as well, "we would sort of press-gang our SHAEF-accredited correspondents who lived, ate, worked and sometimes slept at the Scribe Hotel to come up to the Rue de Berri and sit on the desk to help out."[28]

Hawkins also had another, less work-related reason for often crossing over to the Scribe. He said in his memoirs, "Not only was it desirable for me to keep up contacts there; I also discovered that a well-timed visit to the Scribe bar frequently removed one of the most annoying aspects of life in Paris at that time—the problem of getting a hot bath. Friendly colleagues, who had warm rooms and hot water at the Scribe, invited me to use their tubs, and I was only too happy to accept."[29]

Hawkins and his Paris paper faced unexpected competition some two months after the war ended when the *New York Post* began publishing its afternoon Paris edition in July 1945. Paul Scott Mowrer, the editor of the four-page tabloid, with eight pages on weekends, had for years well before the war led the Paris bureau of the *Chicago Daily News* and later became editor-in-chief of the Chicago publication. In 1933, he had married Hadley Hemingway, Ernest Hemingway's first wife. When Paul Scott Mowrer, who was the older brother of Edgar Mowrer, took the new job in Paris, Hadley joined him there. William L. Shirer noted in his diary in late October 1945 that he had glimpsed Martha Gellhorn and Hadley having aperitifs together in the Scribe bar.

The *Post* was put out from rented space in a building where the French paper *Le Populaire* was published before suspending operations during the occupation. Most of the new paper's staff shifted over from *Stars and Stripes*, as had happened with the Paris *Herald Tribune*, while others came directly from New York. Helen Kirkpatrick recalled that the *Post* also tried to recruit all the foreign staff of the *Chicago Daily News*. "So when this pressure from the *New York Post* came along," she said, "I very stupidly succumbed and went along with Paul Scott Mowrer." She had just been offered a Nieman Fellowship in journalism at Harvard but allowed Mowrer to talk her out of it. She also regretted moving to the *Post* because "it wasn't a great paper. It was a New York paper and that's about all you can say for it."[30]

Eric Hawkins, on the other hand, found the *Post* a strong rival, especially while the war in the Pacific provided both papers with good copy. He believed the *Post* nearly equaled the *Herald Tribune*'s daily circulation of forty-five to fifty thousand during the period.[31] But with the American military presence in Paris dwindling and the morning *Herald Tribune* once again firmly entrenched in the city, the *Post* folded six months after its launch.

CHAPTER EIGHT

∼

The Hottest Noncombat Spot

In a diary entry in September 1944, Harry Butcher noted in passing that he was leaving his room in the Scribe for one in the Raphaël, a small, elegant hotel on the Avenue Kléber that SHAEF used primarily for transient visitors. In the Scribe he got no rest because correspondents kept pressing him about their needs. For his own he had to keep his distance, this despite now residing in a place that "stays colder than a refrigerator and my bed is so damp it never seems to dry."[1]

Butcher doesn't indicate whether he knew that the Raphaël was in an area where many of the Nazi leadership in Paris, including top Gestapo figures, lived during the occupation. The hotel's red-carpeted English Bar was a setting for drinking parties—and conspiracies. Some members of Operation Valkyrie, the July 1944 plot to, among other things, kill Hitler, had gathered in the bar and a suite above to plan the action and later flee its failure. "The Hôtel Raphäel," a historian has written of the plotters, "had been their primary operational headquarters for certain organizational meetings."[2]

Leaving the Scribe may have improved Butcher's rest but could do nothing about events that kept upsetting relations between SHAEF's PROs and the press. At best, the relationship was always fraught because of fundamentally opposed roles: correspondents reporting the war and the military, in its censorship authority, stopping whatever it judged as news that aided the enemy. Another way of describing the inevitable friction, this from the correspondents' angle, was to hold that the military considered war news its property and provided it, or didn't, as it saw fit.

Walter Cronkite recalled that while working for the United Press in Britain and the country still under threat of invasion, correspondents had to write their stories in a large pressroom of the UK's Ministry of Information while censors were present. "Few hours passed there," he wrote, "without a near violent scene as an indignant reporter argued with an unmovable censor." If a story only conveyed news the Germans would have reason to already know yet the story was killed, the assumption of the reporter—as Cronkite phrased it—"was that either (1) the censor was stupid, or (2) he or she was covering up a purely political decision. Not infrequently both answers applied."[3]

However enflamed the battles between correspondents and censors, they were conducted in a setting in which censors always had the final word. Correspondents couldn't be in war zones unless they were accredited, and accreditation meant agreeing to military censorship. No doubt many correspondents approved of the ultimate barrier as understandable wartime restraint—and practiced self-censorship before encountering it. Andy Rooney wrote of the latter:

> While censorship was seldom onerous we all understood that pessimistic reports, reports of great losses, or negative stories about our own men were seldom passed. Actual censorship—that is, times when the censors forbade a reporter from transmitting a story he had written—were rare because reporters knew what they could and could not write. It was the case of self-imposed censorship again. Military people are convinced that they always have to be winning the war in stories sent home.[4]

Others held that censorship allowed military brass, Eisenhower included, to speak more openly to the press than they otherwise would because they knew blue pencils governed what made the news. Yet for both correspondents and the PROs an awareness of having opposed missions was never far from their mind. An insoluble problem on the military side was that after copy was passed by censors and transmitted, it could be rewritten by editors in home offices and misleading headlines stuck on it.

In the *New Yorker* just after the war ended, A. J. Liebling alluded to an added form of censorship that preceded self- or blue-pencil censorship based on "political, personal, or merely capricious reasons." "But the worst form of censorship," he explained, "was the preventive kind exercised by Public Relations, which . . . acted on the principle that an inactive correspondent was potentially a source of less bother than a correspondent who was going somewhere." In other words, PROs could prevent correspondents from reaching fighting zones and writing critical dispatches by holding them in "Algiers, Naples, or Paris, as the case might be." He mentioned no instances in which correspondents were in fact rendered inactive—and made clear he was speaking of the "higher echelons of Public Relations." "To give Army Public Relations the only credit due it," he concluded, "some of the younger officers in the field were helpful, hard-working, and at times even intelligent."[5]

⌒

At a point just before the liberation of Paris, Harry Butcher found himself thrust into the center of contention. In what he regarded as a troubleshooting assignment, he was asked by Eisenhower to get involved with the PRD while its commanding officer, General Davis, was ill and had been replaced in London by his deputy, Colonel R. Ernest Dupuy. An experienced newsman who spoke French and after the war became a prominent author and military historian, Dupuy had commanded an artillery battery in World War I. In 1942 he helped create in the United States *The Army Hour*, a popular Sunday-afternoon radio program on NBC stations in which each week he gave war updates. As a public-relations officer with SHAEF in Britain, he read over radio the official announcement of the Normandy landings.

With Dupuy in place as the acting PRD head in London, Butcher flew there to join him. He acknowledged thereafter—in a diary entry in London on the day Paris was liberated—a host of problems making the PRD "quite the hottest noncombat spot in the Supreme Headquarters organization. The opportunities for error are very high, indeed."[6] An immediate failing was Dupuy's inability in London to confirm in SHAEF's name that Paris was indeed liberated.

French announcements kept pouring in that the city was free, but poor telephone connections within SHAEF left Dupuy helpless in a series of news conferences. As he recorded in a journal entry, he was "henpicked by British and US press, everyone got on the bandwagon to congratulate the French. SHAEF alone held to the facts. Madhouse. Accused of everything up to contradicting the King. When I found out he had sent a message of congratulations [to the French] I called up his secretary at Windsor, informing him."[7]

A more serious gaffe from the PRD's standpoint took place in Paris in the early hours of liberation. A group of six correspondents, split evenly between British and American, followed Leclerc's entry into Paris, and upon reaching a clandestine station of Radio Nationale de France they talked operators into allowing them to broadcast. Swept up in liberation frenzy and facing an open microphone, the six weren't inclined to follow censorship procedures. James McGlincy of United Press broadcast first, followed by Larry LeSueur of CBS,

Paul Manning of Mutual Broadcasting, Seaghan Joseph Maynes of Reuters, and Robin Duff and Howard Marshall of the BBC. LeSueur later laid claim to making the first broadcast—and said he sought to get it passed by censors at the Scribe but none had yet appeared.[8] The six were finished broadcasting when John MacVane of NBC swept in with a script bearing a censor's stamp.

MacVane had left a First Army press camp, and like the other broadcasters he took the congested road to Paris with French troops. He found the Scribe already teeming with correspondents, nearly all boasting that they had been the first to enter the city. His plan was to be the first to file a story with an approved stamp, and he camped out in the hotel until censors arrived. With two companions he then hurried off at night to an underground station he had learned about from French police, only to find it occupied by American and British broadcasters who had already sent their reports. MacVane was beaten on a major story but, as he later reflected, had the "cold comfort of moral satisfaction" of having followed censorship requirements.

After making his belated broadcast, MacVane and his companions returned to the Scribe, where through open windows they heard crowds outside lustily and repeatedly singing the "Marseillaise." Uppermost in MacVane's mind at the time was a bath in his room to rid himself of fleas from sleeping in fields. As for the miscreant broadcasters, Jack Redding, the senior PRO then in the Scribe, banished them from the Continent for a period but allowed them to work in Britain, a punishment MacVane dismissed "as a kind of vacation."[9]

An official statement put out by SHAEF said that "certain extenuating circumstances were taken into account" in deciding on the penalty. Among those listed were street fighting that limited movement to the Scribe, "the ready proffer of broadcasting facilities by the radio station involved," and the fact that the material broadcast gave no aid to the enemy.[10] In his diary, Butcher agreed that nothing the six said would have been stopped by censors, which did nothing to narrow the gulf between PROs upholding the rules and correspondents cheering their enterprising peers.

～

Within the Scribe there were times of good feeling between the opposing sides. British correspondents held a big birthday bash for Brigadier William Turner. John O'Connell of the *Bangor Daily News* hosted a convivial dinner featuring what remained of moose meat sent by his paper for soldiers from Maine. In October 1944 an Allied Press Committee was formed in the hotel, with the members chosen by the correspondents, to help mediate disputes with PROs.

Still, in the hotel, with PROs, censors, and correspondents together in large numbers and close quarters over a lengthy stretch of time, disputes were frequent and combative. Collie Small of the United Press deftly noted the gap between the sides in an article in the *Saturday Evening Post* in November 1944. He wrote that while the hotel bar was where "correspondents gather nightly to plot ways of poisoning the censors," the censors "also drink at the Scribe bar, but from different stools—like big-league umpires and ballplayers."[11]

The lighthearted remark came within a lengthy story, datelined Paris, in which Small recounted the large-scale surrender of German troops within enemy territory south of the Loire River. "Army public-relations officers, who never tire of devising new ways to torture weary correspondents," wrote Small, "announced prematurely that 20,000 Germans were surrendering at nine o'clock the following morning. Naturally there would be a special mass expedition of correspondents to the scene."[12] Small was among them, jeeping from Paris at five in the morning with Charles Haacker of Acme Newspictures and Fred MacKenzie of the *Buffalo Evening News*.

But three hours after making the announcement, Small noted, the PRD "frantically announced it was all a horrid mistake, and for everyone to stay as far away as possible because the Germans might not surrender after all. Unfortunately, the three of us left between announcements."[13] As it happened, the twenty thousand Germans, cut off by rapid American advances, did surrender. Fortunately for Small and his jeep mates—and numerous others among the press—they were on hand to cover perhaps the strangest capitulation story of the war.

Ernest Dupuy had only high praise for the PRD's efforts to support the coverage. He proclaimed that the surrender "was staged in the light of proper press, radio and newsreel coverage with outstanding results. I consider this to have been one of the superlative performances of our SHAEF public relations operations. . . . It was propaganda in the purest sense of the word, so far as its impact concerned both the Allied world and Germany."[14] The leader of the American infantry platoon to whom the Germans surrendered, Lieutenant Samuel Magill, was rewarded with a pass to Paris—and a bylined story in *Life*, "We Took 20,000 Germans," which the magazine said was "as told to *Time* and *Life* correspondent Mary Welsh."[15]

⌇

Together with censors on the different bar stools in the Scribe, it was possible for much of the postliberation period to find Britain's Harold Acton. Before transferring to Paris in October 1944, he worked for SHAEF censorship in

London. From there he balanced, as he wrote, the correspondents' view of censors as "pedantic spoilsports" with his of the newsmen as "myopic in matters of security." He added, "It was amazing how much 'off the record' information they tried to smuggle through during peak-hours of our activities." Acton on the other hand described his own after-work nights as "haunted by the dread of having overlooked the number of a group or the name of an Air Marshal which should have been omitted."[16]

Among further broadsides aimed at correspondents was that they played hunches about war news that often originated with out-of-touch editors back home rather than following war-zone briefings. But the fundamental failing of both correspondents and their editors was that, as Dupuy flatly declared in a letter to his wife, they were "silly asses who don't know what war is" and failed to realize "the press has been better served in this campaign than ever before."[17]

In the flood tide of complaint from the other side, correspondents charged the PRD with inconsistent standards among censors at the various press camps, lack of a sense of news urgency, and censorship based on political and policy needs rather than security. Such nonsecurity censorship typically meant highlighting certain military units and generals and stopping anything that might ruffle harmony among the Allies.

A deeply quarrelsome matter was news blackouts during important battles. Correspondents granted the need for withholding information at such times but chafed when censors at one location lifted the ban but not at others, leaving some newsmen scooped by competitors. They chafed as well at censorship so exhaustive that it left approved reports hardly worth the costs of transmission.

In early September 1944, Ernest Dupuy flew from London to Paris and the Scribe—in part at the urging of Butcher, who thought the officer's endless jostling with the London-based press had left him needing a rest or a change of atmosphere. The Paris atmosphere was surely different, but Dupuy's work therein would prove far from restful.

At Le Bourget airport in Paris he found some runways restored but others still pocked with bomb craters. Hangers and other buildings had been gutted by air attacks. The road into the city was strewn with scorched German vehicles. In the Place de la Concorde were signs of recent fighting. But beyond such scars, the city that Dupuy knew well from earlier days seemed unchanged. On the corner of Rue Scribe, the large white sign "Old England" for the shop below the Grand Hôtel stood out just as it had in pre-occupation days.

Inside the Scribe, Dupuy faced an immediate problem when he met with PROs Jack Redding and James Quirk. "You've got to make a decision, pronto," Redding informed him. "Five correspondents have gotten here all the way through France from the Seventh Army down south. They have no orders, are in fact AWOL. And they want to file their stories. I've suspended them, holding their copy waiting SHAEF action. Three of them are here now and will want to see you."[18]

Among the AWOL five was the AP's Edward Kennedy. After the Allied invasion of southwestern France in August 1944, he flew from his post in Italy to France. With a jeep, trailer, and driver provided by public relations and accompanied by correspondents from the *Chicago Times*, the International News Service, and British and Australian publications, he journeyed through France and even briefly into Switzerland, thanks largely to the help of French Resistance fighters. In Paris, Kennedy was now one of the three meeting with Dupuy. When the colonel asked for their travel orders, they admitted they had none. Kennedy still made a case for the group staying in Paris, but Dupuy said they would remain suspended and be returned to Italy as soon as possible. He allowed, though, that their dispatches about traveling through France could be transmitted after censorship. But they could write nothing about Paris.[19]

It later developed that Kennedy did go back to Italy, but only to settle his affairs with the AP before returning to Paris as head of the service's French operations. It may have helped Kennedy's cause with the PRD that Dupuy was aware, as Kennedy at the time was not, that he had been picked to head the AP from headquarters in Paris. Months later, Dupuy and everyone in the PRD leadership would have profound reason to wish that Kennedy had stayed suspended and been removed from France.

Disciplining a few correspondents was a straightforward matter compared with the overall state of affairs Dupuy found within the hotel. Butcher called it general turmoil and ascribed it to the persistent "champagne atmosphere" of freed Paris. Barney Oldfield of the PRD noted round-the-clock crowding in the hotel. "There were 500-odd men and women based in the rumpled hostelry," he wrote. "The lobby milled with humanity, day and night, like a refugee collecting point. Work and play were common to the same room at the same time."[20]

In late September, a month after the liberation, General Frank A. Allen Jr., a former tank commander who had become the chief of intelligence of the Sixth Army Group but with little experience in public relations, was named the new head of the PRD with a mandate to bring order to the Scribe. Bypassed in the shift perhaps due to his age, fifty-eight, Dupuy got a consolation Legion of Merit award and stayed on with the PRD. Butcher commented in his diary that Dupuy had said, without rancor, that "he not only got decorated but got the ax."[21] To himself in his journal, Dupuy professed relief at passing on to General Allen duties that he summed up as "this fantastic business of being responsible for news from Britain to the borders of Germany. It was intriguing but also quite a chore."[22]

After Allen was introduced to correspondents on September 25, he produced quick results, at least in the judgment of *Time* magazine. A story in early November credited "squarejawed, battle-seasoned" Allen, widely known as "Honk," with changing things for the better for "grumbling Allied newsmen based in the disheveled Hotel Scribe." *Time* rolled on: "By last week the milling throng was gone from the Scribe lobby; censors, PROs, wireless men were settled and working in designated rooms; correspondents were eating regularly." For his part, Allen was quoted as having "honked" in the magazine's paraphrase that "chief credit should go to rayon-smooth naval Captain Harry Butcher . . . aide and close companion of General Eisenhower."[23]

Barney Oldfield, taking in the new broom's work from the PRD side, agreed with *Time*. He said that Allen, acting as a tough old soldier, ordered the Scribe "policed up, and spruced up." Together with Butcher, "he got the place"—in a notably moderate turn of phrase—"running in less irregular fashion." Oldfield added, "The censors, public-relations officers and communications men were assigned to offices. The mess began to run right. One of the best and most cheering developments was the increase of Press Wireless sending power by its boss, Stanley Grammar."[24]

With Allen's appointment, Butcher returned to Paris and took on jobs ranging from upgrading transmission facilities in the Scribe to finding nearby billets for enlisted men and women working in the hotel. Already PROs had spilled out beyond the Scribe to walking-distant billets in the Hôtel Chatham and office space in the American Express building at 11 Rue Scribe. For generations of Americans, the Paris address was an acutely inscribed part of their tourist or expatriate existence. It was where they collected mail, cashed travelers' checks, shipped baggage, or simply gathered to share news. In *Tropic of Cancer*, the author Henry Miller—who came to Paris in the early 1930s and worked on one of the Paris-American newspapers—wrote, "For

Photo 8.1. Correspondents at work in the Scribe's former reception area.
Source: National Archives

five days I have not touched the typewriter nor looked at a book; nor have I had a single idea in my head except to go to the American Express. At nine this morning I was there, just as the doors were being opened, and again at one o'clock. No news."[25] The building's prewar life was not lost on Colonel Dupuy. He told his wife that his work space was in the building where in the past they had picked up their mail. "I never thought that I'd have an office there," he added, "and be looking out from its windows on the fantastic traffic scenes, with the traffic cops as futile as ever."[26]

Evaluating his own recent past in a diary entry on December 6, Butcher decided he "hadn't had a better time during the war than in the past couple of months as head of communications for the Public Relations Division of SHAEF." A primary reason for his sunny view was recognition by some correspondents that "press traffic moves more rapidly now out of Paris than before the war."[27] It was also moving in large volume. Oldfield reported that in the period after Allen's appointment the Scribe's censors "were pawing over an average of more than 3,000,000 words a week . . . 35,000 still pictures, and 100,000 feet of movie film every seven days."[28] He also quoted a *Time* correspondent in Paris, Sherry Mangan, who had written that "the wonder is not that an occasional piece of copy gets stuck in censorship, but that so much gets through as quickly as it does."[29]

Yet if living and working conditions were enhanced in the Scribe, squabbles between correspondents and their PRO keepers growled on. Edward Kennedy said of Allen's reign that he "attempted to weed out some of the deadwood that cluttered up the organization. He had little success; the incompetents and misfits had the tenacity of barnacles. More arrived."[30]

For Kennedy, the PRD was a bloated bureaucracy that no one could entirely put arms around. He said he tried and failed to learn the full number of its personnel in the European theater, though he was certain it was in the thousands. He granted that there were "many highly capable and conscientious men in this great complement," though most of those carped about the bureaucracy nearly as much as the correspondents.[31] While reporting in Italy, Kennedy on occasion had gotten around what he called "the main Public Relations set-up" with the help of "Underground Public Relations," made up of unorthodox PROs who could ease the rules because they had the backing of equally unorthodox generals.[32]

With Allen in place as the PRD's head, Eisenhower told Butcher that he could come back to his role as the commander's aide when he "felt the reorganization was set and the division was operating smoothly." Butcher's diary response was to chuckle since he doubted that "any public-relations office can operate smoothly. There are a half-dozen crises every day."[33] Dupuy said the same in a different way: "We have earthquakes at least once an hour in this PR div."[34]

～

Toward the end of 1944 and on into the new year, two particular eruptions flowed into headlines in the American and Allied press. The German counteroffensive into the Ardennes in Belgium in mid-December, known latter as the Battle of the Bulge, resulted in a forty-eight-hour blackout of information at the Scribe. SHAEF held that the suppression was necessary for military security while correspondents countered that it was really a cover-up of military missteps in the fighting. It was also preventing the public from having an adequate sense of the progress of the war.

During a raucous briefing in the hotel with General Allen on December 19, George Lyon, a former newspaper editor who was now the US Office of War Information's representative to SHAEF, sided with the correspondents. "May I say," he challenged Allen, "that SHAEF policy in this matter is stupid—and that's no reflection on you, sir. Everybody across hell and 40 acres knows what's going on. The American people are entitled to know what's going on."[35]

The blackout resulted in sweeping rumors of German advances from the Ardennes. Butcher took note in his diary of a story making the rounds within the Scribe about an experienced correspondent who returned from the battle and told everyone he would keep going to the United States because the Germans would be entering Paris just as they had in 1940.[36] In an entry on December 23, Butcher mentioned that George Lyon had come to his office to tell his side of his "SHAEF is stupid" remark appearing in American publications. It had stemmed, he said, from his feeling that correspondents were being talked down to during the briefing rather than getting a frank explanation for the delay of news. Dupuy, looking back with regret on the blackout affair, believed that SHAEF "never fully recovered the public relations ground lost in the Ardennes offensive. The shadow of lost confidence hung forever after over all our press relations."[37]

In early January, briefings in the Scribe raged again over a hold on news of significant command changes on the Western Front involving British Field Marshal Bernard Montgomery and American General Omar Bradley. Correspondents in the field and at the hotel were told that the information was off the record, yet stories of the shifts appeared in the United States in *Time* and United Press reports. According to a Time Inc. spokesman, correspondent James Shepley of the magazine had flown from France to New York with a story that was subsequently approved by censors at the War Department in Washington. They had, however, overlooked a paragraph that disclosed the embargoed information.[38]

At a stormy session with Paris correspondents, Allen held that despite the story's publication abroad, SHAEF could not release it to them because it had been given out in confidence. He maintained as well that the holdup in announcing the command changes was based solely on military security. Commanders had distinct methods of fighting, and telling who was in charge of a particular group could give the enemy knowledge of tactics and troop deployments.

Butcher got a similar response when he went to Eisenhower and, as he noted in his diary, "suggested that since the news was all over the place, an announcement should be authorized to prevent further speculation." Already, he added, London newspapers were inferring that when the American military was in trouble, Montgomery rode to the rescue. Eisenhower nonetheless resisted release of the new command structure since the information would help the Germans "better plan their tactics."[39]

～

News stories of squabbles in Paris soon swelled to roundup opinion pieces sharply critical of SHAEF operations. In early January 1945 the *Chicago Tribune* ran a Paris dispatch by Larry Rue with a question-and-answer opening: "What's wrong with headquarters [SHAEF] as far as its release of news is concerned? The answer seems to be a little of everything."[40] That same month Gladwin Hill of the *New York Times* published an account in *Editor & Publisher* magazine that bore the headline "SHAEF a Headache to War Reporters" over a lead sentence that read, "The five little letters SHAEF means hot war news to newspaper readers but to some 100 war correspondents [in the Scribe] their first connotation is two parts vertigo and one part migraine."[41]

In Larry Rue's report, various Paris correspondents declared their irritation with SHAEF in snippets of comment. Noel Monks of Britain's *Daily Mail* declared that SHAEF's operations in the Scribe were a "mad-house." Drew Middleton of the *New York Times* said that recent briefings in the hotel were the "worst I have listened to in six years of war." Rue summarized the recent PRO-press conflicts that had arisen and concluded that SHAEF was "extremely weak on its main function—supplying news and timing releases." Rue cut PROs some slack, however, by pointing out that briefing officers in the Scribe, trying to get current information about American, British, Canadian, and French fighting groups, had too little time to fully acquaint themselves with "what has and hasn't been released at briefings at army and group headquarters or what is being published."

Gladwin Hill's indictment of Supreme Headquarters was more sweeping. He took note of the fact that correspondents worked, slept, and ate in the same Paris hotel where SHAEF's news operations were centered. Sometimes correspondents spent days before they left the Scribe. "It's like," he wrote, "a big convention that just goes on week after week and month after month with the nervous strain proportional." Much of the strain was caused for both PROs and correspondents in trying to figure out what exactly was going on at battlefronts. There was always what Hill called "the unhappy time lag of 24 hours" in official information from the front to SHAEF, an interval that he thought would probably persist. The ultimate reason for the gap was that "the Army is not geared to move information like news organizations." Added to the time issue was "inadequate evaluation" by briefing officers in the Scribe when presenting information to the press and the failure to match release dates at the front and at the hotel. Hill also questioned the system, "or lack of system," for selecting the Scribe's briefing officers. He said he knew personally of officers seemingly drawn at random from replacement pools who "lacked understanding of [military] operations to an extraordinary degree."[42]

～

Airing of correspondents' grievances in news stories in the United States appeared to get Washington's attention. In a diary entry on January 12, 1945, Butcher said that SHAEF released an announcement that day that "Steve Early is being loaned to us by the President for temporary duty." He added that he had requested him, with General Allen's agreement, for help with the PRD's ways of briefing correspondents.[43] Two days later, a story in the *New York Times* said that Stephen Early, President Roosevelt's long-serving press secretary, was going to SHAEF headquarters for several weeks to "survey the arrangements for handling war news and make recommendations which the Army apparently hopes will improve a troublesome situation."

According to the story, Early had been invited by Allen, but it was clear the European trip had Roosevelt's approval—and perhaps, as some speculated, it was little more than a gift from the president for his press secretary's tireless service. Or, as Ernest Dupuy in Paris privately suggested, Early had wangled the trip because he had been a captain in World War I and couldn't bear missing out on the current one. In any event, the *Times* went on to sort out reasons for unrest among correspondents, a key one being the blackout of information during the Battle of the Bulge.[44]

Early reached Paris on February 20 and declined housing in the Ritz to stay with Butcher and make his temporary office in the cold Raphaël. He was introduced to correspondents at a Scribe press conference, then spent days listening in on briefings in the hotel—"our activity being most subject to criticism," Butcher observed. Early also followed one dispatch through the steps of filing, going through the copy room, censorship, and then commercial transmission to New York and receipt. The entire process took seventeen minutes.[45]

In early March, Early and Butcher traveled to Eisenhower's new forward headquarters in Reims and later to the field headquarters of Generals Patton and Bradley on an extended inspection trip of 1,200 miles through France, Germany, Luxembourg, and the Netherlands.[46] At Patton's headquarters, James Quirk was the PRO in charge of arrangements for meeting the general. "Coming down to spend the night with me," Quirk commented in a letter home, "are Steve Early and Captain Butcher, General Ike's Naval aide. I don't know that they want anything. They are most probably just bucketing around the front." It was Quirk's job to get them good billets and, after his press camp's usual evening briefing, put on a special drinks and dinner party, and afterward invite some correspondents to meet with the visitors. Quirk added that he was getting "a little tired of visiting firemen but they are part of the job."[47]

Together with Allen, Early toured other press camps, then made a hurried flight to Britain to visit a son recovering from war wounds. After the press secretary left for home on March 21, Butcher thought one change in PRD briefing practice that Early recommended to the War Department might prove useful. In cases where information was delayed for security reasons, correspondents should be given quotable material for their stories so readers would have some sense of the reason for the holdup. "We are also," Butcher recorded in his diary, "going to try to avoid the use of the term 'blackout.'"[48]

CHAPTER NINE

~

The Great Parisian Magnet

Charles Collingwood's CBS script about the Scribe becoming like no other hotel in the world had such appeal for Harry Butcher that, "as one of the few kind things ever said about PRD," he quoted from it at length in a diary entry. (Collingwood later informed Butcher that his broadcast never reached New York. The reason, Butcher assumed, was "atmospherics.") What seemingly pleased Butcher as well—he made no diary notation one way or the other—were the unkind things the correspondent equally laid out about his fellow newsmen.

"In theory," said Collingwood of the Scribe's correspondents, "they are all supposed to be covering the war, but Paris is a great magnet and many seem to be here just because they want to be in Paris. This is a great trial to the Public Relations Officers who are supposed to provide facilities for war coverage. They call the nonworking correspondents the 'lunatic fringe.'"[1] The fringe newsmen were of course covering the war, but doing so within the comfortable confines of the Scribe rather than, as PROs intended, from somewhere on the Western Front. The evident paradox was that the array of living and working services offered in the hotel by the PRD encouraged correspondents to extend Parisian sojourns and continue filing dispatches with such imposing datelines as Supreme HDQ., Allied Expeditionary Force, Paris.

Collingwood—who at the time was rotating CBS broadcasts from the hotel with Larry LeSueur and Richard C. Hottelet—could well have offered himself as an example of a fringe correspondent. While LeSueur and Hottelet would eventually track the war into Germany, Collingwood largely stayed put in Paris. He had good professional reason for doing so: in Paris his chances of actually getting on the air were better than if he was off at some distant front. Transmission could fail anywhere, but the established setup for broadcasting from the Scribe made it less likely.[2] Personally, Collingwood was also having a grand time in Paris. "I like the city and I like the life," he informed his parents in a letter. "There is always something to look forward to . . . friends to see, an exposition . . . a shop where they say there are some nice things, a gallery where there are some good pictures."[3] There was as well his busy social calendar. William Walton said of his friend that "a new Charles was born in Paris. He was invited to very fancy soirées, with roomfuls of famous people. It was a world he found terribly fascinating. Charles began to get very fine feathers in Paris."[4]

Others made the same point about the Parisian hold on newsmen. Ernest Dupuy noted that "the newshawks now in Paris didn't want to leave for the front" since they had "a tremendous mass of news to cover in the city."[5] Barney Oldfield, equally commenting from the PRD's side, wrote that "the war left Paris behind, but the war correspondents hadn't the heart to do likewise."[6]

What some did do, while staying well clear of harm's way, was interview Allied troops flocking to Paris as a designated site for rest and relaxation. When pressed, newsmen who employed the tactic insisted that information gleaned in face-to-face encounters with soldiers got them closer to the war than did official SHAEF briefings in the hotel. Oldfield's mocking dismissal of such street reporting was that "being born among us was the journalist mendicant, who would pluck at the sleeves of soldiers on leave in Paris to get stories."[7]

In the enduring argument about the news values of what Drew Middleton of the *New York Times* defined as the sharp end of the war up front and the big picture at the Scribe, the views of correspondents shifted—at least as they found their way into publications back home. "Sobered from their Paris liberation news jag," Dwight Bentel wrote in *Editor & Publisher* magazine some two weeks after the liberation, "correspondents in France reluctantly returned to the comparatively dull business of covering the war this week only to discover that the story had gotten out of hand." He pointed out that combat fronts in France and the Low Countries were moving so fast that when newsmen caught up with them, they couldn't send reports because they had "outrun their communications."[8] In a dispatch from Belgium in early September 1944, the *New York Sun*'s Wilfred Heinz revealed his own troubles:

This is the story you have been trying to write now for three days and it is still difficult. There have been times when you have been moving so fast that you have been unable to set up your typewriter, and there have been other times when, although you could set up the typewriter it was useless to write because there was no way to get the story back.[9]

Another problem with reporting from the sharp end of the war was, again according to Bentel in *Editor & Publisher*, the "wet blanket" that SHAEF kept tossing over "practically all of the news that was hot and informative." Prime examples were the rapid thrusts of General Patton's armored force that presumably kept the Germans from knowing its exact location, hence producing a SHAEF "security blackout" that gave rise to rumor and speculation that included stories of German surrender. At the same early September period, the *New York Herald Tribune* reported that news sent back to Paris from front lines was usually twenty-four hours behind real time and often much more.

~

Paris in the postliberation period was short of food and cigarettes, short of coal for heat and electricity, short of public transport—short of virtually everything needed for everyday life. Yet what it singularly had was itself, the magnificent and largely undamaged city that appealed as much as ever to the Western mind and imagination. Correspondents and PROs alike marveled at the good fortune that stationed them there, if only for a time. Thor Smith quoted a PRO colleague's phrasing of a common feeling: "Yeah, it's a tough war here in the silver fox holes of Paris."

Ernest Dupuy took a break from his official duties to put on paper his impressions of the city as glimpsed from a room within the Scribe:

Am sitting here overlooking the boulevards, with a Paris sun shining and traffic wheeling by. It's mostly American traffic, and the streets are filled with soldiers. This place is an amazing sight. . . . Paris is filled with bikes—men, women and children ride bikes—passengers sitting on the handle-bars, sitting side-saddle behind the cyclist, children in baskets. Women in afternoon gowns, fantastic hats on heads, pedal along, wearing long white gloves! . . . Yesterday took a quick reconnaissance of our old haunts . . . all look the same except for traces of barricades, bullet-pecked walls and German debris. . . . The flower women are in front of the Madeleine.

Dupuy didn't blink from noting dark moments in his amazing city. One day he saw a crowd gathered in front of the Scribe and learned that "a collaborator had been picked up and the cops rushed him into the lobby to save him from lynching. I shall never forget his face as they finally took him away." He recorded that "hoodlums several times justled some of our RAF girls [who worked in the Scribe] because they alleged their uniforms were German." While walking Parisian streets he noticed that police wore empty holsters. Only in front of their stations did he see armed men. "An unarmed Paris police force," he told himself, "added up to one thing only—the authorities did not trust them." He also logged rumors among both Parisians and correspondents of American officers living in high style in elegant apartments, of the military wasting food while the French starved, and of Germans with French hostages holding out in the Paris sewers. "Good for fiction, that," Dupuy commented in his journal about the sewers, "and oddly enough, it may be true. The story goes that the French know it and have the exits guarded but will do nothing because of the hostages."[11]

～

For a spell after the liberation, Paris was a gift for correspondents in that editors and producers back home found the city eminently newsworthy. Readily available were stories about people who had endured the occupation, the crosscurrents of French politics, and the revival of Paris fashion after the Germans tried to reduce its prominence. And there were always stories at hand about Paris's risqué nightlife or, if a correspondent knew it from the past, simply comparing the city's present with the past.

Tania Long of the *New York Times* took the latter route for a piece for her paper's Sunday magazine. She had lived happily in Paris as a child and later as a student at the Sorbonne. Now back as a war correspondent with her husband and *Times* colleague Raymond Daniell, the beauty of familiar streets was breathtaking. Yet she couldn't ignore signs of war. There were no private cars or buses, and the metro wasn't running for lack of fuel. Burned German tanks were pushed onto sidewalks. On the Place de la Concorde were barricades the FFI had used. On the Boulevard Saint Michel were heaps of rubble and glass. Montparnasse where she once lived seemed nearly dead. Nightclubs had closed due to lack of electricity, and outdoor cafés had few customers since there was little to drink but ersatz coffee. Overall, Long decided, Paris was "barely functioning as a city." Still, the sight of children playing and Allied flags hanging from buildings and people repeatedly shaking her hand encouraged her to write, at her story's end, that the spirit of the city was unchanged.[12]

Iris Carpenter turned out a similar then-and-now story about a Paris fashion event she attended. "The show differed," she told her *Boston Globe* readers, "from those I remembered the last time I saw Paris three weeks before the war only by the fact that prices were higher and materials of poor quality." "Pleats," she anticipated, "will highlight the Autumn fashion trend. Pleats are used every way than can be thought of—on sleeves, for yokes to define the hips, and just as trimming."[13]

Noel Busch, a *Life* editor now acting as a war correspondent, took on the demanding subject of a cover story about de Gaulle, datelined Paris, which appeared in the magazine on November 13, 1944. His lengthy profile, "De Gaulle the Prophet," traced the French leader's career from his early military days to his long exile in Britain to his triumphant return to France. Busch followed this large undertaking with a breezy "Notes from Paris" column in *Life* on December 18. One of his tidbits dealt with the Scribe: "After adding up his accounts at the bar of the Hôtel Scribe, appropriately named hostelry reserved for German correspondents during the occupation and American correspondents during the liberation, the bartender proudly revealed that, while wine and beer consumption was identical, US correspondents drank up exactly as much brandy in a day as their enemy colleagues had in a month."

An article on the *Chicago Tribune*'s front page by Robert Cromie was full of similar morsels about Paris on the Sunday after the liberation. Among other things, he had an especially fine view of Rue Scribe since, as readers were informed, he was overlooking it while writing in his hotel room in the Grand. The exuberance of the liberation had died down, he believed, but the street was still crowded by Frenchmen inspecting American vehicles. On the previous day, his soldier driver, going out to his jeep parked at the curb, found three young girls washing it. "That was their way," Cromie paused to explain, "of expressing thanks."[14]

If Paris was the great magnet holding correspondents from moving on, the Scribe was a key element. It not only accommodated SHAEF correspondents for work and housing needs but also, as Harry Butcher pointed out, served as their social center. The wood-paneled bar in the basement lounge was amply, if irregularly, stocked and amply attended. Butcher probably understated its role in the hotel when he wrote that "the Scribe Bar is a chief attraction." He was more fully on target when, in an entry on November 8, 1944, he recalled that when American election returns were put on a loudspeaker in the hotel at night there was little interest. Most correspondents were instead "primarily absorbed in their jobs of covering the war and of recovering from the effect of the Scribe Bar, where the unending process of swapping stories goes on—referred to as 'picking one another's brains.'"[15]

Butcher nevertheless thought that the pay-as-you-enter SHAEF mess established in the hotel's former dining room was "perhaps more popular than the bar" and recorded its modest cost for breakfast at ten to twenty francs and lunch and dinner at twenty to forty francs that appealed at a time when black-market food in Paris cafés came with sky-high prices. (In 1944, an American dollar was worth fifty French francs.[16]) The only problem Butcher found with the mess was the throngs it drew. He noted that "correspondents and officers who find old or new friends amongst the French, or former employees of the [local newspaper] bureaus, are crowding the Scribe's dining room." Though the mess was profitable, he held that "we cannot indiscriminately feed everyone whom the correspondents or our own staff wish to bring as a guest."[17]

Along with the mess, the hotel provided a military-style post exchange—or as Butcher called it, a "GI's country store"—for the needs of occupants for their weekly rations of cigarettes and other necessities and his own for cigars. But for many it was the quality and quantity of food in the mess that left the strongest impression. When the Parisian writer Simone de Beauvoir came to lunch with a French journalist, she called the mess the *Restaurant du Scribe* and exclaimed that "it was an American enclave in the heart of Paris: white bread, fresh eggs, jam, sugar and Spam."[18]

Barbara Loxton, a South African field artist, said in a letter home in November 1944 that she was billeted in a "very comfortable hotel where all the war-correspondents are, a boiling cauldron of newspaper life, very interesting and quite extraordinary." "The joint," she added about the Scribe, "is run by the American Army and though their ways, manners, speech and outlook is strange and baffling to begin with I find they are helpful and accommodating and very ready to arrange things without a super abundance of red tape." She reserved higher praise for the mess where the food was "marvelous and very plentiful, American rations cooked in French fashion."[19]

Yet the basement lounge bar was seldom overlooked in recollections of the Scribe. David Scherman, a *Life* magazine photographer who kept a room in the hotel for two years, said "the bar in the basement was for months European headquarters for the world press, its patrons a name-dropper's paradise of once-and-future newspaper, wire-service and radio celebrities."[20]

Ned Calmer, who in prewar Paris worked on two Paris-American newspapers and later joined CBS as one of Murrow's stalwarts, drew on experience of the Scribe and its bar in his 1950 novel *The Strange Land*. After a briefing session on the floor above, a crowd descends to the bar where an American officer is sipping cognac and musing about "the good old Scribe bar. Before the war I must have passed this hotel a hundred times without ever dreaming of coming inside for any reason under the sun. Now it's in midstream of world history."

As the bar fills up, the officer wonders if others feel his sense of the room's importance: "The sergeant-clerks, the Wacs, the COM-Z small fry, the play-it-safe correspondents, all the thousand and one with the snow jobs and, of course, their local girl-friends, who like them never had it so good. Do they feel the meaning of this room?" As the officer defines it to himself, the feeling is awareness of being "released from the past. The old responsibilities have crumbled in rooms like these in London and Paris." For the people about him flushed with cognac and cigarette smoke, the meaning of the Scribe's bar is that "anything goes."[21]

The COM Z mentioned in Calmer's novel, both its small and otherwise-sized fry, presumably came in goodly numbers to the bar. The short form of Communications Zone, Com Z arrived in Paris with the liberation, established its headquarters in the Hôtel Majestic near the Arc de Triomphe, and rapidly became a ponderous presence in the city. For a time it seemed, at least to Ernest Dupuy and other Scribe PROs, that the logistical operation also intended to absorb all communications activity in the city. But with briefing, censorship, and transmission facilities entrusted to SHAEF's PRD, the Scribe and Com Z went forward, as Dupuy phrased it, as "separate organizations." When Com Z needed its own public-relations office in Paris, a PRO formerly with the Associated Press moved over to take charge.[22]

With the D-Day landings, the army's Services and Supply branch had been renamed the Communications Zone. From headquarters in Valognes in Normandy, the group moved—as Harry Butcher wrote—pell-mell into Paris. Eisenhower, Butcher added, groused about what those in combat zones might think about the "supply people living in the luxury of Paris." He thought about ordering Com Z's commander, General John Lee—warmly treated in a *Time* cover story on September 25, 1944, as an old-fashioned and self-important but effective leader—to move his operation entirely out of Paris, but decided it was too late to do so. He settled for instructing Lee to banish from the city any American personnel not needed for essential tasks.[23] According to Dupuy, Com Z headquarters had at this early point already mushroomed to some eight thousand officers and seventeen thousand enlisted men working in and about a fortified area around the Majestic.[24] Rumor had it that General Lee lived apart in a fine penthouse apartment.

～

However meaningful the basement bar was for life in the Scribe, the hotel's day-to-day business as a press camp took place on the floors above. As reconfigured by workmen, the ground-floor reception area held long tables, giving correspondents and their typewriters common work space. The marble-columned ballroom became an information room, wall-mapped from floor to ceiling. Here, in a setting holding about a hundred people, SHAEF briefings, press conferences, and VIP talks took place, news releases were handed out, and a reference library was maintained.

On the hotel's second floor were transmission facilities and office space for, along with other activities, travel booking for correspondents to outlying press camps and transportation within Paris. Six connecting rooms on the floor formed the hub of censorship operations, with a seventh a copy room where military clerks logged in stories filed by correspondents, had copies made, moved stories on to censors, and logged out stories when censors were finished.[25]

Censors worked—using as guidance a two-hundred-page mimeographed "bible" plus updates—at large tables designated for ground censors, air censors, photo censors, and French liaison censors. Correspondents were allowed only in a separate room for meetings with censors who had stopped or ordered cuts in their reports. While British and Canadian censors were graded as military captains, American censors were typically lieutenants. Once copy was passed, correspondents went to a Signal Corps office to have it stamped for transmission or broadcast on a first-come-first-served basis.[26] By October 1944, three commercial transmitters in the hotel—Press Wireless, Radio France, and MacKay Radio—connected Paris with America. Three other lines, one commercial and two military, linked the city with Britain, with one of the military lines soon replaced by a BBC transmitter. In the early days a substantial amount of approved press material was also flown back to London.

On the third floor some hotel rooms were turned into broadcasting studios, and one area became a secure MP-guarded war room with more floor-to-ceiling maps. Within this space PROs prepared for briefing sessions by contacting units in the field for current information. The subsequent daily briefing with correspondents in the information room ordinarily took place at 10 a.m., 3 p.m., and 10 p.m. American or British staff officers mounted a low platform at one end of the room and from a rostrum used long pointers to track military progress on the vast colored maps. Colonel Dupuy usually supervised the briefings, responded to correspondents' questions, and gave off-the-record background information.[27] Other SHAEF officers attended now and then with less time-based material that could be drawn on for lengthy roundup stories.

Day or night, urgent alerts were signaled in the hotel's upper four floors with a booming klaxon—or, as christened among correspondents, the "hog caller"—that sent figures spilling down to the former ballroom in various states of dress. One blast of the horn meant a normal news release, three the signal for big spot news. On hearing the alert, correspondents had no certain way of knowing the news value of the information, yet they couldn't risk missing anything, especially if they were hotly competitive wire-service reporters. Harold Acton reported that when briefers took questions, the sessions, either regular or alerts, could turn into boisterous affairs in which correspondents "often betrayed a shameful ignorance of geography and the lecturer was sometimes heckled as if he were a slippery politician juggling with the facts."[28] Correspondents countered by insisting they had to stay vocally vigilant to correct frequent briefing errors and, especially with air force accounts, challenge claims of damage.

Attendance at briefings varied due to time constraints on newsmen. Wire services came to all sessions, while mornings drew writers for evening publications, afternoons attracted British and Commonwealth morning men, and evenings predominantly attracted American morning reporters. Dupuy believed the average turnout across all briefings was about thirty newsmen, a number he found strikingly low given the hundreds living in the hotel. He ascribed the figure to more correspondents covering Paris happenings than military operations.

When Butcher staged what he called a symposium on communications, he estimated that forty correspondents attended. Appearances by top SHAEF figures drew standing-room-only crowds, though for the most part correspondents—appraising names of coming speakers posted on a blackboard—made their decision to show up on assumptions about immediate news value. Dupuy acknowledged that correspondents were often presented with more war material than they could reasonably handle. In any case, if the audience for a special speaker was expected to be embarrassingly low, PROs packed the crowd with their own people, secretaries, and off-duty briefers.

There was never a problem with attendance during the supreme commander's press conferences, the usual glut of jeeps and military cars cleared from the front of the hotel and MPs positioned. After mounting the briefing platform, Eisenhower usually lit the first of several cigarettes, a signal to deferential correspondents to light up as well. Harold Acton found that most newsmen were chain smokers, and when cigarette rations were limited, de-

Photo 9.1. Eisenhower addresses newsmen in the Scribe's former ballroom.
Source: National Archives

spondency could be so intense that, as one correspondent told him, "it would take him hours of cerebration to formulate a message he would normally type in a few ticks."[29]

The avuncular NBC radio commentator H. V. Kaltenborn got his first look at Eisenhower during a Scribe press conference. The commander's candid answers to questions about military matters surprised him until he grasped that everything he heard was off the record, with PROs afterward providing a few approved quotes to work into news stories.[30] Officers made clear to the cast of international correspondents that for briefings and press conferences censors followed the American definition of "off the record": for background only. Dupuy made it standard procedure that such instruction include an all-inclusive statement hammering home the point: "Off the record, confidential, for background only, and not for publication." The repeated warning, he noted, was "stuffy but necessary."[31]

The occasional press conferences and regular briefings gave newsmen added excuse for covering the war from the distance of the Scribe. Attached to frontline units, they were limited to a narrow slice of action, whereas guided by hotel briefers and the ballroom maps, they got, in theory, broader and more nuanced reports of land and air operations. Staying in or near the hotel also meant correspondents had more rapid access to censors and reliable transmission equipment than they would have in the field. For broadcasters, transmission was crucial. Radio equipment was subject to hazards everywhere, but more so in combat areas, leaving correspondents uncertain if their scripts would ever get on the air or fussing that competitors at the Scribe were having no trouble getting through to London or New York.

A further benefit of staying at the Scribe, again in theory, was greater awareness of what other correspondents were reporting. But this could be two-edged, with the unending process of swapping stories leading to parallel dispatches. The Scribe, said Barney Oldfield, "from the very first day, became a fanciful place, its lobby filled with aimless human tides, everyone afraid to leave it for fear of missing something, everyone afraid also that anything he could find there would fail to measure up under the eyes of his editor or program director."[32]

Oldfield was hardly a detached observer since at the time he was trying to get PROs to nudge correspondents in the Scribe—"the laggards in Paris," he called them—to occupy some of the available press camp spaces with the Ninth Army on its push into Germany. Briefings at combat press camps, he argued, "were more war-flavored, as well as closer to the fighting and the men who fought, than the briefings at SHAEF." This reality, he went on, caused battlefield newsman to heap scorn on the work of the Paris stay-at-homes. They believed it only fair that they should have priority with stories garnered up front under dangerous conditions. But in the system they labored under, briefers in the Scribe relayed the frontline information, and the resident correspondents could reshape it or expand on it and get their work quickly passed by censors.[33] But if close to combat was the better place for war correspondents, Oldfield had to concede that among them "bed and board at the front was not too gay a thought."[34]

Edward Kennedy agreed with Oldfield about the limitation of war reporting from the rear, but as the AP's chief in France he had to stay in Paris. With the regular briefings and the wire service's need to keep updating stories, he spent days on end never leaving the Scribe. He felt himself as removed from the battlefronts as he would have been in Chicago. The briefings, he complained, "lacked the breath of life, usually lacked the essence of good reporting, and not infrequently lacked the whole truth. They represented SHAEF's official line."[35]

But if frontline dispatches were superior, they didn't fill the demand of the AP's client papers for wide-ranging accounts of military events. Over time, Kennedy's Paris bureau developed a system of gathering reports transmitted by AP correspondents at the various fronts, or sent directly to New York and then directed back to Paris, and using them together with SHAEF briefing material to write roundup stories that Kennedy thought more accurate and interesting than relying wholly on the briefings or frontline accounts.[36]

～

Briefings were such a familiar feature of the hotel's work that newsmen fell into routines. Dupuy believed that at any ordinary night session, briefers saw in the front row the same lineup of print correspondents seated in the same chairs. He named and lightly sketched them. Directly in the middle were "usually beaming round-faced Drew Middleton" of the *New York Times* and "grave and witty" John O'Reilly of the *New York Herald Tribune*. To their left would be Bob Cooper of the London *Times*, "punctiliously polite—and sometimes touchy, too," and "little Anderson, delicate, sensitive," of the *Manchester Guardian* whose "news scalpel at times probed dangerously close to the briefer's nerve centers."

Holding up the front row's right side was *Newsweek*'s "ironical" Joe Evans, "the beard he wore in London stripped." On the ends of the right side were the AP men—Ed Kennedy, "nervous and worn" from four long years of war, and Jim Long or Ned Bealmear. On the end of the other side were "stout" John Gilbert of the London *Evening Star* or Stanley Bishop of the London *Daily Herald*.

For the inner rows Dupuy shifted to football jargon. "Roving in the secondary defense" were Reuters's "quizzical" Marshall Yarrow and Marcelle Poirier of the Agence France-Presse, "as thirsty for Boche blood as she was attractive, always doing a job of Monday-morning quarterbacking." "Drumthumping" Larry Rue of the *Chicago Tribune* would be "lurking in midfield" and "far back in the end zone, conveniently close to the door," was James Kilgallen of the INS, "a cold cigar clutched in his mouth, cap covering his bald dome like a rabbi's shammoka." They all, said Dupuy of the newsmen, comprised for the PRD a "tough team to buck."

Dupuy also named and labeled a host of other print and radio reporters who were regulars or near regulars at briefings—among them, "sensible, sound" Mark Watson of the *Baltimore Sun*; the "Diana of the linotypes" Helen Kirkpatrick of the *Chicago Daily News*; and "urbane" Douglas Williams of the London *Daily Telegraph*. Dupuy held out special notice to a newsman who spent more time at the front than at Paris briefings. Nemo Canabarro Lucas, who wrote for *A Noite* in Rio de Janeiro and was SHAEF's only Brazilian correspondent, spoke Portuguese, Spanish, and French but limited English. In the Scribe, a Portuguese speaker censored the flood of copy he sent to Rio. Dupuy found the correspondent "inquisitive as a cat" and said he "couldn't help liking Nemo and trying to help him, since he was after news, and went wherever he could find it."

An incident illustrating the Brazilian's wide-ranging pursuit of stories took place during the Battle of the Bulge. He had jeeped from a Ninth Army press camp toward the fighting when he was stopped by American soldiers struggling to construct a roadblock with German troops just ahead of them. As Dupuy wrote, the American "commander, rushing from gun to gun, was stopped suddenly in his tracks by the debonair Nemo, who tapping him on the shoulder, bowed profoundly, then waved his arm at the scene of feverish activity to demand—'Explain, please?'"[37]

Dupuy's duties as General Allen's deputy held him in Paris and the Scribe, but he yearned for trips to the front to get, as he put it, "the 'feel' of the action." He also thought it important to provide details to correspondents at the hotel about particularly intense engagements. During the grim fighting in the Hürtgen Forest in early November, he recorded that he and Thor Smith "lit out for the front."[38]

As Smith wrote home about what became a ten-day journey across five countries, Dupuy's presence made it more interesting because of his command of French, his knowledge of territory he had seen in World War I, and his familiarity with top generals. Dupuy and Smith were present during the start of a Third Army offensive, moving from division to division and sitting in on tactical planning, which Smith found "an invaluable experience for me . . . finding out just how it is done."

With field glasses they watched actual fighting as troops moved across a valley, tanks following; prisoners brought back; and artillery strikes by both Americans and Germans. From a hill they looked down at a small town still in enemy hands. That evening they learned that a place they visited was shelled a half hour after they left, with two GIs killed. Another day they saw heavy bombers attack German-held Metz. It appeared to Smith that the entire air force was involved: "Group after group, wave after wave of Forts and Libs . . . and later Marauders . . . came piling over. It was a thrilling, chilling sight. The announcement later said 1,200 planes, and I'm sure I saw every one of them."[39]

CHAPTER TEN

~

Latecomers

As the Allies closed in on the German heartland, prominent writers and newsmen on the home front scrambled for correspondent bylines before the war curtain dropped for good. The *New York Herald Tribune* sent both its sports editor, Stanley Woodward, and its book editor, Lewis Gannett, on limited-time combat tours. In Britain while waiting to accompany a secret airborne operation, Walter Cronkite met up with Woodward. Told to assemble at press headquarters in London, Cronkite came outfitted in full combat gear. Woodward, who had turned out stories for the *Herald Tribune* since reaching Britain, was in the paper's London office when the coded message about the mission was left on the desk of Ned Russell, the paper's airborne reporter. With Russell at the moment away in Paris, Woodward chose himself as the replacement.

Security for the mission was so tight that even PROs didn't have all details, leaving Woodward to appear at press headquarters in his full dress uniform. While in a car taking them to the headquarters of the American 101st Airborne beyond London, Cronkite whispered to Woodward what little he knew: they would parachute somewhere, possibly behind German lines. An astounded Woodward, Cronkite later wrote, "stared long and hard at me through his bottle-thick glasses."[1]

The officers' mess at headquarters had a bar, and when the commanding officer, General Maxwell Taylor, took press members to his quarters for a briefing, Woodward was missing. Having last seen him at the bar, Cronkite assumed members of the 101st had talked the older and overweight sportswriter out of the flight. Cronkite learned from the briefing that the flight would be aboard gliders. He knew their deadly nicknames—flying coffins, tow targets—and would have backed out of the mission save for derisive colleagues he would have to face later. At least a glider flight, as he sought to console himself, "ought to be a nice quiet way to die—no roaring engine, just a nice silent glide into eternity."[2]

The airborne mission was the first phase of Operation Market Garden, a daring and ultimately disastrous plan to land three divisions of troops in the Netherlands to secure a bridge over the Rhine River at Arnhem. In the second phase, the British army would use the access to cross the river and turn into Germany. Cronkite was with a group of some fourteen men who came down onto a patch of earth near the town of Eindhoven, then crawled to cover under German fire. He was searching for a wooded area where a group headquarters with a radio transmitter was supposed to be when he stumbled across Woodward on the edge of a ditch. "Nobody told me," he murmured to Cronkite, "that it was going to be like this."[3]

Behind his glasses Woodward's eyes were bloodshot, and his clothing was ridiculous. Cronkite learned later that at the bar in Britain, Woodward had passed out, after which drinking companions outfitted him in combat gear—far too small, a rope rather than a belt, but decent boots—and gotten him aboard a glider. In the headquarters in the woods, Cronkite used a typewriter he had strapped on his back to punch out a story of some three hundred words, after which Woodward borrowed it to write fifty words. As Woodward recalled, the signalman handling the two stories transmitted only his since the limit for filing was fifty words, giving him, as he put it, "credit for an underserved global scoop on the operation."[4]

As the campaign progressed, Cronkite wrote that Woodward "turned out to be a good sport and one terrific correspondent in the few days he was at the front."[5] Woodward later summed up Market Garden as the greatest adventure of his life. After returning to Britain, he spent a week rolling out copy about the airborne invasion that for days led his New York paper.

～

Barney Oldfield said of Lewis Gannett that he "went off to war to encounter grosser adventures than those offered by the fiction which went across his desk at the Herald-Tribune."[6] In a dispatch sent to the paper from Germany, Gannett used the contrast with newsreels rather than fiction as a means of getting at war's reality. With a correspondent from Yank magazine he was up front to observe an infantry operation when a battalion post came under unexpected heavy German shelling. He huddled with soldiers and officers in a cellar as shells kept coming. He wrote that actual combat "did not look at all the way it does on newsreels, and it did not sound like the precise schedule of operations outlined to the correspondents the night before. It was a muddy, muddled war." When at last he crawled from the cellar, he admitted he "had been as thoroughly scared as I ever had been in my life." Before heading back from the front, he needed "half an hour to screw up enough courage to sit down in the jeep and drive."[7]

The British correspondent Michael Moynihan, who had met up with Gannett in the Netherlands, considered the bespectacled and bookish critic the American he felt the most empathy with during the war, this despite Gannett's addiction to poker.[8] Gannett also became one of Moynihan's favored jeep companions while searching for stories on the way into Germany. Another chosen jeep mate was Moynihan's British colleague Noel Monks, whom he portrayed as given to looking on the bright side of things—"even seeming to bear no grudge against the unspeakable Hemingway for having stolen his wife."[9]

∼

In his 1933 book *Down and Out in Paris and London*, George Orwell mentioned a desultory effort he once made to get a job in the kitchen of the Scribe. After arriving in Paris in mid-February 1945 for a three-month stint as a war correspondent, the then modestly known British writer was billeted in the hotel. Though afflicted with seriously poor health and the new father of a recently adopted infant son, he was determined to view conditions in Germany for himself.

Reporting for both Britain's *Observer* and the *Manchester Evening News*, Orwell first began sending regular dispatches from the Scribe that dealt with such usual subjects as the look of the city, French newspapers, and French politics. "If it were not for the ever-present American soldiers," he said of Paris in a report, "one would hardly take this for the capital of a country at war."[10] In a personal letter sent from the hotel—his room number recorded as 329—he remarked that he was now wearing a beret but wouldn't be sending anyone silk stockings from Paris because the Americans had bought them all up.

He made no mention of facilities within the hotel or trips to the bar. Fellow correspondents or PROs seem to have had little contact with him in or beyond the hotel—or awareness of his presence. Hemingway was an exception. An admirer of Hemingway's fiction, especially *For Whom the Bell Tolls*, Orwell one day went to the Ritz, found the author listed in the register, and went to his room. He introduced himself by his given name, Eric Blair.

Hemingway, busy packing bags, replied, "Well, what the fucking hell do you want?" After Orwell reframed his name as George Orwell, Hemingway changed his tune to "Why the fucking hell didn't you say so?" and proposed a drink together. They drank and talked, but only briefly before Hemingway had to leave.[11]

While at the Scribe, Orwell made by mail some late changes in the proofs of his novel *Animal Farm*.[12] He also spent time with the Oxford philosopher A. J. Ayer, who was then working as an attaché in the British embassy in Paris and impressing important guests with his grasp of French existentialism.[13] With Harold Acton, whom he had known slightly during school days at Eton, Orwell often shared meals.

Among Malcolm Muggeridge's duties with British intelligence was keeping tabs on P. G. Wodehouse, and he took Orwell from the Scribe to meet the middle-aged writer of the Jeeves and Wooster stories at the Hôtel Le Bristol. The Germans had placed Wodehouse and his wife there following earlier radio broadcasts from Berlin by the writer that were interpreted in Britain as serving the Nazi cause. Orwell soon took the Wodehouses to dinner and later wrote an essay defending the author as a political innocent.

After his own wife died suddenly in Britain during what had seemed routine surgery, Orwell went home for a period before returning to the war. In a letter to a friend written from the Scribe, he said, "I came straight back here after Eileen's death and have felt somewhat better for being at work most of the time."[14] He doggedly remained at work, "bumping about in jeeps" through a devastated Germany that, as he remarked in an *Observer* report on April 8, made him doubt the future of civilization.

⌒

Edna Ferber, the author of such popular American novels and plays as *Show Boat*, *Giant*, and *Dinner at Eight*, flew to Paris in April 1945 to write about the air force for the North American Newspaper Alliance (NANA). In World War I she had been chosen by the American Red Cross to write articles but failed to get a French visa because, so she was told, her deceased father was born in Hungary. In Paris she expected to stay with correspondents at the Scribe but was put up at the Ritz with VIPs and top military brass, leaving her somewhat embarrassed by its luxury but delighted by meals of military rations transformed by French cooks.

From Paris, Ferber went on excursions to Belgium and Germany, the latter causing sharply worded complaints in a NANA dispatch about the Russians preventing American correspondents from entering Berlin. "There can be witnessed in Europe today," she wrote, "the sight of a great nation known as the United States of America standing, hat in hand, in the outer office waiting for permission to walk into Berlin."[15] Back in Paris after Germany, she noted the heavy presence of Americans, in and out of uniform, "swirling around the Scribe" and other prominent venues. Among those she singled out for mention were the film producer Mike Todd, "smoking a large dark cigar and wearing a vague uniform that resembles a skiing costume," and Gertrude Stein, plodding along with a large French poodle.[16] Along with Alice B. Toklas, Stein had abandoned Paris for the French countryside during the occupation.

∼

In sending Lewis Gannett and Stanley Woodward abroad, the *New York Herald Tribune* was rewarding veterans of its pages. Sending Marguerite Higgins couldn't have been more different. In June 1942, Higgins—young, attractive, ambitious, flirtatious, fluent in French, and with degrees from the University of California and Columbia University—was just staring out as a reporter in the New York paper's city room. But already she was also campaigning to become a war correspondent. By the following year she had talked her way into becoming one, in part by appealing directly to the wife of the paper's owner. In 1944, at age twenty-four, she traveled to Britain on the *Queen Mary*, converted into a troopship and carrying along with the soldiers a group of other correspondents that included the *New Yorker*'s Janet Flanner.

After the vessel paused on its midnight departure, a ladder from a tugboat brought up a small missing correspondent outfitted in a uniform and helmet. When the helmet slipped off, Higgins's blonde hair was apparent. Years afterward, Flanner recalled the arrival: "It was my first encounter with Marguerite Higgins. She looked so sweet and innocent. I immediately thought of Goldilocks and wanted to protect her. If I'd known then what I know now I'd have thrown her overboard."[17] As they came in contact with Higgins in Europe, other female colleagues shared Flanner's disenchanted view of the younger and energetic reporter who, among other things, wasn't inclined to defer to those with more experience.[18]

After time in London and more campaigning to get to Paris, Higgins at length reached the city in February 1945. "1 Rue Scribe," she excitedly jotted in her journal, confirming that she had actually reached the location of the correspondents' press camp. And she added, "I, war correspondent Higgins, am a colleague of war correspondent Ernest Hemingway. How about that?"[19] But within the Scribe it was crushingly evident to her that she was an accredited war correspondent without any knowledge of war. The lobby of what she called "this frayed middle-class hotel" was "as clamorous and bustling as a wartime railway station. Helmets, musette bags, mud-caked typewriters, bedrolls were strewn about waiting to be claimed by correspondents going to or coming from the front."[20]

Many newsmen wore badges of combat groups they had been with, while she stood out as a newcomer in a pressed uniform bearing only a correspondent's insignia. Moreover, the correspondents all seemed to know one another and treat with no special regard those among them with bylines that awed her. That first night at the Scribe she made a journal entry about meeting the figure with the most awesome byline of her generation:

> Hill introduced me to Hemingway tonight. Hemingway was sitting on the couch in the basement lobby of the Scribe near the correspondents' mess. Beside him was a girl whose close-cropped hair looks like Maria in For Whom the Bell Tolls. Hemingway is rather fat and has a beard. Nobody seems to pay much attention to him. In fact, reporters around the Scribe seem to make a point of not paying special attention.[21]

The Hill she mentioned was Russell Hill, a Herald-Tribune colleague Higgins greatly respected because of his extensive war experience. Just recently he had been released from a hospital after a jeep he was sharing with Richard Tregaskis of INS and the New Yorker's David Lardner struck a land mine near the German border. Both Lardner—one of Ring Lardner's four sons who was on his first day in a combat zone—and the jeep driver were killed instantly.

Meeting Hemingway lifted Higgins's spirits since he treated her as a fellow correspondent. Thereafter Hill took her to the Scribe's bar for a dose of everyday reality. He told her it was fortunate for the paper that the weather had cleared enough to get her from London to Paris since there was local work to do. One of the paper's big names, Sonia Tomara, who had been handling French politics and the diplomatic beat, was in the hospital. John O'Reilly, head of the paper's Paris bureau, was back home for a while. And Geoffrey Parsons Jr. was fully occupied with reopening the Herald Tribune's Paris edition. This meant that Hill would handle all the military stories and Higgins would deal with local matters in Paris. When she seemed taken aback, Hill asked, "Don't you think you can do it?" Higgins replied that of course she could, though she was filled with doubt—and the dismaying awareness that what she wrote in Paris wouldn't be war correspondence.[22]

She dug into her assignment, which amounted to again working as a city reporter whose beat was now Paris. It helped in making contacts and developing sources that what she wrote also appeared in the Paris edition of the Herald Tribune. Parisians and international figures in the city grew accustomed to her byline. She also began writing about Paris fashion for *Mademoiselle* magazine. By her own account, she became a writing "cyclone of energy," churning out two or three stories a day and filing up to 3,000 words at night.[23]

Yet her life was never only work. A biographer wrote of Higgins's time in Paris that "the ambience of the Hotel Scribe was not conducive to celibacy even if Marguerite had been inclined to it."[24] A woman correspondent who shared a room in the hotel with Higgins gave her slant on Higgins's after-work hours: "I remember her surrounded by men; she was attractive and very popular. Of course there were people who said she used her femininity to get what she wanted. I suppose she did sometimes. What did it matter? One had to admire her for what she accomplished. Who cares how she lived or who she slept with?"[25]

Russell Hill's view was more restrained. "The question always comes up," he said, "about her sleeping with men to get stories. She really didn't need to. It was enough just to roll her eyes." He added, "I shared many intimate moments with Maggie but always had the feeling that love wasn't all that important to her. Maggie's primary drive was ambition. She wanted to get to the top of her profession and eventually did."[26]

Seven weeks after getting to Paris, Higgins looked like she was finally on her way to the war. Correspondents had drawn lots to join a parachute drop near the Rhine River, and she won one of the places. But Hill and Geoffrey Parsons wouldn't allow her to go. With John O'Reilly back in Paris and handling some of her duties, Higgins was all the more fearful the war would end without her.

Then she caught a break. Just after the Rhine was crossed the Eighth Air Force said it would fly two jeeps and six correspondents to the front to observe areas inside Germany that were heavily bombed. Two PROs would go along, as would two sergeants—one for communications and another for scrounging. Since the group wouldn't be attached to any ground forces, there would be no press camp. The scrounging sergeant would have to find what was needed for sleeping and eating.

Three women were already chosen for the junket: Helen Kirkpatrick, Lee Miller of *Vogue*, and Margaret Bourke-White of *Time-Life*. This seemed to Higgins to forestall any argument against women in battle zones. Geoffrey Parsons, though, made a case for himself. He had been a correspondent since 1940 but, as he told Higgins, had "never yet heard the sound of a bullet fired in anger."[27] This could be his last chance.

The night before the mission was to set off, Parsons phoned the Scribe room Higgins and Hill were using as an office and said there was a crisis at the Paris *Herald*. If she wanted, Higgins could go in his place. The next morning, in March 1945, she was on the plane to Germany.

She spent some six weeks as a combat reporter. In 1945 she received the New York Newspaper Women's Club award for the best foreign correspondence of that year, a prize based largely on her story of the liberation of the Dachau concentration camp. After the war's end, Russell Hill became the *Herald Tribune*'s bureau chief in Berlin, with Higgins as his assistant. In 1947, at age twenty-six, she took over the bureau.

CHAPTER ELEVEN

~

Upstairs

The upper levels of the Scribe served as offices and storerooms but primarily as private housing for brief or long stays by male and female correspondents. In other press camps the sexes were ordinarily kept separate as part of SHAEF's stated concern for the safety of women near battle areas. After shifting to Paris and the Scribe, SHAEF accepted that cloistering women was no longer worth the bother.

Assigning rooms in the hotel was an unenviable task because it meant dealing with fussy French clerks, correspondents who expected breakfast in bed, and mix-ups that landed men and women together in a room. Along with housing, correspondents needed vehicles. Running the hotel's transport pool required having jeeps and taxicabs always at the ready. Colonel Dupuy wondered how the PROs in charge of billeting and the motor pool "kept their sanity"—and left it at that "they did, somehow."[1]

Private rooms ranged from modest accommodations to grand suites. James Quirk learned that the head of the Gestapo in Paris previously occupied his suite and that for a year it was never used but kept in readiness for Hermann Göring in the unlikely event that he grew weary of the Ritz. Quirk's living room was about thirty-five square feet and grandly furnished. There were two bedrooms with double beds and two bathrooms, all equally grand. The hotel provided him with breakfast and dinner served in the room, though the food in the immediate days after the liberation was military rations splendidly served and with choice wines, as long as he could afford them.[2] The room William Walton shared with Charles Wertenbaker was equally large, had a high ceiling with a crystal chandelier, and featured two windows leading to an iron balcony overlooking Rue Scribe.

∿

Boyd Lewis of the United Press, who came to the Scribe in late January 1945 to manage the wire service's European operations after combat stints with Canadian and American forces, mentioned only that his fourth-floor room was comfortable and adequate for entertaining. He wasn't a bar regular but instead drew on his weekly liquor ration to accumulate enough champagne for parties in his room—when he could find the time.

After frontline reporting, covering the war from the rear nearly amounted to culture shock. Up front Lewis had reported, as he put it, on "operations at close hand."[3] He got glimpses of what war looked like, talked with men who had been under fire, jeeped back to press camps of varying quality to file dispatches based on his experience of the day, ate dinner, and then slept peacefully through the nights. At the Scribe the war existed on great SHAEF maps with crayoned lines showing the back-and-forth of battles across a broad sweep of operations. Covering the hotel's scheduled briefings, working on feature stories, and directing UP reporters in the field was a treadmill of work that occupied his days until early morning.

Lewis's private life was virtually nonexistent. "It seemed ridiculous," he said of himself, "to be living in 'Gay Paree' like an overworked monk," though that—as he kept his wife up to date in letters home—was his chosen fate. As he put it elsewhere, he was "working like a monk in a city which was a virtual banquet of feminine availability."[4] Maintaining the monkish life was all the more demanding when loud noises came from the room next door, which the occupant explained to him were caused by his "having the best time any 59-year-old man ever had in Paris."[5]

Lewis's room in the hotel wasn't always his alone. After a briefing one morning he found the door open and the chambermaid's cleaning tools parked outside. On his balcony she had gathered a group of French civilians of differing ages to watch a military parade passing on the street. Some of the guests glanced in Lewis's direction but quickly went back to waving hands and cheering on the passing units. Lewis shrugged off the situation: when there was a parade, the balconies apparently belonged to the people. "It would have made no difference, I'm sure, if I'd been in bed or on the Johnny," he later wrote. "They would just have streamed through the room smiling and 'bon jour-ing' to my balcony."[6]

∿

Room 412 in the Scribe, Lee Miller's, was noteworthy both for its stunning American occupant and impossible clutter. As a correspondent and photojournalist for British *Vogue*, she wrote dispatches on a portable typewriter on a table in the room, developed photos in the bathroom, and stored five-gallon jerry cans of gasoline on the balcony outside as an enticement for military transport.[7] *Life*'s David Scherman, who occupied a room next door, described the look of Miller's as "a cross between a garage sale and a used car lot. Guns, bayonets, camera equipment, crates of flashbulbs and cognac, flags, rolls of leather and other assorted loot erupted from every corner and from under the armoire."[8] Scherman thought cognac bought by the crate and prolonged evenings in the Scribe bar were Miller's ways of staving off "stone-wringing," her term for the anguish of writing.[9]

Before the war Lee Miller was known for photography, both as subject and practitioner. Classically tall, blonde, and blue eyed, she had been a successful model in New York and had appeared on the cover of *Vogue* in 1927. Soon thereafter she went to Paris to study photography with Man Ray, to become his lover, to join in Surrealist escapades, and to continue modeling, now for French *Vogue*. After interludes of running her own photo studio in New York and marriage to an Egyptian and life in Cairo, she was living in Britain with her future second husband, the artist Roland Penrose, when war broke out.[10]

She joined the staff of British *Vogue* as a photojournalist and began adding text to her pictures, including a feature story about Edward R. Murrow with a photo she took of him at his typewriter. She mingled with other American correspondents in London, including David Scherman, who became her close friend, eventual lover, and colleague in wartime photography.

In late July 1944 the fashion magazine sent Miller to France to report on the postinvasion work of nurses. On another assignment she found herself in Saint-Malo in Brittany, a town thought by Allied intelligence to be secured but wasn't. She photographed combat troops in action and Germans in surrender, but when SHAEF learned that a woman correspondent had been in an active fighting zone she was ordered to remain in a press camp in Rennes. With other women correspondents she was later transported to liberated Paris and the Scribe. She knew she wouldn't count as the first woman journalist in the freed city but, as she put it, "I'll be the first dame photographer, I think, unless someone parachutes in."[11]

She quickly contacted Paris friends to find out how they endured the war, Picasso among them, and got involved in French *Vogue*'s coverage of new fashion trends. For the magazine she also took photos of such visiting celebrities as Marlene Dietrich and Fred Astaire and interviewed and photographed the French writer Colette. She left the Scribe long enough to visit war zones in Luxembourg and Belgium but was anxious to follow the fighting front into Germany. Hearing Eisenhower in the hotel's ballroom outline the difficulties of crossing the Rhine intensified her desire, and David Scherman's, to leave the Scribe for the war.

⁓

While Miller and Scherman were still housed in the hotel, John Morris, a *Life* photo editor, came to Miller's room one evening for a drink and discovered Scherman alone in her bed, reading. Coming for a drink the next evening, he discovered Roland Penrose alone in the same bed, reading.[12] Howard K. Smith's first visit to Charles Collingwood's Scribe room differed, among other things, in the number of occupants in his bed.

Smith and his Danish wife had spent the war in neutral Switzerland until, with the Allies closing in on Paris, they headed for the city. The former UP reporter and then CBS radio voice in Berlin was eager to return to reporting and find a safe place for his pregnant wife. In liberated Paris the couple went at once to the Scribe in search of a room. From the lobby Smith called Collingwood's room and was told to come right up. Inside, the Smiths, disheveled by travel and rain, were greeted by a dazzling Collingwood in a red silk dressing gown over red silk pajamas and smoking a cigarette in a long ivory holder as he lay propped up in bed. On one side of the bed was a bucket of iced champagne, and beside him on the other side was a young blonde woman. After he whispered to her in French, the woman smiled and said good-bye. In the room the Smiths noticed a half dozen or so Picasso paintings set about that Collingwood told them he had recently won in poker games.

Then Collingwood got to work. He phoned the front desk and got the couple a room in the already filled hotel. With another call he made arrangements for Smith to get SHAEF press accreditation the next day. For the night at hand he proposed cocktails and dinner, but the Smiths were eager to get settled in their own room. In following days Smith was quickly moved into the company of Collingwood and other CBS correspondents broadcasting from the Scribe.[13]

He found that his new radio role required little effort compared with the legwork for stories he was used to. There was no need to leave the hotel. It was possible, he wrote, to remain in bed until mid-morning, get to a briefing in the information room, write it up, go up another floor to broadcast it to the United States, and by early afternoon be "free to have an elaborate Parisian lunch and take your girlfriend/wife walking in the Bois in the afternoon, or to go back to bed. Evenings seemed to be one long party for journalists in newly liberated Paris."[14]

The Smiths' time in the Scribe was short lived. A PRO, learning that the pregnant woman with Smith was his wife, delivered the news that rooms couldn't be used as family quarters. Girlfriends or evening pickups might be ignored, but wives had to go. The Smiths found new lodging in a pension, and Howard Smith himself was soon to leave Paris and the easy life of the Scribe—though keeping a room in case he was needed for a broadcasting emergency—for a press camp with the Ninth Army in the Netherlands.

The early CBS figures associated with Murrow had largely turned away from combat reporting, leaving the field to newcomers like Smith. He now spent his days in jeeps with other correspondents touring frontline positions in foul weather conditions. With transmission facilities uncertain, Smith often felt he was, as he put it, "carefully writing a script and dropping it in the nearest manhole, and that was the end of it."[15]

The seeming futility of writing broadcasts was offset for Howard Smith by the consolation of nights spent in a press camp at Maastricht organized by Barney Oldfield. "Blond, good-looking, always cheerful," Smith said of the former Hollywood publicist and press agent, "Barney was what God meant when he allowed the term 'PR' to be coined. Resolved despite everything to have a happy camp, he had requisitioned a good hotel and acquired a good local cook, a band and a pretty girl to sing or just sit and be looked at."[16]

Boyd Lewis of the UP equally praised Oldfield's camp. The transmission setup within the Dutch hotel included four American commercial agencies sending dispatches directly to London and New York. Lewis even thought well of the camp's censors—"friendly but tough censors could clear a piece in minutes"—but personal pleasure came when he casually mentioned to Oldfield that the hotel's music was short on classical pieces. Soon there appeared on occasion a trio of aged men in evening dress playing Bach and Vivaldi.[17]

However appealing they might be, press camps had limited life. As the war thrust forward, new ones followed, with the Scribe in Paris always the great exception. Correspondents were inclined to say that any sort of camp would suffice since all they needed was a place to eat and sleep, transportation, and transmission facilities. Oldfield was skeptical. "They were a comfort-loving lot," he observed of newsmen, "and since the Ninth Army had provided clean sheets twice weekly in Maastricht . . . and various other fillips, none but the unwise would want suddenly to wean them of this creamy diet."[18]

Nonetheless, Maastricht was left behind for other sites. In the next Ninth Army camp, correspondents lived in rooms that held from six to nine men who slept on folding cots without mattresses. Yet for the first week in the new camp the orchestra was brought from Maastricht, with the result, as Oldfield wrote, that "the break was not too pronounced" for the correspondents.[19]

CHAPTER TWELVE

∼

Downstairs

In Ernest Dupuy's considered opinion, the Scribe's lower-level bar served two primal needs of correspondents. It was where they voiced their myriad complaints with censors and PROs, and it was where they decompressed with colleagues and competitors:

> There—down in the basement—was the sounding-board and safety-valve; the "medicine hat" of SHAEF's war correspondents, whence all the big winds started. It was also a real oasis of relaxation. One will long remember the narrow bar with its absurdly high stools, the red-leather over-stuffed easy chairs and the shop-talk after "thirty," in the midst of good companionship.[1]

He might have made even larger claims for the hotel's drinking place, as does the character in Ned Calmer's novel when he suggests it harbors some deep meaning. But as it happened the bar's lasting renown came not in words but paint when *Life* field artist Floyd Davis chose it as the setting for a vivid caricature of war correspondents at play.

Now in possession of the Smithsonian Institution's National Portrait Gallery, the oil-on-canvas painting with the unvarnished name *Bar in Hotel Scribe* was first displayed as a double-page spread among a gallery of eighteen paintings by Davis and his field artist wife, Gladys Rockmore Davis, in *Life* on July 16, 1945, some two months after the war ended. An accompanying story, "Paris 1945," by Charles Wertenbaker, bearing a Paris dateline, didn't mention the Scribe or the painting, despite the writer's own visible presence among the bar's twenty-three identifiable correspondents, including the artist and his wife. "How the once-gay city has fared during its first year of liberation," said an editorial note with the story, "is described here in paintings by two LIFE artist-correspondents," going on to attribute the various paintings in the issue to the particular Davis that created the work. "Accompanying the paintings," the note ended, "is a report by Charles Christian Wertenbaker, chief of 'Time' and LIFE's European staff."

The report opened with some details of the liberation and then turned to consider what life had been like in Paris from that lofty point to the war's end. As Wertenbaker sketched it, much of the period had been, at best, difficult. There were scarcities of basic needs. People still got around largely on bicycles or on foot. When winter came early in 1945, the cold seemed especially severe. Wertenbaker wrote, "The girls in the Folies-Bergère had to get drunk before they would strip. Many a well-dressed Parisian did not take a bath for five months. All Paris caught a cold in October and coughed with it until April or May."

American officers and GIs in the city saw little or nothing of what beset French citizens. And with the spring and warmth their lot improved. With the end of the war in June there was restrained celebration. "If there was one mood," said Wertenbaker, "that hung over V-E night it was the mood of hope." Yet his article closed on a somber note. Driving in the center of the city on the evening of victory, he saw at the quay across from the Chamber of Deputies some lilac fixed about a small tablet set in a wall. The tablet read, "Here fell, on August 25, 1944, Claude Billard, FFI of Loiret, 21 years old."

~

Most of the Davises' paintings in the magazine are scenes of renewed Parisian life. But there are also dark studies treating the past: a widow placing a wreath under her husband's name on a Nazi execution wall; a Nazi torture chamber with empty wooden caskets; a GI looking at a shop window pasted with large swastikas as a warning against trading with a collaborator. Floyd Davis's Scribe painting leaps out as a colorful cartoon with a large cast of characters. A caption read,

> Every other day the bar served brandy and then the place was crowded with correspondents who drank the brandy, they insisted, to keep warm. The Scribe was a confused place, which will appear in innumerable future war books, plays, movies. Spruce correspondents rushed out to the front to get stories. Disheveled correspondents rushed back from the front to file their stories. At any time reporters could be heard complaining about censors, brass hats, editors.

None of the rushing or complaining is suggested in the painting. With the possible exception of Ernest Hemingway, no one seems in a conversational mode. None of the standing newsmen holds a drink or a cigarette, while a seated Janet Flanner has both. The holder of a captured Nazi banner and Hemingway are among the few animated figures.

Though four Allied flags hang above the bar and a charcoal portrait of de Gaulle is placed on a far wall, the tightly grouped correspondents are mostly Americans. Among them, a white-coated French waiter passes through, an indifferent lone enlisted man sits on a high stool at the bar giving his back to the scene, and across the bar are a French bartender with shifty eyes and a mysterious woman, her partly covered head turned to the soldier. Davis and his wife are tucked away at a table in the far left foreground, wrapped in winter coats, sketch books on their table and its edge listing the artist, date, and location of the completed work: "Floyd Davis '44 Paris."

Floyd M. Davis served in the navy in World War I. Without formal training as an artist, he built a successful career as a magazine illustrator, with work appearing in the *Saturday Evening Post*, *Red Book*, and *Collier's*. In Britain as a *Life* war correspondent, he flew in July 1943 in the first American bombing raid of Hamburg, his aerial paintings of the massed planes appearing in the magazine later that year.[2] In liberated Paris, he and his wife formed a rare team of married accredited correspondents, his work emphasizing military subjects, hers customary life.

Seated together in the painting's center foreground are a petite Flanner; a glum, eye-patched William L. Shirer (a skiing accident in Europe years before cost him vision in one eye); and a bulky, domineering Hemingway. Davis perhaps placed the three together because their prominence was a cut well above most other correspondents in the painting. He also may have known that their Paris days went back to the fabled 1920s, with Flanner and Hemingway starting out as writers and Shirer as a cub newsman on the *Chicago Tribune*'s Paris edition.

Janet Flanner had fled France for America with the start of the European war. When the *New Yorker* queried her about returning as a war correspondent, she told the editor, William Shawn, that she doubted she would be of use to the magazine if "there is a big bloody push, with Paris bombed, gas, measle [*sic*] germs in parachutes, etc., which some, indeed, may now envisage." She went on: "The kind of work I can do wouldn't be that kind of

Photo 12.1. *Bar in Hotel Scribe.*

Source: Floyd MacMillan Davis, 1944, Oil on canvas, National Portrait Gallery, Smithsonian Institution

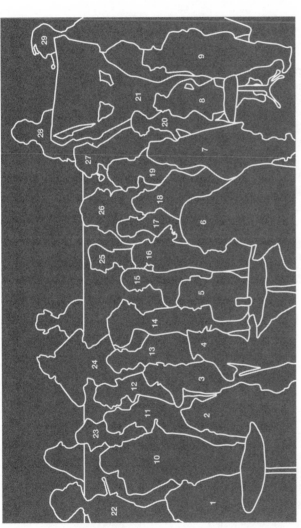

Photo 12.2 *Bar in Hotel Scribe* key

1. Floyd Davis, *Life* field artist
2. Gladys Rockmore Davis, *Life* field office
3. David Scherman, *Life* photographer
4. Janet Flanner, *New Yorker* correspondent
5. William Shirer, CBS newscaster
6. Ernest Hemingway, *Collier's* correspondent
7. A. J. Liebling, *New Yorker* correspondent
8. Merrill Mueller, NBC correspondent
9. H. V. Kaltenborn, NBC correspondent
10. Richard de Rochemont, *March of Time* producer
11. Bill Reusswig, King Features illustrator
12. Ham Green, *American Legion Magazine* correspondent

13. Bob Cromie, *Chicago Tribune*
14. Hugh Schuck, *New York Daily News* correspondent
15. Will Lang, *Time* correspondent
16. Lee Miller, *Vogue* photographer
17. Graham Miller, *New York Daily News* correspondent
18. Donald MacKenzie, *New York Daily News* correspondent
19. Robin Duff
21. Ralph Morse, *Life* photographer
26. Charles Wertenbaker, *Time-Life* correspondent
28. Robert Capa, *Life* photographer
29. Noel Busch, *Life* correspondent
20, 22–25, 27. Unidentified

reporting; for that work would be needed . . . a writer who is male, young, fighting-minded; my age, sex, Quaker upbringing would make me a poor leg-man in those conditions."[3] When she did finally reappear in a liberated Paris that had been spared a big bloody push, it was late in 1944. As one of the *New Yorker*'s war correspondents, she took a room at the Scribe and kept it through the end of the war.

With her white hair, habitual cigarette, colorful neck scarves, and glass of something near at hand, Flanner became a familiar presence in the bar. In letters to friends she complained of sitting alone in her room, but among the hotel's press, Genêt, the *nom de correspondance* of her "Letter from Paris" in the *New Yorker*, was nearly as famous a writer as Hemingway and equally a center of attention. She made many friends among the correspondents— Helen Kirkpatrick was one of them, and another magazine reporter, Monica Sterling of the *Atlantic Monthly*, became especially close—though she lacked patience with those who hadn't known Paris before the war. Part of her af-fection for Hemingway, whom she met frequently at the Scribe and Les Deux Magots café, was their prewar bond. She told a friend, "I've seen a lot of him & love him far more even than ever."[4]

Visitors flowed in and out of her hotel room, which at times presented a problem. She enjoyed breakfasts and gossip in the hotel's mess while also wanting to be back in her room in time for warm morning baths. One morn-ing she found Hemingway soaking in her tub, an interlude she later related with amusement.[5]

The esteem of other correspondents couldn't entirely lift the unease Flan-ner felt about wartime reporting. Back in Paris after a trip to the front in a jeep with a Scot she met at the Scribe, she sought out Hemingway for advice about writing what she had seen. He told her, she recalled in a letter, to write "it the way you saw it. . . . There is never any other story." She claimed this the best advice she had ever heard, though she told Hemingway the problem was that she hadn't seen anything. "That is always all," was his enigmatic response.[6]

When Flanner resumed her regular column for the *New Yorker* in Decem-ber 1944, writing again as Genêt, she ignored the Scribe and its inhabitants while often giving close attention to French newspapers. She doled out spe-cial praise for a new young journalist on the previously underground paper *Combat*, Albert Camus. In January she took on added work of writing and delivering broadcasts from the Scribe for the Blue Network, the forebear of the American Broadcasting Company.

～

Like Flanner, William L. Shirer had spent the war in America after leaving his Berlin post in 1940. He appeared in Paris only after the liberation. "Bill Shirer is here," Harry Butcher wrote in his diary on November 22, 1944. "Ed Murrow is also here." The close relationship between Shirer and Murrow was showing strains because Murrow and others of his CBS team thought Shirer should have covered the war up close rather than from New York. But Shirer's dour look in the Davis painting may have stemmed more, as Butcher reported, from CBS's poor record at the time in getting its broadcasts through from Paris to New York. The multiple problems—atmospherics, line breaks, power failures—were mostly on the reception side in New York, but this did nothing to soothe Shirer in the Scribe.

With his weekly broadcasts on Sunday nights, Shirer had "all his eggs in one basket," Butcher noted, and especially so since CBS wouldn't allow him to record his remarks when transmission conditions were best in Paris and rebroadcast them in New York. The CBS bias against recordings, he added, left Shirer "hurting all over—right down to his toes."[7]

When Hemingway ventured from the Ritz to the Scribe—outfitted in the painting with a visible correspondent's patch on his uniform and a folded newspaper jammed in his pocket—it was typically to claim attention at the bar. Lyn Crost of the Associated Press remembered first seeing the man she would marry, the AP's Edward Kennedy, when he was together with Hemingway in the bar and both were "dead drunk and could hardly stand up."[8] Britain's Malcolm Muggeridge also glimpsed Hemingway in the bar, finding him "somewhat drunk, as we all were, and with a number of hand grenades rather absurdly attached to his person."[9]

Another story linking Hemingway to the bar involved the film correspondent William Saroyan, who was drawn to the Scribe because of its "writerly" name and crowd of journalists. When the two ran into one another in the bar and Hemingway didn't seem to remember him, Saroyan said, "In London you had a beard, but even without it I haven't forgotten you. Did shaving it off make you forget me?" Hemingway turned away but the remark stuck with him.

Nights later, Hemingway was drinking in the bar with group captain Peter Wykeham-Barnes, an RAF pilot he had flown with in Britain who was now on leave in Paris. After consuming what Barnes called "quite a quantity of grog" at the Scribe, they retired to the Hôtel George V for dinner. When Hemingway spotted Saroyan at another table, he called out, "Well, for God's sake, what's that lousy Armenian son-of-a-bitch doing here?" After Saroyan's

companions had their rejoinders, a full-out brawl resulted in the hotel management and the police tossing everyone into the night.[10]

Placed off to Hemingway's side is a bulky A. J. Liebling. As observed earlier,
he left Paris and the war and went home in late 1944, never to return. Yet
in his writing, he returned to Paris and the Scribe if not the war. A collection of work called *Mollie and Other War Pieces* included "Day of Victory,"
which in a foreword he said was done in the summer of 1946 in celebration
of the second anniversary of the liberation of Paris, "of part of which it is an
unofficial report." He elaborated about its unofficial stature by labeling "Day
of Victory" a "pseudo-short-story . . . in which fact is turned to fiction by
changing the names of the actors and perhaps juggling a bit with details."[11]

The result is a satirical dismantling of a type of war correspondent Liebling
encountered in Britain and then in France: unprepared, pretentious, covering the war from the boozy comfort of hotels and cafés. Liebling said as much
directly: he lent his chief character in the story "some of the characteristics
of correspondents I disliked."[12] The time of the story is the day after the
liberation, the subject one Allardyce Meecham, a former New York drama
critic. He is age forty-three, red-haired, and awkward—in his own eyes, "an
unimpressive representative of a victorious army."

Meecham is first glimpsed descending five flights of stairs (the lift isn't working) from his billet in the Scribe to the lobby. Reaching Paris early that morning, he found correspondents who, so they held, entered the city well before the
Germans surrendered. Now in the lobby swarming with victorious correspondents and PROs, he hurries through to keep from overhearing more thrilling
accounts. He is outfitted in a tanker's combat jacket and an officer's dress-pink
trousers, a mismatch caused by his feeling that the GI pants he ordinarily wore
with the jacket were too dirty for Paris. On his head is a helmet liner.

In the street outside the hotel there are cheering crowds and affectionate
women, and he soon has lipstick plastered over his face. At the Café de la
Paix a waiter brings him a glass of wine, which suggests that Paris is returning to its usual ways, and he makes a note of this as a lead to a story he will
write. He knows his newspaper will use wire services for coverage of liberated
Paris, so what they will want from him, he reflects smugly, is "something
more subtle."

He moves on to a bar where drinks are on the house for an American,
then to a restaurant for a meal. Here he finds a drunken American colonel
who has a pretty girl with him, and they soon become a party of three hunting for a girl for Meecham.

Ultimately, girl found, the foursome go to a hotel, drink champagne, and all is tranquil until there is small-arms fire in the streets and the colonel begins firing his pistol at what he thinks are snipers on a roof. The colonel is subdued by the women but not before a bullet hits a mirror in the room.

The pseudo-story ends abruptly with Meecham's cabled report reaching an editor's desk in New York. It is, as expected, a garbled, clichéd invention, which concludes, "This was prometheus unbound period it was throbbing heart-warming day of victory period burnedout tanks lay scattered about streets in front cafe de la paix like bits broken glass."[13]

⌇

Depicted at waist level with the bar in the painting's upper right corner is somber, unshaven Robert Capa overlooking his gathered colleagues while wearing his favored headgear, a helmet liner. The intrepid photographer had seen his share of World War II action in Italy and Normandy, but in Paris, a city he loved and considered home, he was content to remain. *Life* magazine was equally pleased to have him there. When the New York office told him to remain in Paris for the time being, Wertenbaker cabled in reply, "I am delighted that Capa is to remain in Paris, and so is Capa."[14] One reason for Davis placing him at bar level may have been, as Capa relates in his autobiography, due to the close relationship he developed with the Scribe's bartender, named Gaston in the book.

On a day Capa designates in D-Day fashion as liberation day plus seven, he tells Gaston how to mix a potent pick-me-up, "Suffering Bastard"—today's Bloody Mary—needed not only for his physical condition but his downed mood. He feels that the "noble art of war photography . . . had expired in the streets of Paris only six days before" and hence believes that going back to the front again would be a "dull prospect" of repeating himself with war pictures he had already taken.[15] Gaston understands this lament because his own heroic war, fought during the occupation with the French Resistance, is equally over.

Capa was never, though, in seclusion in Paris. With his knowledge of the city, he guided correspondents and PROs to black-market restaurants, horse racing at Longchamp, the casino at Enghien-les-Bains, and other palaces of entertainment. For his boss, Wertenbaker, he helped ease the problem of transportation in Paris by buying on the black market four used cars for *Time-Life*. Haggling about prices and then getting the vehicles actually running took long hours. "You don't just buy a car in Paris," Wertenbaker enlightened his New York office about the purchase. "You practically buy it part by part."[16]

On another occasion in the Scribe, the bar empty, Capa has Gaston reading a newspaper account of General Patton crossing the Saar River into Germany. This prompts him to declare pointedly that "every real newspaperman was already off to the front."[17] But what finally edged Capa off his bar stool were cables from *Life*'s New York office that agreed with Gaston. In early October 1944 Capa began a series of back-and-forth ventures from Paris to fighting areas. In December he joined Charles Collingwood of CBS and Will Lang of *Time* in covering the Battle of the Bulge.

In late March 1945 Capa accompanied a high-risk daylight parachute drop of troops behind enemy lines as part of a massive crossing of the Rhine close to the German town of Wessel, cameras strapped to his legs and a flask of Scotch in his breast pocket. Until evening he photographed fierce fighting, then sought to get back to Paris with his pictures. It wasn't until the following day, after spending a night sleeping rough in a rolled-up parachute, that he crossed the river and hitchhiked to Paris.

The April 9, 1945, issue of *Life* gave eleven pages to the pictures and captions Capa transmitted from the Scribe. Triumph was soon followed by frustrating failure to photograph the German surrender, the only war event that Capa thought could surpass the liberation of Paris. He was on a trip to London for a personal matter when *Life* picked for the duty Ralph Morse, portrayed in the Davis painting just below Capa as a madly grinning figure stretching out a captured Nazi banner. The closest Capa got to the war's end came in April in Nuremberg when he ran into the soldier-driver who had taken Wertenbaker and him into Paris for the liberation. His photo of Hubert Strickland, arm raised in a burlesque Nazi salute in front of a large wreathed swastika in a stadium where Hitler often stood, was used on the cover of *Life* on May 14, 1945.

Along with Gladys Davis and Janet Flanner, Lee Miller is the only other known woman correspondent in the painting. Though located in the center of the composition, her small frame is tightly squeezed between two men. With her blonde head turned to the side, she seems poised for a picture, or simply attention. Nearby and staring straight ahead is a small, bespectacled, camera-toting David Scherman, Miller's partner in reporting and one of the several *Life* figures that *Life*'s Davis put in the painting. Directly up from Hemingway, his prominent head at bar level, is Davis's European chief, Charles Wertenbaker. At the upper right, forming a triangle with Capa and Morse of *Life* and looking as if he and his pipe have just arrived in the bar, is Noel Busch of *Life*. Striding in at the opposite corner, wearing a green beret, bearing a thick mustache, and with a military baton firmly under his arm, is an unknown British figure. Presumably a military officer rather than a correspondent, his presence is perhaps meant, like the bar's flags, to suggest Allied balance—or to simply balance in the composition Busch's entrance. The lone African American in the caricature, a tiny figure striding ahead just below Ralph Morse, is unidentifiable.

As of this writing, the National Portrait Gallery lacks full provenance of *Bar in Hotel Scribe*. A handwritten note in its files says the field artist and correspondent John Groth donated the painting to the Overseas Press Club of America in 1974. The organization, based in New York, auctioned it that same year to an unknown buyer. In 1979 the painting was reproduced—half on the front cover, half on the back, and with a key identifying the figures— in a fortieth-anniversary edition of the club's annual publication, *Dateline*, which also reprinted some of the best work of correspondents from past issues. An editor's note by the author and broadcaster Lowell Thomas, an early president of the club, indicated that the painting's owner at the time was Ernest Hemingway's widow, Mary Welsh Hemingway.[18] The National Portrait Gallery purchased the painting in 1988.

PART III

LEAVING

The Hotel Scribe, in Rue Scribe, Paris, which became the Paris home of war correspondents and headquarters of the valiant public relations forces of Supreme Allied Headquarters immediately after the liberation of the city and which was the scene of some of the heaviest verbal battles of the war, will be evacuated tomorrow.

John O'Reilly, *New York Herald Tribune*

CHAPTER THIRTEEN

~

Jeeping to Berlin

In February 1945 General Eisenhower shifted his headquarters from Versailles to Reims, the cathedral city some eighty miles northeast of Paris where French kings were once crowned. For the Scribe's correspondents, the move was yet another signal that the war was rapidly winding down. Daily briefings in the hotel reported the collapse of German armies in the field, the massive surrender of troops, and the unstoppable advance of the Russian Red Army.

Newsmen assumed the final goal of the Western Allies was the taking of Berlin, the only dateline that could compete with D-Day and the liberation of Paris. A further assumption was that the Russians could well reach the German capital first, so SHAEF correspondents might be flown in on press junkets rather than trekking through Germany in jeeps.

With American military forces halted at the Elbe River within Germany and the Russians just across the water, some correspondents had already set off for a Berlin dateline. For the AP's Don Whitehead, reaching Berlin first would form a scoop bracketing his entry into Paris, and he and his frequent jeep mate, Lee Carson of the INS, gave it a try. As Carson recounted the venture, after a Russian colonel invited them to visit across the river, they just kept going, driving a captured Mercedes the military had painted to give it some semblance of an official car.

After some forty-five miles of movement they realized they had no idea where they were. When Carson spread a map on her lap to try to figure their location, the wind whipped it away. A few miles later, a gasket blew on the Mercedes, and they had to flag down a Russian truck. After an exchange of information with hand signals, the driver agreed to tow them. "He towed us through the whole Russian Army," said Carson. "We ran right across their line of march. The Russians were simply furious."

A young Polish girl who spoke Russian helped them find a mechanic who fixed the car, and they again forged ahead. Eventually they came upon serious fighting between Russians and Germans. "Then both sides opened fire," Carson said, "and we hit the dirt." They had no choice but to stick with the Russians, though with Carson wearing a red bandanna over her hair a Russian had to crawl to her and tear it free because it was directing sniper fire. The Berlin jaunt ended with the Russians holding the two correspondents in custody for three days before releasing them.[1]

Virginia Irwin of the *St. Louis Post-Dispatch* and Andrew Tully of the *Boston Traveler* fared better with the Red Army. On April 25 the pair were in Nuremberg covering the taking of the Nazi party birthplace and talking about when all of Germany might fall. Tully gave it about a month and then casually suggested to Irwin, "Let's keep going to Berlin." "She didn't blink an eyelash," Tully wrote. "'O.K.' she said. So we started—just like that."[2]

Together with their military driver they jeeped to Torgau on the Elbe and there enticed Russian soldiers operating a ferry—by shouting "Jeep" and making swimming motions—to carry them across. Here they joined an American group for a planned celebration of the meeting of the Allies on the Russian side of the river. After much food, drink, and dancing, Irwin considered that their only options were to get fully drunk or get moving. "We 'ran' off the map," she wrote of the journey, "and had to navigate by guess."[3]

None of the three in the jeep understood Russian, and all road signs were now in that language. They bore with them one of the homemade flags the Russians had put up marking the way to Torgau, and when they encountered Red Army troops they saluted, called out that they were "Americanski," and pointed to their flag. The soldiers, many riding in wagons filled with hay, lumbered along singing songs, downing vodka, and seeming to Irwin like "holiday-makers going on a great picnic." One bad moment came after they were stopped by a stern female MP. When she demanded papers, Irwin and Tully produced their SHAEF identification cards, which after careful scrutiny were accepted.

The correspondents reached the outskirts of Berlin at nightfall on April 27, three days before Hitler killed himself in his bunker in the capital. After convincing a French-speaking Russian major commanding an artillery unit of their identity as reporters, they became his guests in a requisitioned house within Berlin's city limits. They were led, one at a time, to a bathroom to clean themselves—and the major instructed an orderly to see to fresh flowers in Irwin's room. Late that evening the Russian unit put on a banquet with massive amounts of food and drink while heavy guns roared nearby and the house shook. Dancing followed the banquet, with Irwin, the sole woman present, dancing with each officer until in the early morning she gave way to exhaustion.

Irwin, Tully, and their soldier driver spent three days and two nights in Berlin, but faced with continued fighting they were unable to penetrate the city center. Everything they witnessed, Irwin wrote, seemed unreal: German dead on sidewalks or in front of shattered homes; Russian horses freed from carts running wild in the streets; the incessant pounding of artillery; and the unrestrained joy of Russians settling the score for Leningrad, Stalingrad, and Moscow. Tully wrote that "the entire center of the city was a no-man's land." He added, "It was the most desperate fighting I have ever seen—surpassing for pure violence and desperation the battles for Metz and Frankfurt and Nuremberg. At least it seemed that the German military automaton was heeding his mad dictator's orders to fight to the death."[4]

The correspondents' link with the Russians ended decisively when they were back on the Elbe and were refused ferry passage across the river. After shouting for help, two American boats came to their aid. At the nearest press camp at Weimar, Irwin and Tully learned that their stories about entering Berlin would not be cleared by censors. After catching a plane for Paris and the Scribe, they learned that General Allen had suspended them for their unauthorized Berlin trip and they could no longer file dispatches of any sort. In a note to her paper's publisher, Joseph Pulitzer Jr., Irwin asked—leaving Berlin unmentioned to escape the blue pencil—to tell her mother she was safe and asked for a thousand dollars if she was to remain in Europe for any length of time. Pulitzer complied with both requests.[5]

Being in trouble with the PRD was nothing new for Irwin. After reaching Paris following the liberation, she was eager to leave the Scribe and get as far up front as she could. "The public relations boys," she wrote at the time, "thought we gals ought to be happy [at the Scribe]. There we had a bed with clean sheets, maid service, bathtubs that ran water. . . . But I was itching to see what our Joes were doing."[6] After some weeks in Paris she got a three-day pass to visit the headquarters of the Nineteenth Air Command of the Ninth Air Force and stayed on until nearly Christmas. PROs in Paris began searching for her, but she kept avoiding them. Even her newspaper wasn't always sure where she was.

Irwin specialized in feature stories with a humorous touch but also got close to the action. Through the fall, winter, and then spring of 1945, she was with the American Third Army in France, Belgium, Holland, Luxemburg, and Germany, living and eating like the troops. Her publisher cautioned against taking chances and told her to come home if she wished. Yet on one occasion she accompanied troops to within two blocks of a German mortar and within range of small arms. "I can now say with the best of the male correspondents," Irwin said of the experience, "that I've been in the front lines. That's about a mile closer than any other woman correspondent has been or I'll eat my correspondent's beret dry without any butter."[7] She would see more action, and with it more stories carried on her paper's front page, but her major splash in the *Post-Tribune* was yet to come.

⌒

Seymour Freidin and John Groth did reach central Berlin. Barney Oldfield reported that Freidin, a correspondent of the *New York Herald Tribune*, crossed the Elbe for a "soiree" with the Russians and then kept going through Germany, presumably with Red Army cooperation.[8] Oldfield didn't mention that accompanying Freidin was Groth, attached to the Ninth Air Force and equally committed to viewing up close the fate of a city he had known a decade earlier.

The soiree was between top American and Russian officers in the river city of Wittenberg, with some correspondents also in attendance. Groth and Freidin learned from the Russians that fighting to reach inner Berlin could not last more than a day or two. Groth knew that Irwin and Tully had already reached the outer edge of Berlin but, as best he was aware, no one had gotten into the center. When a Russian captain they were drinking with claimed he could get them there, the two newsmen hustled him into Groth's jeep, and they set off.

Freidin had encountered Russian troops earlier. On May 1, the *Herald Tribune* carried his story, datelined Apollensdorf, Germany, about forward elements of the American 125th Infantry meeting forward elements of what he called an elite Russian division in which no two men wore similar uniforms. After some moments of eyeing one another, members of the two sides were exchanging headgear amid the unintelligible babble of conversation. "The Red Army soldiers," Freidin noted, "were singularly unimpressed by rank. They drove 'liberated' German motorcycles recklessly past their officers and ours, and appeared to enjoy hearty laughs in watching people duck out of the way of vehicles."[9]

The helpful Russian captain guided Freidin and Groth only as far as his own military group. Left on their own on the road, the traffic entirely Russian, the two Americans followed a convoy that allowed them a distant view of the Red Army on the march. Along with militarized vehicles of all manner and condition were a staggering number of horse-drawn conveyances, farm wagons, carts, herds of cattle, and endless lines of men walking, riding bicycles, and upon horses. At every stop, Russian soldiers and officers surrounded the jeep and there were cigarette exchanges. The Russians seemed to accept that the continuing presence of the Americans meant they had been approved somewhere by someone.

Near the town of Luckenwalde there was firing as the Russians mopped up some German resistance. Beyond the town the convoy stopped when a tire blew on one of the trucks. The captain of the convoy came to the jeep and tried to make conversation despite the language barrier. The only thing that worked was Freidin's Yiddish. "The Russian captain," wrote Groth, "was elated that one of the first Americans he should meet was a Jewish boy on his way to Hitler's Berlin."[10] He told the correspondents to hold their position with the convoy and he would guide them to within ten miles of Berlin's center.

After camping out a night in a German home, the next day, May 3, 1945, Groth and Freidin entered Berlin in the early afternoon. They drove through a chilling rain into the core of the demolished and still burning city, observing some of the final fighting within Tiergarten Park.

As they left Berlin the two correspondents were held up on the Unter den Linden by overjoyed Russian troops and officers who wanted to pose for repeated photos with the first Americans they had seen. Hurrying back to American lines on the Elbe to get their dispatches written and transmitted, the newsmen came across at Luckenwalde a gathering of American prisoners of war just freed by the Russians. As Groth recalled, they felt they could do nothing else but spend a night with the men and talk of home. The next morning four of them came back with Groth and Freidin. Lacking a formal arrangement with the Russians for returning prisoners, the correspondents shared some of their clothing and insignia with the men to help ensure they wouldn't be stopped, with the effect of six correspondents finally passing from Russian into American-held territory.[11]

SHAEF responded to the Berlin excursion by stopping the stories of Groth and Freidin, while at the same time admitting that their accounts of Russians taking Berlin had no bearing on military security. The two were also stripped of accreditation and ordered from the war zone. Back in Paris, Geoffrey Parsons of the local *Herald Tribune* paper intervened by submitting Freidin's story to French censorship, where it was passed for publication.[12] After it appeared in the Paris paper on May 8, SHAEF censors allowed the reports of both Freidin and Groth to be filed to New York, and they appeared the following day in American papers.

The opening paragraph of Freidin's story on page one of the *New York Herald Tribune*, carrying a Berlin, May 3, dateline, closed with the decisive battle in the Tiergarten:

> Over the rubble that remains of the most bomb-leveled city in the world, the red banner of Soviet Russia flew triumphantly this afternoon as exultant Russian soldiers swept into the hedgerows of the Tiergarten opposite the Reichstag and subdued the last of the Nazi defenders.

The opening of Groth's story, circulated by the AP and printed in the *New York Times* and other papers, read,

> Hitler's legacy—the broken, smoking chaos of Berlin—sprawls under the vivid banners of the Red Army today. German tears and hunger mark the end of the Nazi empire.

After protests from their publications and other newsmen in Paris, the two correspondents eventually got their credentials back but were suspended for a month and ordered to the UK.[13]

The suspensions immediately became part of a larger press story appearing in American newspapers of correspondents in addition to Groth and Freidin who were punished for unauthorized entry into Berlin. Virginia Irwin, Andrew Tully, and Tom Downs of the *London Evening News* were among the violators singled out, as were two sergeants writing for *Stars and Stripes* and *Yank* magazine. In an opinion piece in the *New York Times*, Gladwin Hill complained about an "epidemic of suspensions." He reported that correspondents were now greeting one another by saying, "What! Haven't you been suspended yet?" Hill held that there never had been a clear agreement against correspondents going to Berlin. In addition, he noted that Berlin, like Paris before, was a magnet for newsmen, and if SHAEF couldn't get them there, they would certainly go themselves—and do so with "enthusiastic welcome from the Russians."[14]

"I think it has been the greatest exhibition of bungling I ever saw in my life," Irwin said of her suspension. "They [SHAEF] treat you as if you were a half-witted child." Tully observed that he was "going to raise hell when I get home." Downs held that he never got into Berlin but only flew over it with a pilot in a British Mosquito. Freidin said he was astonished that he wasn't told about his suspension until after his story had appeared in Paris and New York. The two army reporters, it was noted, would be treated with unspecified military discipline.[15]

After a period of uncertainty in Paris, Irwin and Tully insisted that censors either cleared their Berlin stories or they were disaccredited and sent home, from where they could get their work to their papers. General Allen promptly ended their accreditation and ordered them home, without adding that the stories had already been passed for publication.

On May 9 the *Chicago Tribune* ran the delayed Berlin dispatches of both Irwin and Groth, circulated by the AP, in a prominent unified story headlined "The Day Berlin Fell; Wreckage, Tears Mark End." The major press play of Irwin's Berlin reporting had come the day before in her St. Louis paper. Her delayed account shared the front page of the *Post-Dispatch* on May 8 with a banner headline proclaiming the end of the war. "Post-Dispatch Reporter Gets into Berlin" ran a second eight-column headline just below, accompanied by a photo of Irwin at a typewriter and the first of her three-part Berlin story over the next days that recounted in detail the journey from the Elbe with Tully and the jeep driver. For a suspended war correspondent, the big display in her hometown paper was sweet triumph, as was a reported bonus of a year's pay from Joseph Pulitzer.

CHAPTER FOURTEEN

~

Last Scrap of the Press

When it came, the war's end was sudden and startling, and the dateline wasn't Berlin. In a brightly lit second-floor, wall-mapped SHAEF war room in a technical school in Reims, General Alfred Jodl, seated at a central table and flanked by two other Nazi officers, signed for the German High Command the unconditional surrender documents. Eisenhower's chief of staff, Bedell Smith, and two other Allied officers representing France and Russia and seated across the table then affixed their names to the documents. Eisenhower had determined in advance to deal with the Germans only through his staff and to avoid the war room until the surrender was complete.[1] When at length he joined others in the room it was for a round of congratulatory photos. Eventually he cabled to the Combined Chiefs of Staff an elegantly concise message: "The mission of this Allied force was fulfilled at 0241, local time, May 7th, 1945. Eisenhower."

While the shooting war ended in Reims, in Paris the Scribe's correspondents and the PRD remained locked in communications combat that overshadowed news of the Berlin suspensions and all else. During the period just before the surrender there were waves of elation between both sides that victory was at hand. In the hotel's bar, Edward R. Murrow, over from London in late April, gathered his CBS stalwarts about him and spoke exuberantly of the future. "We've seen what radio can do for the nation in war," one of the group heard him say. "Now let's go back to show what we can do in *peace!*"[2] Yet echoing through the Scribe at the same time was a minute-by-minute "death watch," in the words of Gladwin Hill in the *New York Times*, that kept everyone in a state of high anxiety. Stories coming in made clear that German forces were in complete disarray, but it wasn't clear whether any high officials among them were capable of agreeing to surrender.

SHAEF and the PRD heightened tension when, as Hill's full-blast prose had it, the Scribe's "orderly thrice-daily press conference system itself disintegrated into a nightmare series of extemporaneous assemblages for important announcements heralded by hoots from the klaxon-horn system throughout the correspondents' working, sleeping and eating quarters in the Scribe. This reduced the hardiest to a state of jumping jitters."

Hill barreled on: "Fifty times or more in the past ten days and nights the horns hooted and the correspondents rushed from typewriters, meals, drinks or beds, primed for word of the surrender, only to be let down by less important announcements—the junction with the Russians, the German's northern surrender, the German's southern surrender . . . until finally someone remarked: 'The next announcement will be of Colonel Dupuy's junction with SHAEF.'"[3]

Osmar White, a correspondent for Australian papers, added that the Scribe's rattled nerves caused the American wire services in the hotel to employ French youths to literally race flash news to offices on upper levels. Correspondents with less time-bound needs made bets on who would gain a two-second scoop after a military officer barked "Go!"[4] Edward Kennedy had once observed that such rat-race journalism practice by the wire services "was imbecilic by any sensible standard." But it was what he and others were paid to do, and he acknowledged that the "fierce competition was heady stuff. I admit I liked it."[5] Boyd Lewis, also paid to do it, said—somewhat tongue-in-cheek—that "some of the biggest battles of World War II were not between the Allies and the Germans but between the United Press and the Associated Press. . . . A beat of a few minutes would get a reporter kudos from his home office; a similar beating by the opposition brought a stinging 'rocket.'"[6]

The surrender in Reims only heightened agitation among the Paris-bound press, now over three issues surrounding the deed: the secretive selection of a small group of pool correspondents to witness it, excessive delay in releasing the news to the world, and unauthorized disclosure by one of the hotel's most prominent newsmen. Barney Oldfield summed up "the Scribe's end of the war" as "more wordy, violent and vituperative than the end of the conflict in Germany." He added that "even though the real struggle ended in Central Germany, the last scrap of the press was fought in Paris, the city it had attained in force and had refused to leave."[7]

⌒

When the surrender seemed definitely at hand, Harry Butcher in Reims phoned General Allen in Paris and suggested that a pool of fifteen to twenty correspondents should be flown to Reims to view the capitulation as representatives of the international media. The number finally settled on was seventeen, culled from an earlier list of Allied news outlets put together to cover the expected fall of Berlin.

The Reims list included representatives of the Associated Press, United Press, International News Service, Reuters, and Exchange Telegraph wire services; French, Australian, and Russian news agencies; American, British, and Canadian radio networks; and two army newspapers, *Stars and Stripes* and Canada's *Maple Leaf*. No positions were allotted for individual commercial newspapers, magazines, or radio stations, on grounds that communications outlets around the world would receive adequate coverage from the pool representatives. Margaret Ecker, representing the Canadian Press, was the lone woman selected. Also put together for the surrender was a pool of still photographers, newsreel operators, and radio technicians.

Colonel Dupuy at the Scribe was content with the pool arrangement. "For the man in the street," he maintained, "Allied world news coverage was guaranteed." He acknowledged, however, that two "ringers" among the chosen seventeen were controversial.[8] Britain's Exchange Telegraph handed over its slot to Price Day of the *Baltimore Sun*, with the *Sun* later trumpeting Day's surrender story, under a six-column-wide headline, as the only one by a correspondent of an individual paper. The Canadian Broadcasting Corporation, when its own radioman wasn't available, nominated Gerald Clark, a correspondent of the *Montreal Standard* and one of the Canadian newsmen that first reached the Scribe with the liberation of Paris.

The ringers were an irritant for the press, but the larger issue was the singling out without consultation of seventeen correspondents to attend the surrender. The number seemed too small for such a historic event and the means of selection too capricious. Helen Kirkpatrick aimed her finger at General Allen:

> A general who had been assigned as the Poohbah for the press corps in Paris, by himself and without consulting any correspondents, set up a pool of correspondents to go witness the surrender. On what basis he made his choices, none of us ever knew. Obviously they had to make choices, but they could have consulted the press corps—we had a sort of loose organization—to see that the major newspapers and magazines and wire services were involved. But he didn't do that.[9]

Edward Kennedy of the AP was in bed at the Scribe on May 6 when an aide of Allen's told him the service could send one correspondent to report on an unspecified event. Kennedy guessed it was the surrender and named himself. The UP picked Boyd Lewis, while the INS went with James Kilgallen. Gerald Glark of the Montreal paper, just back at the Scribe after covering the meeting of the Western Allies and Soviet forces in Germany, was relaxing in the hotel's bar as a PRO burst in, searched the crowd, and then rushed to him. "Thank God I've found you!" he said. "We need a Canadian."[10]

The Australian representative among the national news services, Osmar White, had covered the Pacific war in New Guinea and written a book about it before duty in Europe following the American Third Army. He was temporarily back at the Scribe when a friendly master sergeant of the PRD, a previous information source, took him aside and said, "This is it, buster. No announcement here, but there's a Dakota [transport plane] readied for the press. Strictly limited. Agencies and national reps only. Get weaving and remind them Australia's been fighting this fucking war, too."[11]

Sixteen Paris correspondents—Charles Kiley, the Stars and Stripes representative, was already in Reims—were bused to a small airport outside the city, where General Allen joined them. Gerald Clark reported that the plane was in the air before Allen cleared his throat and they learned for certain their destination.[12] "We are going to a mission to cover the signing of the peace," said Allen. The stories they wrote would be off the record until heads of Allied governments announced the surrender to the world and SHAEF then allowed newsmen to release the story. He asked correspondents to pledge on their honor their agreement with the procedure. There were no objections. Edward Kennedy later observed that what Allen asked for was nothing more than common SHAEF practice since newsmen frequently got stories they wrote in advance but were embargoed until a given time.[13]

Aboard the plane with the correspondents were two censors, Lieutenant Colonel Richard Merrick, the head American censor, and his British counterpart, Lieutenant Colonel George Warden. Since Reims lacked transmission facilities to handle the heavy load of dispatches and broadcasts certain to follow the surrender, it was understood that correspondents would return to the Scribe and deposit their dispatches at the copy center. First reports would be fifty-word bulletins that would largely duplicate the bare bones announcements of Truman, Churchill, and Stalin.[14] Next reports would add some further matter and finally full descriptive pieces. As usual, all outgoing material would move according to priority of filing.

While the plane to Reims was still aloft, Boyd Lewis hatched a plan for handling his surrender story. He would be the last passenger to board the plane leaving Reims. He would grab a seat close to the door. Once landed in Paris he would dash for the nearest jeep. A bottle of gin would persuade the driver to break Paris speed rules. He would arrive first at the Scribe with all his written material. "The glory would go to him," he knew, "who first got the fully fleshed story to home papers."[15]

⌒

Following the forty-minute flight to Reims the correspondents were driven to SHAEF headquarters in the redbrick École Professionelle and led by Allen into a ground-floor room. Here they were briefed on negotiations going on with two German officers in an upper area. Allen shifted back and forth, giving updates on what was taking place, until finally announcing, "Well, gentlemen, I think this is it." About the moment, Gerald Clark recorded,

> Now, after an anxious watch of more than eight hours, I did not feel any flush of excitement. . . . Perhaps, finally, it was all taking place too quickly. We mounted a flight of stairs to a door marked "War Room" and saw at a glance that it was not a large room—about forty feet long and thirty feet wide. But it was impressive. Spotlights shone from the whitewashed ceiling onto the maps that covered the walls—maps the Germans would have sacrificed divisions to have examined earlier in the war.[16]

The seventeen were held in a chalk-lined area of the room against a wall. The line reportedly was drawn by photographers to keep the press out of pictures, though *Life* carried one that clearly revealed the tightly packed band.

After General Jodl, his military aide, and Admiral Hans von Friedeburg were led to the room's central table, the ceremony of signing the surrender documents was over within minutes. As the Germans departed, silence filled the war room until Bedell Smith said to those at the table, "Thank you, gentlemen." Allen then led the correspondents to a narrow hallway where they glimpsed the Germans meeting for the first time with Eisenhower and his deputy, Marshal Tedder. Sitting behind a small desk, Eisenhower, speaking in, as Osmar White wrote, "a quiet, clear, tired voice," asked if the Germans understood and agreed to abide by the terms of the surrender.[17]

Returned to the lower room, the seventeen set to work on typewriters. They wouldn't leave from the Reims airport until dawn—and, as Allen informed them, their stories wouldn't be released until the following day. To both Allen and the correspondents it seemed senseless to restrict news of such magnitude. Harry Butcher's view was that the surrender story was certain to leak no matter the precautions, and he suggested to Eisenhower that newsmen start filing their stories early the next morning. Eisenhower replied that he was under orders from the Combined Chiefs of Staff to await disclosure by Truman, Churchill, and Stalin. When Allen raised the same issue with him, Eisenhower lectured him, "These are my orders, and by God, they are yours, too."[18]

～

Back at the Scribe, the snubbed correspondents were an unruly mass. One of the more relentless reporters among them, Charles Wertenbaker, assuming that wherever Eisenhower was located was where a total surrender would take place, had already made an unauthorized trip to Reims. He was prevented from entering the school building, but glimpsing uniformed Germans doing so he knew what was coming. A plea that since he was on the spot he should be included among the select coming for the signing was ignored. In his dispatch "Surrender at Reims," appearing in *Life* two weeks after the event, he made his absence from the war room part of the story of German capitulation. "We watched the windows," his closing paragraph began,

> but the War Room had no window on the street and MPs barred us from the courtyard. Through the double doors leading to the court I thought I could see on one of the trees light shining from the War Room. I watched that tree. Suddenly it was lit by a brighter flash, then another and another. These would be the lights from flash bulbs. . . . At 5 minutes past 3 Bedell Smith walked down the corridor, swinging his swagger stick, but holding himself stiffly as if his stomach hurt him, and as he got in his car he said, "*Fini la guerre.*"[19]

Stationed with Wertenbaker at the moment were what Butcher called a "hornet's nest of correspondents" who had found transport from the Scribe and were loudly determined to be merged with the seventeen. The group included such press heavyweights as Raymond Daniell of the *New York Times* and Helen Kirkpatrick of the *Chicago Daily News*, yet they with other so-called illegals were held outside as well. While waiting beneath the war room before the surrender, Gerald Clark glimpsed through a window the illegals pressing to the glass. "Ironically," he noted, "one of the first persons I was able to pick out in the exterior darkness was a frustrated Matthew Halton of the Canadian Broadcasting Corporation."[20] Irony arose from the fact that Clark, as the Canadian representative with the seventeen, would eventually deliver a broadcast for Halton's CBC. When the surrender was complete, the outcasts were allowed a peek inside the war room to get scraps of detail for their future stories. Kirkpatrick carried a tape measure about the room, seeking evidence that the space could have accommodated more reporters.[21]

∽

During the flight of the select newsmen back to Paris, the AP's Kennedy reflected on what seemed the utter absurdity of holding back news of the war's end. "I knew from experience," he later wrote, "that one might as well try to censor the rising of the sun. The war in Europe ended after six years and the Allied governments deciding to keep it a secret for thirty-six hours—it was as though the heads of the governments had jointly lost their minds at the last moment as a result of the strain. I was certain that a flash of sanity would soon come."[22]

One earlier experience that might have crossed Kennedy's own mind involved General Patton slapping and berating two soldiers in hospitals in Sicily in August 1943 when he believed they were faking illnesses. Kennedy stumbled upon the unreported story when, after a home leave, he arrived in Morocco and heard gossip about it. He learned that correspondents in a press camp in Sicily had agreed not to pursue the story but sent a delegation to Eisenhower with a petition that he order Patton to apologize to the men or else lose his command. Both Eisenhower and Patton had complied.

Yet with his arrival in North Africa, Kennedy pushed the matter further. In the company of Harry Butcher, he went to see Eisenhower in Algiers and argued that the Patton affair would eventually get into print and the long delay would suggest that the army had suppressed the news. The way to handle the story now was to let correspondents release it while including information about Eisenhower's decisive treatment of Patton. "He agreed with me in principle," Kennedy wrote, "but couldn't bring himself to the point to approving publication of the story." Eisenhower let it be known, Kennedy added, that he would view any attempt by a correspondent to publish the story as an embarrassment to Patton, to himself, and to the war effort.[23]

The story became public in November 1943 when the Washington columnist Drew Pearson disclosed it during a radio broadcast, sparking the kind of uproar on the home front that Kennedy anticipated. Eisenhower's headquarters first blanketed the story with censorship before grudgingly allowing publication. Kennedy got out a story himself but, as he recalled, he was "rebuked by the Associated Press for not having informed the home office on the situation before Pearson scored his beat."[24]

∽

During a mid-morning press conference on May 7 in the Scribe's information room conducted by General Allen and other PRD officers, there was no last-moment change of plans. About a hundred angry correspondents were present, both those who had made their own way to Reims and those who had remained in the hotel. Allen and company gave out detailed information about the surrender that correspondents could work into reports but held firmly to the SHAEF order about the release date of dispatches, now set for 3 p.m. Paris time on May 8.

Allen repeated that he agreed with the correspondents that the news should be immediately released, but there was nothing he could do. His hands were tied. So were those of newsmen like David Walker of Britain's *Daily Mirror*. "This must be the greatest single Press fiasco of all time," the veteran correspondent angrily cabled his editor. "While the peace news has been broadcast all over the world, British and American newspapermen's copy still lies here pending the permission of officialdom. Even in their defeat, the Germans can laugh at us for our confusion, and for those who have been abroad on war stories since 1938 and 1939, this is the final humiliation."[25]

Up in the relative calm of his hotel office, Kennedy was reading reports that de Gaulle was writing a victory address, that loudspeakers had been put in position at 10 Downing Street in London, and that Allied troops had been informed about the surrender. Then he learned that German army radio in Flensburg had announced the surrender to its troops, and he believed this could not have been done without SHAEF's approval. He would later insist that, before knowledge of the Flensburg broadcast, "no idea of breaking the news before the official release time had entered my head."[26]

After telegrams came in from the AP in New York and London giving him the text of the German announcement, Kennedy decided to act. He would subsequently hold that what he did came down to a moral question. Did his duty as a reporter require "subservience to a political censorship which was contrary to the principle of a free press and in violation of the word of the government and the Army or action which I believed right and which I knew would bring plenty of trouble upon my head?"[27]

His answer was to first telephone Allen to tell him he was releasing the story, but a secretary said the officer was too busy to speak with him. He next confronted Richard Merrick with the same story and the texts of the Flensburg disclosure. The chief censor's response was to shrug his shoulders and say to Kennedy, "Do as you please."[28] Merrick's clipped reply was presumably

Photo 14.1 In calmer times, Edward Kennedy (right) buys weekly rations at the Scribe's PX.
Source: National Archives

based on his certainty that the Scribe's iron wall of censorship would stop
any premature story.

Kennedy knew of a military telephone line to London that was, he later
said, a "gaping loophole" in the hotel's security. He noted that he had used
the line many times before "with the knowledge of public relations officers
and sometimes at their suggestion," though never as a means of avoiding
censorship.[29] After asking an AP staff member, Morton Gudebrod, to place
the call, Kennedy dictated a brief surrender report to the AP's London office.

Typically carried in print versions with Kennedy's byline, the full AP story
swiftly circled the globe. The *New York Times* ran it below a rare full-page,
four-line banner headline. Hours would yet pass before London, Washington, and Paris announced that VE Day would be May 8, 1945, thus allowing
release of all surrender stories while according Kennedy what many considered the greatest scoop of the war.

As Kennedy expected, his action unleashed on him the fury of SHAEF,
General Allen and the PRD, and his fellow correspondents. The two other
American wire-service men among the seventeen, Boyd Lewis and James
Kilgallen, were exceptionally bitter. As he had intended, Lewis was the first
to get from the Paris airport to the Scribe and have his surrender report filed
number one. Kilgallen came in number two and—reportedly after dropping
his portable typewriter to slow the progress through the hotel's revolving
door of the competitor just behind him—Kennedy number three.[30]

The filing order was pointless after Kennedy broke the story. There
was momentary satisfaction for correspondents when SHAEF withdrew
his accreditation and he was expelled from Europe, the Associated Press
as a whole was suspended from filing in Europe, and in mid-May Kennedy
returned to the United States. Still, following what Barney Oldfield called
a "steadily erupting geyser of wrath" in the Scribe, correspondents gathered in the information room to consider Kennedy's deed. "You realize,
gentlemen, that you have taken the worst beating of your lives," said Drew
Middleton of the *New York Times*. "The question is, what are you going to
do about it?"[31]

The action taken was a letter to Eisenhower signed by fifty-four correspondents lamenting that by respecting the rules they had "suffered the most
disgraceful, deliberate and unethical double-cross in the history of journalism."[32] In a letter to his wife from the Scribe, Colonel Dupuy was more suc-
cinct: the "AP 'scoop' was carried out by a skunk."[33] Harry Butcher confided
to his diary that, now distant from the PRD, he was fortunate to escape the

thoroughly messy aftermath of the Kennedy affair that General Allen had battled through.[34]

Raymond Daniell lashed out at SHAEF, the PRD, and Kennedy in a *New York Times* story on May 9 headlined "Fiasco by SHAEF at Reims Is Bared: Reporters Barred from Seeing Historic Signing of the German Surrender." On May 10 the *Times* printed the full text of a formal statement by Allen about what he called the alleged scoop of Kennedy and the AP. Allen restated what he told newsmen on the flight to Reims, that everyone save Kennedy had observed the pledge he asked for and that Kennedy's violation caused SHAEF to break an understanding with Russian allies that could have led to a chain of events that would have been "deplorable."

The same May 10 issue of the *Times* carried a long story by Gladwin Hill in Paris under the headline "Peace Jeopardized by AP, SHAEF Says." After reviewing Allen's statement, Hill paused at the end to say that SHAEF correspondents were generally satisfied with the statement. He added that a number of them, though, took issue with Allen's remark that correspondents in Reims had not gotten the surrender story "in the ordinary course of their [reporting] activities within this theatre" but it had been "obtained by the courtesy of SHAEF headquarters" and his personal relationship with the press. Hill responded in his own words: "The American public, whose war it was to such a great and tragic extent, had the inherent right to be represented through their news organizations at the formal ending of the war."

Coupled with Hill's story under the subhead "Kennedy Defends Himself" was an AP dispatch from Paris in which Kennedy refuted Allen's charges. A notable point of disagreement was with Allen's assertion that the surrender story had to be held "until the Russians were satisfied that the surrender was genuine." This was an astonishing position, said Kennedy, "in view of the fact that Soviet Russia was a signatory of the Reims agreement." Kennedy only indirectly challenged the claim of SHAEF's "courtesy" to newsmen by holding that Allen must know "that the purpose of correspondents in this theater is to report news, and certainly as the head of public relations he should realize that the signing of the end of the war was news and, since he himself conceded there was no question of military security involved, it was legitimate news."

In the *New Yorker* on May 19, A. J. Liebling rose to Kennedy's defense against the piling on of colleagues like Raymond Daniell. Liebling allowed only that, on the plane to Reims, Kennedy might have refused any agreement with General Allen, though—he added pointedly—this would have meant missing an event no newspaperman would ever choose to miss. In any event, Liebling concluded that the Kennedy explosion probably hadn't harmed anyone beyond Kennedy, who was "one of my favorite reporters, I might add." Liebling noted for the record that surrender stories by Drew Middleton of the *Times* and John O'Reilly of the *Herald Tribune* appeared in New York papers some twenty-four hours after Kennedy's AP dispatch in the *Times* and were essentially simply duplicates of it.

More troubling in the Kennedy row, Liebling believed, was SHAEF's PRD bypassing all American newspaper reporters and allowing only three US wire-service representatives—Kennedy, Lewis, and Kilgallen—to "one of the memorable scenes in the history of man" and then making them promise to tell about it only when General Allen said they could. "*No* correspondent of a newspaper published in the United States," Liebling emphasized, "was invited to the signing."[35]

～

In a news story appearing two weeks after the war ended, *Time* said the response to Kennedy's action by AP member papers in the United States was almost equally divided between scorn and support. Tom O'Reilly, a columnist for *PM* quoted by the magazine, pointed fingers at both Kennedy and SHAEF: "Kennedy was guilty of breaking a release date, which, in the newspaper business, is practically crime No. 1. . . . But never before in history had anybody been so dumb as to try to put a release date on the end of a continental war." *Time* closed the piece with a broad swipe at the military's view of the press throughout the war and beyond: "So long as all U.S. newsmen in Europe are obliged to wear Army uniforms, carry Army credentials, depend on the Army for transportation and send their dispatches by Army courtesy—to do business, in fact, only as 'guests' of the Army—the U.S. public could not expect to get all the news it was entitled to from Europe."[36]

The European suspension of the AP was soon lifted, and Wes Gallagher, a crusty veteran of the wire service and Kennedy's long-running rival as a correspondent, hurried from the Elbe River to replace him as head of the Paris bureau. One of his first acts was to meet with Eisenhower in Reims. "If I'd been Kennedy," Gallagher told the supreme commander, "I'd have done the same thing—except that I'd have telephoned you first." Eisenhower responded, "I would have thrown you in jail." To which Gallagher replied, "That wouldn't have stopped the story."[37] His point, he later clarified, was that once a source breached a story, all sources were free to release it.

CHAPTER FIFTEEN

~

The Guns Were Still

George Orwell, back in Paris and writing about VE Day for Britain's *Observer*, mentioned the "much discussed misdemeanour of one of the news agencies" but didn't name the Associated Press or Edward Kennedy. He noted that the surrender had leaked out via German radio and that the information had been repeated on French radio, causing some early singing and parading in Paris streets and airplanes dropping colored flares. The official celebration began the following morning. "Bands of youths and girls," he wrote, "marched to and fro in military formations, chanting, '*Avec Nous! Avec Nous!*' ("*With Us! With Us!*"), and gradually swelling their numbers until by midday the crowds were so enormous that many of the main streets and squares were quite impassable." Orwell pushed through to a loudspeaker in the Place de la Concorde to hear the announcement of the war's end. After de Gaulle came on and proclaimed, "The war is won. This is victory," people didn't cheer but listened intently to the rest of his remarks. Afterward they stood in silence while the national anthems of the Allied nations were played.[1]

In her "Letter from Paris" in the *New Yorker*, Janet Flanner also emphasized the way Parisians marched on victory day: "In Paris the war ended the way it began—with marching. It began with the French soldiers marching off to the war and it ended with the French civilians marching into the peace."[2] She added that some of the hundreds of thousands were still marching at dawn the following morning. Simone de Beauvoir, on the other hand, called attention to the difference between VE Day and the liberation of Paris. "This victory [over Germany]," she wrote in a memoir, "had been won a long way off; we had not awaited it, as we had the Liberation, in a fever of anxiety; it had been foreseen for a long time, and offered no new hopes. It simply marked the end of the war; in a way, this end was like a sort of death."[3]

James Quirk, writing home to his wife about the victory as he experienced it in a press camp with Patton's Third Army in Czechoslovakia, described a last meeting between correspondents and the general that ended with a class picture on the steps outside his headquarters. Overall, wrote Quirk, there was "no jubilation, no celebration," about the war's conclusion. The whole army seemed "downcast and dispirited," as he did as well. "I can only wonder," he said, "what I shall get up for tomorrow."[4]

Don Whitehead was with the American First Army in Germany when he learned the war was over. The GIs, he said in an AP dispatch on May 7, were asking themselves, "Where do we go from here?" "It is a strange ending to a strange war," he wrote of his own feelings, "an ending nobody could have quite visualized and without the dramatic conclusion most of us had pictured. Suddenly the war just melted away into nothingness and the guns were still."[5]

There was still plenty to do at the Scribe. Ernest Dupuy said in a letter home that reporters in the hotel "are thinking up all sort of angles and the telephone is ringing constantly. We in PR have several problems—the war is far from over for us."[6] Among issues he ticked off were the occupation of Germany, the handling of displaced people and prisoners of war, and the demobilization of German forces. Harry Butcher wrote that he expected the German surrender "would mean a letup in work, but instead just the reverse has happened."[7]

Just as postwar problems remained for the military victors, so did censorship for the press. In "Military Censorship Retains Curbs on News from Europe," a front-page story in the Paris edition of the *Herald Tribune* shortly after VE Day and reprinted in the New York edition, Geoffrey Parsons caustically noted that military security is "still the phrase used by the censors to justify any steps imposed on the free flow of news from the European Theater." He acknowledged some easing of restrictions and offered an example from his own paper that "last night the censors permitted the transmission to New York of the news that yesterday in Paris was warm and lovely." Before, weather information about London and Paris had been, for security reasons, taboo until several days after the fact.

In a weightier vein, Parsons pointed out that Allied censors had never dealt with the truth or accuracy of stories by correspondents. But now the "newest regulation is that they will stop all 'unauthenticated, inaccurate or false reports, misleading statements and rumors.'" Also banned was the be-havior of American troops in regard to looting or fraternizing with German citizens as well as any speculation on details of the occupation of the country. Finally, Parsons switched his attention to the postwar need of many war cor-respondents relearning how to be genuine reporters. "After five to six years of censorship," he wrote, "they have learned to weaselword their articles through a censorship that objected to the direct verb, the tough or precise adverb, or a direct attribution of sources. The premium was on the vague."[8]

An immediate postwar staffing problem Eisenhower faced up to was General Allen's leadership of the PRD in the wake of the Kennedy affair. Despite at the time blustering in his diary that Kennedy had "caused the damnedest snafu I've ever experienced," Butcher preferred to believe that the newsman's action was a problem only for the press. Yet clearly Allen and the PRD were inescapably involved. Butcher observed that Allen had said his combat time in Italy with an armored division was more pleasurable than his days with Public Relations; now he wanted out of the job and connected with a force going to the Pacific. Eisenhower's first choice to lead the PRD was Butcher himself, with a commitment to stay in the post as long as the general remained in Europe. Butcher responded that he would do whatever his boss wanted.[9]

But as he sized up the job, it would be anything but smooth sailing for whoever was in charge. During the war the single objective had been to win it. That accomplished, correspondents still in Europe would need to compete for news space with riveting battle accounts in the Pacific. Hence, as Butcher saw it, they would turn to critical stories about Eisenhower's handling of is-sues in occupied Germany. "In other words," he told his diary, "the open sea-son is here—each of the Allies will tend to revert to his nationalistic interest and all our operations constitute game to be shot at by correspondents and Congressional committees." If he stayed overly long in Europe, Eisenhower's elevated reputation would likely suffer.[10]

As it happened, Eisenhower decided not to name Butcher to lead the PRD. His reasoning, as Butcher characterized it, was that since "nearly every public-relations officer eventually 'broke his pick,'" after some months he too would be in the "correspondents' doghouse." Eisenhower also decided that Allen, having served his sentence with the PRD, should have a combat command, in this case an armored division in the Pacific.[11] "Gen. Allen was a reluctant shepherd to the press," Boyd Lewis had once said of him. "He was lonely for his beloved tanks."[12]

⁓

Howard K. Smith had been with the American Ninth Army preparing to cross the Elbe and roll on to Berlin when Charles Collingwood informed him by telegram that his wife had given birth to a son. Smith took a flight to Paris to be with his new family but also secured a room at the Scribe in case he was needed for CBS broadcasts. The need arrived in short order when Collingwood became one of the select seventeen to cover the Reims surrender. While Paris was ecstatic with celebration when the war ended, Smith remained chained to a hotel microphone.

Collingwood was lucky when CBS tapped him for its radio slot in Reims. Immediately thereafter, Drew Middleton spotted Smith in the Scribe's lobby and said he had just drawn CBS from a hat containing the initials of the three American broadcast networks. Before Middleton could explain what this new bit of luck meant, Collingwood came by and congratulated Smith. Edward R. Murrow had named him as the CBS man going to Berlin the next day, May 8, to cover a ratification of the Reims surrender demanded by the Russians.

Edward Kennedy recalled, some time after the fact, that during the highly charged press conference with correspondents in the Scribe on May 7, General Allen had disclosed that news of the German surrender might be blocked even longer than expected because of the Russians. They, as Kennedy paraphrased Allen, after having "induced Washington and London to hold up the announcement until the hour set for their own ceremony in Berlin, now were asking that news of the real surrender at Reims be suppressed until some hours *after* the phony surrender of Berlin."

The news, Allen had continued, was off the record, but Kennedy thought the correspondents paid no attention anyway because they were wrapped up in concern about his scoop. As result, he wrote, they had "overlooked one of the biggest stories of the war—one almost as important as the German surrender. It was placed under their noses by no less august an official spokesman than General Allen himself, but not one of them, apparently, recognized it as news."[13]

Now, clearly if reluctantly accepting that the second surrender was newsworthy, the Western Allied contingent heading to Berlin was taking along a small number of international correspondents to act as pool reporters. Hoping to avoid the uproar over selections for Reims, Dupuy had asked Joseph Evans of *Newsweek* magazine, the president of the correspondents' committee in the Scribe, to canvas his members and come up with names. Americans in the eight-member press group picked for Berlin were Joseph Grigg of the UP, John O'Reilly of the *New York Herald Tribune*, and Charles Kiley of *Stars and Stripes*, a veteran of the Reims surrender. Joining Howard Smith among the broadcasters chosen was Canada's Matthew Halton. The Berlin delegation was headed by SHAEF's deputy commander, Marshal Tedder, and included American and French generals, Colonel Dupuy and Brigadier Turner of the PRD, and the pool correspondents, plus photographers and *Stars and Stripes* men.

Also in the party were—as Howard Smith phrased it—"a couple of freeloaders, allowed to go along because Ike liked them": Harry Butcher and "Ike's driver, Kay Summersby, she of the romantic rumors."[14] A WAC lieutenant, Summersby was also present in the war room at the Reims surrender, as was Butcher. Her image was later removed from a photo showing her just behind Eisenhower and Bedell Smith as Eisenhower exhibits pens used in the signing. According to Butcher, Eisenhower wanted to go to the Berlin signing to meet the Russians and see the city but accepted the view of staff members that the war ended in Reims, and the Russian insistence on an "encore" was merely "showmanship for the Russian people."[15]

In Reims, General Smith had fretted that, despite its brevity and the limited number of correspondents, photographers, and film men present, the surrender ceremony would have a Hollywood air. In Berlin the Russians had no such qualms. During the klieg-lighted event presided over by Russia's Marshal Georgi Zhukov, some thirty Soviet reporters and about one hundred still and film cameramen recorded every moment of the German capitulation. After the formal ceremony ended at 12:45 a.m., dinner and an epic champagne-vodka-wine and speech-making celebration rolled on well into dawn.[16]

Howard Smith tried to organize his radio material on the plane back to Paris, believing that among the returning hungover party only he and the pilot managed to stay awake. At the Scribe he faced nonstop writing and broadcasting as the pool man any radio outlet could go to for reports of the Russian ceremony. In one ten-hour period he logged seventeen broadcasts from the hotel before collapsing in sleep at his typewriter. Just ahead for Smith was more normal microphone work as CBS's man in Berlin reporting on the occupation and the trials—and in 1946 a steep career leap when he replaced Murrow as the network's chief European correspondent.

In mid-June 1945, Eisenhower, who had come to Paris to be feted by de Gaulle, appeared at the Scribe for a farewell news conference with correspondents. Butcher, accompanying him, thought it only a moderate success since the general had little news to convey, though the AP transmitted a full transcript of his remarks. Eisenhower then set off on a triumphal trip to

Photo 15.1 Eisenhower departing a press conference, with Colonel Dupuy following.
Source: David E. Scherman/The LIFE Picture Collection/Getty Images

the United States. Butcher joined him but did not return to Europe, his war service over.

Two months after the Reims surrender and the ratification in Berlin, SHAEF, now based in Frankfurt, ceased to exist, and military authority was transferred to individual nations. In the Scribe's information room, an American major read to correspondents a terse announcement: "Termination of the combined command and dissolution of Supreme Headquarters, Allied Expeditionary Force, will become effective at 0001, 14 July, 1945."[17] All American PROs and censors were now part of US Forces in the European Theater (USFET) under Eisenhower's command. In August came the announcement that a new American press camp would be set up in the Hotel Grunewald in the old spa city of Wiesbaden and, like the Scribe, have briefing, censors, and transmission services in a single place.

That same month Harold Acton moved from the Scribe to the new location. While distressed at leaving Paris for the grim reality of Germany, he marveled that his American colleagues seemed to welcome the change of setting. "Their cheerfulness and good nature were impervious," he wrote, "to the blanket of hostility, to the ugliness of the flats where they were billeted, each drearier than the last." In September, Acton left his agreeable Americans for a British unit in the German city of Minden and billets in a hotel with his country's newsmen.[18]

With SHAEF's demise there was a flurry of public-relations departure activity in the Scribe—a dance held at the Hôtel Chatham, dinner parties, and rapid liquidation of the officers' personal bar in the Scribe that had been kept stocked, from their own pockets, since reaching Paris. Finally, British, Canadian, and other international figures left for new accommodations, and Americans were shifted from Paris to Frankfurt or, like Ernest Dupuy, left for Le Havre on the first leg of a ship journey home.

Some new correspondents still passed through the Scribe while on their way to report on occupied Germany and the Nuremberg trials. The author John Dos Passos got to the hotel in October 1945 with an assignment for *Life* to write about both. He had reported on combat in the Pacific, and possibly war fatigue caused his notably gloomy view of his Paris surroundings. Neither the Scribe nor the familiar city had appeal. "Here I am in a dreary little room" with a bed that was "damp and lonely straw," he wrote in a letter. Walking Paris's grand boulevards only left him wondering how the French could manage to survive when a meal of US military rations in the Scribe cost him thirteen francs while in non-black-market restaurants it would have been a hundred francs plus ration coupons.[19]

⌒

On December 1, 1945, the Scribe was officially vacated by the American military as a requisitioned building. This prompted a story from Paris by the *New York Herald Tribune*'s John O'Reilly that appeared the following day under a three-column headline reading "Hotel Scribe Ends War Career" and a subhead adding "Famous Paris Headquarters of War Reporters Passed Eventful Years." O'Reilly said the evacuation of the hotel would cause no tears, yet he reminisced at length about reporters who for weeks at a time slept, ate, and wrote stories in the building and only needed to walk twenty feet in open air to reach a barbershop.

Their complaints had been many: the klaxon blasting away at night, the bar that at odd times had nothing to drink but pale wine and tomato juice, the need of correspondents to set morning calls for warm baths, night briefings in the information room that seemed the coldest place south of the Arctic Circle. Still, he believed the passing of the "curious institution" of the hotel, now with worn carpets and a "dusty lonesomeness" descended upon the bar, shouldn't be overlooked when—echoing Harry Butcher's diary observation of over a year earlier—historians wrote their chronicles of the war. O'Reilly ended his own journalistic chronicle with the news that some correspondents planned to stay on in the hotel under civilian operation and "years hence probably will haunt the place, weird figures out of the past."[20]

Continuing press activity in the Scribe, including military censorship and transmission procedures, was now in the hands of the French Ministry of Information. American correspondents still residing in the hotel had sought a compromise in which the US army would play some role.[21] But a story by John Thompson in the *Chicago Tribune* on December 13, 1945, indicated that the French were in sole control. It described a French subsidy for room rentals by news organizations of four hundred francs a day, or about eight dollars, to bring hotel rates more or less in line with those of SHAEF days. Thirty-eight news groups had accepted the subsidy for staff members still working in the hotel, though for unspecified reasons the Chicago paper declined even though it was still leasing a suite in the Scribe until a street-level location came available. Two magazines, the *Saturday Evening Post* and *Collier's*, also declined the subsidy.

～

Lee Miller was typing a story for *Vogue* at a press camp in Rosenheim, Germany, when the war ended. Since leaving Paris and the Scribe, she and David Scherman had photographed and written about German cities in ruin, the concentration camps, and mingling with the Russians on the banks of the Elbe. Ironically, one of their best-remembered pictures from the period was a staged shot by Scherman of Miller having a bath in the tiled bathroom of Hitler's home in Munich, her combat boots and rumpled uniform artfully arranged beside the tub.[22] Miller then photographed Scherman bathing in the tub. After the war the pair made their way back to Paris and the Scribe but only as a temporary haven before leaving again on an ambitious postwar plan to carry on as correspondents reporting on Central Europe under Russian domination.[23]

Scherman was less committed to the venture than Miller, as he also was about their staying yoked together. After both briefly went back to Britain and Scherman continued on to New York, Miller began her travels on the Continent in mid-August 1945. In Paris she connected with Scherman, who was again back in the Scribe, but she found the city dead and the hotel unappealing. "The room and my affairs are a hopeless mess," she complained in a letter, "and I'm incapable of sorting them out."[24] She was suffering from depression and an inability to sleep without pills and alcohol, yet she couldn't relinquish her unfettered wartime life of photography and reporting.

After a stay in Austria, Miller ventured on to Hungary. In due course she joined forces with *Life* magazine's John Phillips and added Romania to her list of countries. The peripatetic Phillips, a *Life* photojournalist since age twenty-one, had covered the European war in Italy, Yugoslavia, and Slovenia. In Austria when it ended, he decided to carry on his work in Central Europe. He was in Budapest when, as he recounted, Miller entered his life in the form of "an American free spirit wrapped in the body of a Greek goddess."[25]

While the two were together in Hungary and preparing to move on to Romania, *Vogue* cabled Miller that it was pulling the financial plug that allowed her to stay on in Europe. At nearly the same time Phillips had gotten a cable from David Scherman urging him to tell Miller that her relationship with Roland Penrose was in danger if she didn't return to London— information she ignored. Further complication set in when Phillips was ordered by an officer of the Allied Control Commission in Vienna to return his jeep and driver, both long overdue. Phillips and Miller argued about her future. He believed she should go home. "That night," he said of her, "Lee understood that Bucharest was the end of the line. Her war was finally over."[26]

The next day Miller took a train to Paris and the Scribe, where a *Life* writer and researcher staying in the hotel, Rosemarie Redlich, found her in a badly exhausted state. As a later writer summed up her condition, Miller was a burnout case.[27] After Roland Penrose came to Paris and took her to Britain, she managed to finish articles about Hungary and Romania for publication. Meanwhile, David Scherman had come to London to work on a photo essay about Scotland Yard and was reunited with Miller. In 1943 Scherman had coauthored *Literary England*, a book developed from a photo essay in *Life* that same year.

Yet before long he abandoned the new British piece, set off to Paris with a scheme for a book about the city's literature, and settled in his old room in the Scribe, from where he could still glimpse the jerry cans on Miller's balcony. When Miller came to Paris to celebrate her thirty-ninth birthday, she lunched with Scherman, but their journalistic collaboration was over. After Miller's return to Britain, where she and Penrose eventually married, Scherman stayed in the Scribe and worked on his literary project with Rosemarie Redlich. (They later married and in 1952 joined as coauthors of *Literary America*, a photo book drawn from travels together in the country.) In the immediate postwar period, however, the hotel struck Scherman as a ghostly presence. In a letter home in April 1946, he said that there were only "a few gnomes still hanging around from the war, nobody told 'em it's over."[28]

~

CHAPTER SIXTEEN

Snafu Revisited

The last scrap of the press was fought at the Scribe in Paris, as Barney Old-field had it, but Edward Kennedy gave the struggle continuing shelf life in America. While working after the war as managing editor of a newspaper in California, the *Santa Barbara News-Press*, he published in the *Atlantic Monthly* in August 1948 an article called "I'd Do It Again," the title encapsulating his certainty that he acted properly in breaking the story of the Nazi surrender. The magazine said in a blurb accompanying the article that Kennedy was for the first time giving a full reply to complaints that he violated SHAEF's release agreement and took advantage of fellow correspondents.

Step by step in his piece, Kennedy rehashed what had taken place in Reims and thereafter Paris, adding only bits of new information. One such was a signed admission he had received from Bedell Smith that SHAEF had indeed told German radio in Flensburg to inform troops of the surrender and to cease resistance. "SHAEF itself," Kennedy emphasized, "had not merely authorized the breaking of the news before the 'official' release time. It had ordered it!"[1]

About his use of the telephone line from the Scribe to the UK, Kennedy repeated that in the past he had employed it several times to reach the Associated Press in London and had done so with the knowledge of the PRD. He went on: "Anyone could call 'Paris Military' from the Scribe and be connected with any telephone in London. Any enemy agent in Paris might have done this. The fact that SHAEF had left this loophole in its supposedly airtight security system is something for the military mind to explain."[2] Kennedy wound up the article by holding that, with the passing of time, feelings about him in newspaper circles had shifted more in his direction. During meetings now with correspondents who in Paris had signed the petition against him, his surrender scoop no longer came up.

⁓

Even before the *Atlantic* piece appeared, *Editor & Publisher* magazine had cleared Kennedy of any wrongdoing. An editorial in its July 12, 1947, issue said it was now beyond doubt that SHAEF had "cooked up on the spot" the excuse that the surrender story had to be held up for a joint Allied announcement. SHAEF had already authorized release of the story via German radio, and the BBC had rebroadcast the report. "Kennedy's name has been cleared," the magazine concluded, "and we believe that his story will go down in the books as one of the greatest journalistic beats in history."

For Thor Smith, who left military life as a full colonel and was again employed by the *San Francisco Call-Bulletin*, Kennedy was anything but in the clear. He seized upon the former correspondent digging up the past in the *Atlantic* as an opportunity to set the historical record straight from the slant of the PRD. When he first took up the pen, it was to propose to the *Atlantic*'s associate editor, Charles W. Morton, a collaborative article by himself and two former high-placed public-relations colleagues, Burrows Matthews and S. G. Pawley, who were also fully acquainted with what happened in Paris.

In writing to Morton, Smith was responding to a notice under the editor's name in the *Atlantic* of July 1948 that said the next issue, in August, would carry an article by Kennedy giving his version of the surrender. Kennedy would set out facts, Morton added, that had been mangled both by his opposition among fellow correspondents and "the Army oafs in charge of the nightmarish press arrangements on that occasion." The article, he promised, would be "rugged stuff."

In his query to Morton, Smith said that the three ex-military officers would give their side of the story, though—an important distinction, as it turned out—not the view of Morton's "Army oafs" but PROs who, in many cases, had more experience as newspapermen than the accredited war correspondents. Smith accepted that the whole Kennedy debacle, as he called it, was caused by the false belief that anything as significant as the war's end could be embargoed—and that he was among those who protested it in advance but had been overruled by chiefs of state. Yet there were still, he assured Morton, "many other angles, the full details of which have never been adequately told."

When nothing seemingly came of his pitch to the *Atlantic*, Smith turned out his own twelve-page manuscript, titled "Surrender Snafu," that now rests, together with his letter to Morton, among the Thor M. Smith papers at the Eisenhower Presidential Library. A handwritten note on the opening page of the manuscript says the article was written in July 1948 and never published.

⌒

Smith begins by pointing out that he was a member of a three-man board immediately appointed at the Scribe in Paris to investigate Kennedy's breach of the surrender embargo. (In a war memoir, Kennedy said that General Allen had granted him a hearing in Paris and "designated three of his subordinate officers for this purpose. Their proceedings consisted of telling me that they'd be glad to take any statement I cared to make. Since Allen was one of the principals in the case, any decision in my favor would virtually have amounted to insubordination on their part toward their commanding officer."[3]) The board finished their work on the night of May 8, 1945, and the following day Smith flew to Reims with the board's report, which among other things recommended an official investigation with the possibility of a court-martial and a full public statement about Kennedy's action.

Smith spent an hour and a half in conference with Eisenhower and Bedell Smith, both of whom were "dismayed at the turn of events, bitterly disappointed, and thoroughly angry" with Kennedy's action. Eisenhower, Smith reports, then personally drafted the public statement that would go out under General Allen's name. (For his part, Kennedy believed Allen and Bedell Smith wholly put the statement together.[4]) Eisenhower subsequently turned over the Kennedy case to General Edward Betts, the judge advocate general of the European theater, whose pragmatic view was that a long court-martial procedure would cause more harm than good and recommended the lesser disciplinary action against Kennedy and the AP's Morton Gudebrod of disaccrediting them and sending them home.

Smith agrees that such a practical procedure was probably the correct course of action. But he insists that Kennedy fully deserved the torrent of anger that came his way from PRD officials and fellow correspondents. Some of Kennedy's "still-injured competitors," he notes, had filed briefs with SHAEF about his earlier record as a war correspondent for "release-breaking and corner-cutting in other military theaters—notably in Cairo and Southern France." In reference to Kennedy telling Richard Merrick that he was going to break the embargo and Merrick saying, "Do as you please," Smith quotes the response of George Warden, the chief censor: "A statement of this nature was made by Kennedy so often that one can scarcely expect Merrick to take action on it."

As for Kennedy's means of contacting London from the Scribe, Smith acknowledges that the open phone line was an astonishing flaw in the PRD's security:

> It wasn't long before some of the smart boys discovered, quite by accident, that it was a simple matter to use a few non-secret telephone code words ("Paris Military," "U.K." etc.), and get connected with their English girl friends at a civilian number in London. In theory, such communication was supposed to be "monitored" for censorship. In actual fact, neither Army Signals nor Censorship had gotten around to such controls in the closing weeks of the war. Naturally, such facilities didn't remain a secret very long to the restless and eager corps of correspondents bedded down in Paris at the Scribe Hotel.

But the most striking part of Smith's article comes toward the end when he takes up possible long-term implications of Kennedy's scoop.

The worst carryover, he believes, would be a "stiffening of attitude on the part of the military in being so free-and-easy with the press on confidential material." That the military was ever casual with the press in sensitive areas might well by dismissed out of hand by former correspondents. Smith seems to anticipate such response when he goes on to explain that by "military" he has in mind "military public relations officers during the war" who were "actually working newspapermen-in-uniform" as against "stiff-necked Army officers of the old school" who scorned the press. During the war such newsmen-in-uniform, he continues, "were constantly in the middle as 'devil's advocates' while trying to sell the regular army on a forthright, frank and 'tell 'em everything' status for war correspondents." In other words, there were always two types of PROs: new-school types who liked and helped the press, and old-school types who wished to wholly stifle it.

Certainly it is true that before and after the Reims surrender such leading public-relations officials as General Allen, Colonel Dupuy, Captain Harry Butcher, and Smith himself—a group of four cited in "Surrender Snafu"— argued against the "fantastic embargo of world-shaking news" that Kennedy upset. And in general there was nothing new in viewing PROs as operating in a middle ground between the military and the press. As observed earlier, Barney Oldfield had praised James Quirk for working effectively in just such hazardous territory for a lengthy amount of time. But depicting a significant number of PROs during the war inclined so far toward the interests of the press as to comprise its devil's advocates seems a revision of how correspondents generally lumped together their military managers as public-relations officialdom.

On the other hand, even such a constant critic as A. J. Liebling mildly tipped his cap to some PROs. As mentioned before, in his defense of Kennedy in the *New Yorker* he remarked, "To give Army Public Relations the only credit due it, some of the younger officers in the field were helpful, hard-working, and at times even intelligent." And Edward Kennedy, as also mentioned before, looked with favor on some elements among the PROs. He wrote, "There were many highly capable and conscientious men in this great complement. Most of these, I noted, complained about their frustrations under 'the bureaucracy' almost as much as correspondents did." While working in Italy before France, he also took note of the presence of underground PROs who went out of their way to aid newsmen.

Since Thor Smith's "Surrender Snafu" never saw print in the *Atlantic* or elsewhere, former PROs and correspondents had no chance to weigh in with responses. Had they, it might only have prolonged all the more the debate about Kennedy's deed. Smith leans in that direction when, at the end of his account, he writes, "And so the pro and con camps continue to re-hash the arguments down through the years." He quotes an unnamed editor in Texas who said he would rather be Kennedy than the American president. Yet he gives the last word to Janet Flanner of the *New Yorker*. After receiving a private suggestion by an unnamed figure at the magazine to salute Kennedy by buying him a Parisian meal, she responded—via radio, Smith says—that it was "impossible to fulfill as for one he [Kennedy] disappeared into bars with enquiry would he be court martialed or shot, and second he sold out everybody in Hotel Scribe including mere weekly correspondent like Genet of New Yorker who along with others would not even buy him a flat beer."[5]

Epilogue

A Hotel like Any Other

The Hôtel Scribe's records give March 31, 1947, as the date it was formally returned to transient civilian life. Becoming again a hotel like any other didn't, of course, erase memories of its wartime existence. As noted earlier, when *Bar of Hotel Scribe* was first reproduced in *Life* in 1945, a caption predicted the hotel "would appear in innumerable future war books, plays, movies." On second thought, the caption writer might have cut *innumerable* as journalistic excess. Still, it was a reasonable guess that the Scribe, given the cavalcade of writers who passed through it, would have some form of postwar life in print.

In his 1948 novel *That Winter*, Merle Miller gives the hotel's bar a small but critical role. Three ex-servicemen are living together in New York and trying to adjust to civilian life during the winter following the war's end. The narrator and central figure, Peter, is drinking too much, as is everyone around him, but doing well as a writer on a weekly newsmagazine much like *Time*. During the war, while on military duty in public relations in Paris, he wrote and published a novel yet is unable to get another one underway. His magazine job is part, but only part, of the reason. Though it is an important publication that provides a fine salary and future advancement, he cannot take it seriously as journalism since everything it prints is bent to the ideological positions of its editor and owner.

In his work on the magazine, the fictional Peter is clearly a stand-in for the author. W. A. Swanberg, in his unflattering 1972 biography of Henry

Luce of Time Inc., *Luce and His Empire*, tells of Merle Miller joining *Time* shortly after his war service in Europe as a writer and editor of *Yank* magazine. He found *Time*, Swanberg writes, "slanted, unfair, and dishonest. He was not instructed to write dishonestly but he came to understand osmotically what was expected." Swanberg goes on to quote approvingly Peter's thoughts about the magazine as Miller assigns them to him in the novel: "No one ever ordered anyone to write anything . . . in a certain way, except, possibly, in the heat of an election campaign. But if you were bright—and you didn't remain on the staff long unless you were—you soon understood the rule."[1]

Swanberg offers as further information about Miller that he left *Time* in disgust and thereafter wrote *That Winter*, a novel that sold well. In fact, it sold so well, Swanberg reports, "that Luce, who lacked time to read it, asked Daniel Longwell to appraise it for him." For many years with Time Inc., and one of the founding editors of *Life*, Longwell "marked the pages Luce might be interested in and noted that while *Time* appeared as background, it was not the book's central theme."[2]

In the novel, Peter's work with the unnamed magazine is simply part of his new life in New York. Far more central to the story is the memory he carries with him of the wartime death of a friend he first met in Paris, Gene Wenisloski, a French-speaking private first class from Mississippi with a wife and children and a member of the same public-relations section as Peter. Gene is chubby, gentle, and competent, and despite dissimilar backgrounds—Peter, a technical sergeant, is from Iowa—and ambitions, a close bond forms between the two.

Peter recalls evenings in the Scribe bar drinking with correspondents, "some of whom were remarkably successful in being able to overlook the fact that I was an enlisted man in the U.S. Army." After several glasses of cognac or champagne, he joins freely in talk with the newsmen. One of them, a broadcaster, tells of trying to get closer to the war, but his network insists on keeping someone based at SHAEF headquarters. Peter notes that many soldiers were like correspondents in wanting to be up front with the action, which causes him to tell of a parachute operation across the Rhine that he nearly joined:

> A few drinks at the Scribe and inevitably someone who had been told in the strictest confidence told a friend in the strictest confidence, and within forty-eight hours all the correspondents as well as all of us who were concerned with Public Relations (always an upper case "P" and "R") also knew. I don't recall when I first mentioned the matter. . . . If only, I said, I could make the landing. But, of course, I couldn't.

One night, sitting next to a colonel he doesn't know, Peter says the same thing after several drinks. "I think I can fix it up for you if your CO will agree," the colonel surprisingly replies. And he does. After the commanding officer also agrees, Peter—now cold sober—regrets what he asked for. Only at the last moment before he leaves for the operation's staging area, his CO picks another man, who as it happens is killed on the mission.[3]

Peter's escape from combat prepares the reader for another mistaken war venture that does take place. Just before Christmas 1944, Peter and Gene Wenisloski read in *Stars and Stripes* about the Germans breaking through American lines in Belgium and decide to go to Liege to see for themselves what is happening. After they improbably convince another colonel, Gene doing all the talking, to provide a jeep, they reach Liege and then plunge on to Spa, the road traffic going mostly in the opposite direction. They never ask for information, let alone advice.

When they get near Spa, Gene wants to turn back to Liege, but Peter—determined now to demonstrate his courage—chooses to keep going. In Spa they learn from a Belgian woman that the US First Army retreated in the direction of Liege. A frightened Gene tells Peter that, as a sergeant, he is their commander and should find them a billet.

But every place they see is deserted until, in a bar in Spa, they come across a drunken and armed American soldier. When he gets back in his jeep, they follow him but become lost and finally decide to return to Spa. They think they are just outside the town when their jeep seems to run out of gas. Peter gets out to check the fuel level when firing starts. He hits the ground and screams at Gene to do the same. After the firing ends, Peter discovers that Gene, shot in the head, is dead. Peter gets the body to a hospital in Liege and, after fainting himself, spends four days in a ward. He never learns whether an American or German bullet hit Gene. "Not that it mattered," he admits. "I was responsible for his death."

Back in Paris, Peter begins a correspondence with Gene's widow, acknowledging his role in her loss and promising to visit Mississippi after his army discharge. *That Winter* gets a happy ending when Peter, free of his magazine job, acts on the promise together with an invitation from the widow to use a beach house in Mississippi to, for as long as it takes, write another novel.

⌣

Ned Calmer's 1950 novel *The Strange Land*—the name, the book's epigraph reveals, is a term of war—gives more attention to the Scribe than Miller's story. It opens during a briefing session in the information room. The time is a Thursday in November 1944, and the scene's narrator, John C.

Wexel, is a well-known American columnist who has just flown to Paris to add war correspondent to his résumé. At present, though, he feels as distant from the war as he did in Chicago. He tells himself, "Here in this gilt salon in the Hotel Scribe, watching people coming in for the regular briefing at SHAEF Public Relations, sitting in this ballroom chair under the swinging chandelier, you certainly would not guess there's a war on, in France or anywhere else."[4]

A newsman Wexel knows, Bates, takes a seat beside him, and this allows Calmer to contrast the two through Wexel's thoughts. Bates makes the journalistic mistake of painting war as unglamorous. Wexel knows better. "People like it the other way. People like it make-believe. And that's the kind of stuff they're going to get from me." Wexel, as the novel's readers immediately surmise, will be treated with unleavened irony. When he finally encounters it, war will have no glamour, yet make-believe will still characterize his writing manner.

The briefing session is a special occasion. Lineups of young WAC stenographers are present. So are three generals. The briefing officer is British and has a suitable Oxford accent. He first announces that there will be no note taking and everything said is off the record. Then he proceeds to outline on maps Operation Uppercut, an Allied offensive into German territory that will get underway at once.

The Strange Land treats six days from the Paris launch of Uppercut to its unsettled conclusion in Germany. Calmer brings into the story soldiers and officers who carry out the mission and tell its grim story in their own voices. There is a WAC lieutenant stationed at the Scribe, Clare Drake, who becomes a tragic figure when a young officer she is in love with is lost in the fighting. An army major, Lowell Harrod, is a voice of sanity and conscience in a story otherwise largely about military shortcomings. From the opening scene onward, Wexel stands out as a one-dimensional portrait of the war correspondent as egotist—or as Harrod simply thinks on first meeting him, "a selfish little man."

Due to an insecure major general who thinks the correspondent's dispatches will make him look good, Wexel gets to the front of the front line during the operation. Before the actual fighting begins, he impatiently ponders what he will write about it: "I haven't got my over-all slant yet, though. First some action dispatches to show I'm still a reporter with the best of them. Then a series of columns I can do at leisure. Probably hitting army waste, inefficiency, sluggishness. . . . The important thing is to be able to say I've been here. In the thick of an offensive in the Siegfried Line. If the offensive ever gets started."[5]

As the reader suspects, the action will turn out far more harrowing than Wexel bargains for. During a confused night he becomes lost and flees blindly from battle through heavily mined territory. When in daylight he comes to his senses in muddy undergrowth, he recalls that he had gone to pieces, had been crazy with fear. "What kind of hellish dream is this whole thing?" he wonders. "What kind of a nightmare have I been living since I left the States? It seems like years have passed."

But nightmare feelings soon give way to the need to create a story to project to others. "Yes, I'll try to make it sound as if I just got lost in the dark. No sense in admitting I was a coward and ran. . . . Why, in due time I might even manage to make this all look like a heroic episode. *Yes, that's it. The angle.* Something about creeping right into the German lines at night to see for myself what the situation was during a dangerous battle."[6] Wexel realizes Major Harrod knows the truth about his flight but believes he is too dignified to challenge his story. As for censorship in Paris, he believes he can get around that by keeping locations vague.

Calmer ends his novel where it began, with a briefing in the information room, though now experienced by Harrod. He finds the room and the Scribe itself unreal since he is just back from the war zone. "Nobody's tired," he muses about the present. "Nobody's anxious. Living is a game of work and play." Seated in a front row of the room are the clean-shaven censorship officers. These are the men, he continues, "who finally transmit the filtered version [of dispatches] to the competitive editors back home who know the public want optimism and take their own part in the process of watering down the truth."[7] During the briefing there are testy exchanges between officers in charge and correspondents, but the situation remains that the Uppercut offensive is stalled for the time being and only slender hope is held out that isolated forward units of troops can be reached in time to save them.

That Winter and *The Strange Land* are novels by writers who were correspondents during the war. *The Race for Paris,* a 2015 novel by Meg Waite Clayton, is a historical novel, and as such it acknowledges a research effort that mentions many of the same sources as my account. Clayton's sources also become figures in her story, typically just as names mentioned—Don Whitehead, Andy Rooney, John MacVane, Lee Miller, Martha Gellhorn—but with Ernie Pyle, for example, they interact with fictional characters. Overall, the story is drawn, as Clayton announces in an opening author's note, from the real-life experience of "women who defied military regulations and gender barriers to cover World War II and the 'race for Paris,' vying to be among the first to report from the liberated city in the summer of 1944."[8]

Two invented characters, Jane Tyler, a newspaper reporter with a Nashville publication, and Olivia "Liv" Harper, an Associated Press photographer, represent the actual women correspondents. The wartime experience of Jane and Liv is framed by a reception in 1994 in the Hôtel de Ville in Paris for the posthumous publication of a book of Liv's war photos and an exhibition of her work. From this opening chapter the novel shifts to the women first meeting while reporting on a field hospital in Normandy in June 1944.

A subsequent chapter introduces Fletcher Roebuck, a well-born British military photographer working with the UK's intelligence service. When first glimpsed in the story, he has come to a US First Army press camp in Normandy where such correspondents as A. J. Liebling and Matthew Halton are present. During a SHAEF-unauthorized jaunt to bomb-leveled Saint-Lô, Liv and Jane connect with Fletcher, who happens to be an old friend of Liv's husband, Charles Harper, the editor of a New York newspaper.

Against his better judgment, Fletcher agrees to help the two AWOL women reach Paris in his jeep and also get their dispatches and photos through censorship and transmission under his name. The novel is two hundred pages along when, on liberation day, Liv calls out from the jeep, "Boulevard des Capucines. And there's Scribe." Greeting the women at the hotel's door is Louis Régamey, the agent for Canadian National Railway, and the hotel's manager. A porter even offers to bring their bags from the jeep to the hotel. "Our Allied uniforms served as the once-required jacket and tie," Jane believes, "although just hours earlier only a German uniform would have sufficed."

Despite their Allied uniforms, Jane and Liv have reason to fret about what awaits them from PROs inside the hotel. They enter with Fletcher into a scene of correspondents tapping away at typewriters and the sound of popping champagne corks. Eventually the women and Fletcher are confronted by a Major Adam Jones, who says he has orders to apprehend Olivia Harper and return her to London—a scene drawn from the actual meeting in the hotel of Lee Carson and Major Frank Mayborn. Major Jones clearly knows who Liv is yet says to her, "I was thinking, ma'am, that you might want to get out of here before I mistake you for Mrs. Harper."

Liv holds her ground. She links her arm with Jane's and tells the major that they both need to get their reporting transmitted. Fletcher, though, intervenes by telling her that nothing can be sent uncensored and censors haven't yet appeared at the Scribe. Outside the hotel he informs the women that there is a wireless facility in Cherbourg and they could transmit to the

United States from there. So they jeep to Orly airfield and find a Piper Cub just ready to leave for the French city. The pilot is instructed to deliver Jane's typescript and Liv's bag of film to the Cherbourg destination.

Back at the Scribe, the two women kiss other correspondents in the Scribe's basement bar as well as strangers in the street. The bar is fleetingly mentioned again in the novel, as is Floyd Davis's cartoon depiction of the room, but no fictional scenes take place therein. On August 27, Paris itself is set aside. Fletcher wants to stay in the Scribe at least another night to sleep in a decent bed, but Jane and Liv are eager to leave. "Stay here with Hemingway if you want, Fletcher," Liv says to him. "Jane and I are going to cover the war."[9]

The two women and Fletcher get as far into the war as Valkenburg in the Netherlands. Along the way romance develops between Liv and Fletcher, Fletcher performs high-risk intelligence gathering in German territory, and Liv and Jane take part in up-front military patrols. Finally, Liv is killed on a patrol while rising from cover to shoot a photo.

The final chapter returns to Paris in 1994 and the issuing of the book called *Against the Fog: The Photographs of Olivia James Harper*. Here various loose ends of the story are tied up. Among them, the reader learns that Jane Tyler married Fletcher Roebuck, lived contentedly in his English manor, and bore children. And there is satisfaction in knowing that while Liv is gone her pictures will endure.

A more common way of recalling the wartime Scribe was in magazine articles and book memoirs. Among these, one of the most evocative of that time and place came from a correspondent who was present from the liberation of Paris through to the surrender in Reims.

In 1984, Gerald Clark, formerly of the *Montreal Standard*, returned to Paris to write a magazine article for the *Canadian Reader's Digest* about the fortieth anniversary of the end of the German occupation. Later he incorporated the article into a memoir. While in Paris, Clark naturally gravitated to the Scribe and its bar, which in turn led him to recount in his article an incident he had witnessed there during what he called the "wonderful fever of liberation" in August of 1944.

His colleague in Montreal journalism, Sholto Watt of the *Star*, was seated at the end of the bar with a snifter of brandy in one hand and a telephone within reach. Characterized by Clark as "an eccentric and a linguist," Watt abruptly picked up the phone with his free hand and, in French, told the switchboard operator that he wanted to place a call to Brussels. The request raised eyebrows among the bar's other drinkers. Didn't Watt know that German forces occupied territory between Paris and Brussels? Did he believe phone lines between the two capitals were still connected?

When a French voice soon answered, "This is Brussels," Watt took a sip of brandy and asked to speak with the German field commander. When a German voice came on the phone, he repeated his request in German. At last, with the German commander himself on the line—and now amid breath-held silence at the bar—Watt drank deeply and said, "This is Sholto Watt of *The Montreal Star*. The jig is up. You might as well quit." He then put down the phone and concentrated on his drink.[10]

Gerald Clark noted in his article that the Scribe's lounge bar had changed since the time of Watt's remarkable phone call. Now named Le Saint-Laurent, in keeping with the hotel's association with the Canadian National Railway, it had on the walls lithographs of old Quebec City and the St. Lawrence River. And now the room's occupants were well-attired men and women having cocktails. The bar itself, despite the alterations, still had its original paneled wood.

From his position there, Clark said he tried to visualize the ring left on the bar's surface by Watt's brandy glass. "But," he concluded, "too many coats of varnish had covered the years since 1944."

Acknowledgments

My thanks to these libraries and archival centers: Hesburgh Library, University of Notre Dame; Christopher Library, Valparaiso University; National Archives of the United States; Library of Congress; Harry S. Truman Presidential Library; Dwight D. Eisenhower Presidential Library; John F. Kennedy Presidential Library; Wisconsin Historical Society Library and Archives; National Portrait Gallery of the Smithsonian Institution; and US Army Heritage and Education Center.

My thanks as well to these individuals who responded generously to my inquiries: Laura F. Manaker, Erin Beasley, Polly Loxton, Julie Daumy, Axel Krause, Jim Armistead, and Lori Wheeler.

An essay drawn from this book appeared in 2016 in *Now & Then Reader*, a digital publication of nonfiction writing.

~

Notes

Prologue

1. John Groth, *Studio: Europe* (New York, 1945), 89.

2. Antony Beevor and Artemis Cooper, *Paris after the Liberation, 1944–1949*, rev. ed. (New York, 2004), 73.

3. Robert Capa, *Slightly Out of Focus* (New York, 1947), 189. For the book's reliability as memoir, see Alex Kershaw, *Blood and Champagne: The Life and Times of Robert Capa* (New York, 2004), 90–91.

4. Quoted in Harry C. Butcher, *My Three Years with Eisenhower: The Personal Diary of Captain Harry C. Butcher, USNR, Naval Aide to General Eisenhower, 1942–1945* (New York, 1946), 744–46.

5. Forrest C. Pogue, *United States Army in World War II: The European Theater of Operations, The Supreme Command* (Washington, DC, 1996), 522. This study and its appendix A, "SHAEF and the Press, June 1944–May 1945," provide basic information about the Scribe as a press camp.

6. A. J. Liebling, *World War II Writings* (New York, 2008), 522.

7. Capa, *Slightly Out of Focus*, 170.

8. Butcher, *My Three Years with Eisenhower*, 671.

9. For example, see Matthew Sweet, *The West End Front: The Wartime Secrets of London's Grand Hotels* (London, 2011), and Amanda Vaill, *Hotel Florida: Truth, Love, and Death in the Spanish Civil War* (New York, 2014).

10. Julia Kennedy Cochran, ed., *Ed Kennedy's War: V-E Day, Censorship, and the Associated Press* (Baton Rouge, LA, 2012), 153.

11. Phillip Knightley, *The First Casualty: From the Crimea to Vietnam; The War Correspondent as Hero, Propagandist, and Myth Maker* (New York, 1975), 330.

12. See Timothy M. Gay, *Assignment to Hell: The War against Germany with Correspondents Walter Cronkite, Andy Rooney, A. J. Liebling, Homer Bigart, and Hal Boyle* (New York, 2012), and Steven Casey, *The War Beat, Europe: The American Media at War against Nazi Germany* (New York, 2017).

13. Knightley, *The First Casualty*, 323.

Chapter One

1. Quoted in Harry C. Butcher, *My Three Years with Eisenhower: The Personal Diary of Captain Harry C. Butcher, NSNR, Naval Aide to General Eisenhower, 1942–1945* (New York, 1946), 745.

2. Lewis Lochner, "Germans Marched into a Dead Paris," *Life*, July 8, 1940, 22ff. The news story is recast in Lochner's book *What about Germany?* (New York, 1942), 134–35.

3. Shirer's experience in France is drawn from Ronald Weber, *News of Paris: American Journalists in the City of Light between the Wars* (Chicago, 2006), 284–86.

4. Canadian ownership of the Scribe is noted in Timothy Balzar, *The Information Front: The Canadian Army and News Management during the Second World War* (Vancouver, BC, 2011), 65.

5. The Scribe's history is drawn from Pierre-André Hélène, *A Legend in the Heart of Paris*, an illustrated 115-page booklet in French and English produced by the Hôtel Scribe.

6. Ronald C. Rosbottom, *When Paris Went Dark: The City of Light under German Occupation, 1940–1944* (New York, 2014), 108–9.

7. Richard S. Malone, *A World in Flames, 1944–1945: A Portrait of War, Part Two* (Toronto, 1984), 67–81. In an earlier book, *Missing from the Record* (Toronto, 1946), Malone essentially tells the same story of the taking of the Scribe. Malone's account in *A World in Flames* is briefly summarized in Balzar, *The Information Front*. Pierre-André Hélène's *A Legend in the Heart of Paris* also states that "Canadians were the very people who, when France was liberated, moved into the hotel first."

8. Quoted in David Halton, *Dispatches from the Front: Matthew Halton, Canada's Voice at War* (New York, 2014), 224. A sound recording of Matthew Halton's broadcast is available in the CBC's Digital Archives under the heading "Second World War."

9. Gerald Clark, *No Mud on the Back Seat: Memoirs of a Reporter* (Montreal, 1995), 78.

10. Maurice Desjardins, "French People Are Overjoyed by Liberation," Canadian Press service, August 30, 1944.

11. Malone, *A World in Flames*, 70. In his memoir noted above, Gerald Clark doesn't directly corroborate Malone's time of arrival at the Scribe but does write that "American and British press groups had learned of the Canadian windfall, and the Scribe became the official billet for all allied reporters." *No Mud on the Back Seat*, 79.

12. Malone, A World in Flames, 99.

13. Malone, A World in Flames, 70.

14. Malone, A World in Flames, 75–76.

15. The figure and Régamey's investment in the Suez Canal was reported by Ralph Allen, "Nazi's Never Knew It, But Paid Canada Rent," *Toronto Globe and Mail*, August 26, 1944.

16. Tilar J. Mazzeo, *The Hotel on Place Vendôme: Life, Death, and Betrayal at the Hôtel Ritz in Paris* (New York, 2015), 18.

17. Filippo Occhino, Kim Oosterlinck, and Eugene N. White, "How Much Can a Victor Force the Vanquished to Pay? France under the Nazi Boot," *Journal of Economic History* 68, no. 1 (2008): 1–45.

Chapter Two

1. John Groth, *Studio: Europe* (New York, 1945), 114.

2. Robert Capa, *Slightly Out of Focus* (New York, 1947), 178.

3. Jeremy A. Crang, "General De Gaulle under Sniper Fire in Notre Dame Cathedral, 26 August 1944: Robert Reid's BBC Commentary," *Historical Journal of Film, Radio and Television* 27, no. 3 (2007): 398.

4. Barney Oldfield, *Never a Shot in Anger* (Santa Barbara, CA, 1989), 107.

5. Groth, *Studio: Europe*, 110.

6. Capa, *Slightly Out of Focus*, 178.

7. Antony Beevor and Artemis Cooper, *Paris after the Liberation, 1944–49* (New York, 2004), n 44.

8. Max Hastings, *Inferno: The World at War, 1939–1945* (New York, 2011), 539.

9. Antony Beevor, *The Second World War* (New York, 2012), 615. For more detail about fighting within Paris, see David Drake, *Paris at War: 1939–1944* (Cambridge, MA, 2016), and Matthew Cobb, *Eleven Days in August: The Liberation of Paris in 1944* (London, 2013).

10. Groth, *Studio: Europe*, 115–27.

11. Oldfield, *Never a Shot in Anger*, 109.

12. Groth, *Studio: Europe*, 131–34.

13. John B. Romeiser, ed., *"Beachhead Don": Reporting the War from the European Theater, 1942–1945* (New York, 2004), 208–9.

14. Romeiser, *"Beachhead Don,"* xxi.

15. Quoted in Joseph R. L. Sterne, *Combat Correspondents: The Baltimore Sun in World War II* (Baltimore, 2009), 112.

16. Don Whitehead, "Embassy in Paris Gets a Phone Call," *New York Times*, August 26, 1944, 5.

17. Crang, "General De Gaulle under Sniper Fire," 399.

18. Crang, "General De Gaulle under Sniper Fire," 399–400.

19. Cobb, *Eleven Days in August*, 29–30.

20. Richard Whelan, *Robert Capa: A Biography* (New York, 1985), 222–23.

21. Charles Wertenbaker, "Paris Is Free!," *Time*, September 4, 1944, 34–36. The report appears as a postscript in Wertenbaker's 1944 book *Invasion!*

22. Quoted in Oldfield, *Never a Shot in Anger*, 111–12.

23. Andy Rooney, *My War* (New York, 2000), 211.

24. A. M. Sperber, *Murrow: His Life and Times* (New York, 1986), 177.

25. This and subsequent biographical information about Kirkpatrick is drawn from Anne S. Kasper, Washington Press Club Foundation interview with Helen Kirkpatrick Milbank, April 1990, 73–75. Hereafter cited as Kasper interview with Kirkpatrick.

26. Kasper interview with Kirkpatrick, 75.

27. Irwin Shaw, "Morts pour la Patrie," *New Yorker*, August 25, 1945, 44.

28. Irwin Shaw and Ronald Searle, *Paris! Paris!* (New York, 1977), 50.

29. Stevens's wartime film work is drawn from Marilyn Ann Moss, *Giant George Stevens: A Life on Film* (Madison, WI, 2004), 101ff.

30. John Leggett, *A Daring Young Man: A Biography of William Saroyan* (New York, 2002), 189.

31. Quoted in Michael Shnayerson, *Irwin Shaw: A Biography* (New York, 1989), 143.

32. Charles Collingwood, "French Armored Division Sent Into Paris by Bradley," *New York Times*, August 23, 1944, 1.

33. Stanley Cloud and Lynne Olson, *The Murrow Boys: Pioneers on the Front Lines of Broadcast Journalism* (New York, 1996), 215.

34. "Press 'Frees' Paris, Scores Two-Day 'Beat,'" *Editor & Publisher*, September 2, 1944, 7ff. See also Cloud and Olson, *The Murrow Boys*, 214–16.

35. William Walton, "Life Correspondents See the New Paris," *Life*, September 11, 1944, 38.

36. Cloud and Olson, *The Murrow Boys*, 218–19.

37. Alan Moorehead, *Eclipse* (New York, 1945), 159–60.

38. Moorehead, *Eclipse*, 163–64.

Chapter Three

1. Quoted in Peter Longerich, *Goebbels: A Biography*, trans. Alan Bance and others (New York, 2015), 453.

2. Hemingway to Mary Welsh, September 11, 1944, in Carlos Baker, ed., *Ernest Hemingway, Selected Letters, 1917–1961* (New York, 1981), 567–68.

3. Michael Reynolds, *Hemingway: The Final Years* (New York, 1999), 102. For whether Hemingway killed any Germans, see William E. Coté, "Correspondent or Warrior? Hemingway's Murky World War II 'Combat' Experience," *Hemingway Review* 22, no. 1 (2002): 88–104.

4. Richard Whelan, *Robert Capa: A Biography* (New York, 1985), 219–20.

5. Hemingway to Mary Welsh, August 1 and 6, 1944, *Selected Letters*, 560, 563.

6. A. J. Liebling, *World War II Writings* (New York, 2008), 931.

7. Quoted in Jeffrey Meyers, *Hemingway: A Biography* (New York, 1985), 403.

8. Hemingway to Mary Welsh, August 27, 1944, *Selected Letters*, 564.

9. Message reproduced in Frederick S. Voss, *Reporting the War: The Journalistic Coverage of World War II* (Washington, DC, 1994), 189.

10. Barney Oldfield, *Never a Shot in Anger* (Santa Barbara, CA, 1989), 109.

11. Hemingway to Mary Welsh, August 27, 1944, *Selected Letters*, 564.

12. Quoted in Nelson Douglas Lankford, ed., *OSS against the Reich: The World War II Diaries of Colonel David K. E. Bruce* (Kent, OH, 1991), 160–61.

13. Quoted in Reynolds, *Hemingway*, 107.

14. Lankford, *OSS against the Reich*, 168.

15. Quoted in Reynolds, *Hemingway*, 107.

16. Andy Rooney, *My War* (New York, 2000), 200.

17. Robert Fuller, "Hemingway at Rambouillet," *Hemingway Review* 33, no. 2 (2014): 69.

18. William White, ed., *By-Line: Ernest Hemingway* (New York, 1967), 383. "How We Came to Paris" is reprinted in *Reporting World War II, Part Two: American Journalism, 1944–1946*, ed. Samuel Hynes (New York, 1995), 242–50.

19. Quoted in Lankford, *OSS against the Reich*, 174.

20. Hemingway to Mary Welsh, August 27, 1944, *Selected Letters*, 564.

21. S. L. A. Marshall, "How Papa Liberated Paris," *American Heritage* 13, no. 3 (1962). All references here are to the chapter in the memoir, S. L. A. Marshall, *Bringing Up the Rear* (San Rafael, CA, 1979), 95–118. For another version of the liberation of the Ritz, in which British troops enter the hotel before Bruce, Hemingway, or Marshall, see Tilar J. Mazzeo, *The Hotel on Place Vendôme* (New York, 2014), 140–43.

22. Marshall, *Bringing Up the Rear*, 113.

23. Marshall, *Bringing Up the Rear*, 114.

24. Marshall, *Bringing Up the Rear*, 117.

25. Marshall, *Bringing Up the Rear*, 117–18.

26. Quoted in Baker, *Ernest Hemingway*, n 639.

Chapter Four

1. "PRO's Trained to Aid Writers on Invasion," *Editor & Publisher*, June 17, 1944, 18.

2. Barney Oldfield, *Never a Shot in Anger* (Santa Barbara, CA, 1989), 34.

3. Biographical information about Quirk is drawn from the James T. Quirk papers at the Harry S. Truman Presidential Library, Independence, Missouri. Quirk's wartime letters to Elizabeth Quirk are located in Box 1: World War II, 1942–1946. Hereafter cited as Quirk papers. Many of the letters were published in Rory Quirk,

War and Peace: The Memoirs of an American Family (Novato, CA, 1999). Subsequent references to the Quirk papers are to letters at the Truman Library.

4. Oldfield, *Never a Shot in Anger*, 209.

5. Quirk papers. All quotations below, pages 42 to 47, come from the Quirk papers.

6. Biographical information about Smith is drawn from the Thor M. Smith papers at the Dwight D. Eisenhower Presidential Library, Abilene, Kansas. Smith's wartime letters to his wife, Mary B. Smith, are located in Series II, World War II, 1942–1945. Hereafter cited as Smith papers.

7. Smith papers. All quotations below, pages 47 to 49, come from the Smith papers.

Chapter Five

1. John B. Romeiser, ed., *"Beachhead Don": Reporting the War from the European Theater, 1942–1945* (New York, 2004), 216–17.

2. Edward W. Beattie, "Paris Opens Arms to Allied Troops," *New York Times*, August 27, 1944, 18.

3. Boyd DeWolf Lewis, *Not Always a Spectator: A Newsman's Story* (Vienna, VA, 1981), 176–77.

4. Ralph Allen, "City Wild with Joy Ignores Bullets' Whine," *Toronto Globe and Mail*, August 26, 1944.

5. Andy Rooney, *My War* (New York, 2000), 204.

6. Rooney, *My War*, 229.

7. Forrest C. Pogue, *United States Army in World War II: The European Theater of Operations, the Supreme Command* (Washington, DC, 1996), 242.

8. Matthew Cobb, *Eleven Days in August: The Liberation of Paris in 1944* (London, 2013), 319.

9. Antony Beevor and Artemis Cooper, *Paris after the Liberation, 1944–49* (New York, 2004), 53–57.

10. Helen Kirkpatrick, "Daily News Writer Sees Man Slain at Her Side in Hail of Lead," *Chicago Daily News*, August 26, 1944.

11. Nelson Douglas Lankford, ed., *OSS against the Reich: The World War II Diaries of Colonel David K. E. Bruce* (Kent, OH, 1991), 177.

12. Quirk papers.

13. Cobb, *Eleven Days in August*, 337.

14. Quoted in David Nichols, *Ernie's War: The Best of Ernie Pyle's World War II Dispatches* (New York, 1986), 354.

15. A. J. Liebling, *World War II Writings* (New York, 2008), 753.

16. Rooney, *My War*, 185.

17. Quoted in Nichols, *Ernie's War*, 351–54.

18. Walter Cronkite, *A Reporter's Life* (New York, 1996), 106.

19. Quoted in Rooney, *My War*, 215.

20. Walter Cronkite IV and Maurice Isserman, *Cronkite's War: His World War II Letters Home* (Washington, DC, 2013), 219.

21. Cronkite and Isserman, *Cronkite's War*, 229.

22. Cronkite, *A Reporter's Life*, 106.

23. John Groth, *Studio: Europe* (New York, 1945), 133, 135.

24. Sketch reproduced in Groth, *Studio: Europe*, 162.

25. Quoted in Iris Carpenter, *No Woman's World* (Boston, 1946), 112.

26. Carpenter, *No Woman's World*, 115–17.

27. Carpenter, *No Woman's World*, 124–25.

28. Irwin Shaw and Ronald Searle, *Paris! Paris!* (New York, 1977), 50.

29. Groth, *Studio: Europe*, 88.

30. Quoted in Lee G. Miller, *The Story of Ernie Pyle* (New York, 1950), 362.

31. Liebling, *World War II Writings*, 987–92.

32. Liebling, *World War II Writings*, 988.

33. Quoted in Carpenter, *No Woman's World*, 109.

34. Gerald Clark, *No Mud on the Back Seat: Memoirs of a Reporter* (Montreal, 1995), 101–2.

35. Quoted in Raymond A. Sokolov, *Wayward Reporter: The Life of A. J. Liebling* (New York, 1980), 174.

36. Liebling, *World War II Writings*, 541.

37. Quoted in Carpenter, *No Woman's World*, 110–11.

Chapter Six

1. Hemingway to Mary Welsh, August 27, 1944, Carlos Baker, ed., *Ernest Hemingway, Selected Letters, 1917–1961* (New York, 1981), 564.

2. Quoted in Carlos Baker, *Ernest Hemingway: A Life Story* (New York, 1969), 417.

3. Biographical information about Welsh comes primarily from her autobiography, Mary Welsh Hemingway, *How It Was* (New York, 1976).

4. Mary Hemingway, *How It Was*, 109.

5. Mary Hemingway, *How It Was*, 109.

6. Mary Hemingway, *How It Was*, 109.

7. Michael Reynolds, *Hemingway: The Final Years* (New York, 1999), 93.

8. Mary Hemingway, *How It Was*, 95–96.

9. Hemingway to Mary Welsh, August 27, 1944, *Selected Letters*, 565. According to Welsh, the letter was actually written on August 26. See Mary Hemingway, *How It Was*, 113.

10. Noel Monks, *Eyewitness* (London, 1956), 226–27.

11. Monks, *Eyewitness*, 234.

12. Monks, *Eyewitness*, 232.

13. Mary Hemingway, *How It Was*, 145.

14. Mary Hemingway, *How It Was*, 126.

15. Quoted in Mary Hemingway, *How It Was*, 117.

16. Biographical information about Martha Gellhorn comes primarily from Caroline Moorehead, *Gellhorn: A Twentieth-Century Life* (New York, 2003).

17. Martha Gellhorn, *The Face of War* (New York, 1956), 96.

18. Harold Acton, *Memoirs of an Aesthete, 1939–1969* (New York, 1971), 151.

19. Richard Whelan, *Robert Capa: A Biography* (New York, 1985), 229. The story is also told in Alex Kershaw, *Blood and Champagne: The Life and Times of Robert Capa* (New York, 2004), 148–49.

20. Reynolds, *Hemingway*, 120.

21. Martha Gellhorn, "The Wounds of Paris," *Collier's*, November 4, 1944, 72–74.

22. Barney Oldfield, *Never a Shot in Anger* (Santa Barbara, CA), 189.

23. Hemingway to Mary Welsh, September 8, 1944, *Selected Letters*, 566.

24. Reynolds, *Hemingway*, 115–16. For more about the hearing, see Robert Fuller, "Hemingway at Rambouillet," *Hemingway Review* 33, no. 2 (2014): 68ff.

25. Reynolds, *Hemingway*, 122.

26. Hemingway to Henry La Cossitt, November 16, 1944, *Selected Letters*, 575.

27. Mary Hemingway, *How It Was*, 140.

28. Mary Hemingway, *How It Was*, 136–39.

29. Mary Hemingway, *How It Was*, 144.

30. Baker, *Ernest Hemingway*, 439.

31. Quoted in Baker, *Ernest Hemingway*, 441.

32. Mary Hemingway, *How It Was*, 142.

33. Mary Welsh, "GI Crime in France," *Life*, March 12, 1945, 17–18.

Chapter Seven

1. Leon Edel, *The Visitable Past: A Wartime Memoir* (Honolulu, 2001), 81.

2. Edel, *The Visitable Past*, 45.

3. Edel, *The Visitable Past*, 78–79.

4. John Pudney, "A Paris Diary," *New Statesman and Nation*, September 23, 1944, 197.

5. Edel, *The Visitable Past*, 218.

6. Edel, *The Visitable Past*, 241–42.

7. Edel, *The Visitable Past*, 160.

8. Forrest C. Pogue, *Pogue's War: Diaries of a WW II Combat Historian* (Lexington, KY, 2001), 201.

9. Malcolm Muggeridge, *Chronicles of Wasted Time: Chronicle 2* (New York, 1982), 214.

10. Michael Moynihan, *War Correspondent* (London, 1994), 77–78.

11. Moynihan, *War Correspondent*, 98.

12. Moynihan, *War Correspondent*, 99.

13. Moynihan, *War Correspondent*, 100.

14. Moynihan, *War Correspondent*, 134–36.

15. Quirk papers.

16. Cpl. John Preston, "Paris—After Liberation," *Yank*, September 24, 1944, 11.

17. Harry C. Butcher, *My Three Years with Eisenhower: The Personal Diary of Captain Harry C. Butcher, NSNR, Naval Aide to General Eisenhower, 1942–1945* (New York, 1946), 676.

18. Smith papers.

19. Smith papers.

20. "New Paris Curbs Face Allied Press," *New York Times*, September 3, 1944, 3.

21. Smith papers.

22. Kasper interview with Kirkpatrick, 75–76.

23. Barney Oldfield, *Never a Shot in Anger* (Santa Barbara, CA, 1989), 115.

24. Harold Denny, "The Times Reopens Its Paris Bureau," *New York Times*, August 29, 1944, 4.

25. Julia Kennedy Cochran, ed., *Ed Kennedy's War: V-E Day, Censorship, and the Associated Press* (Baton Rouge, LA, 2012), 141.

26. Raymond A. Sokolov, *Wayward Pressman: The Life of A. J. Liebling* (New York, 1980), 172–73. The found money is not mentioned in Robert T. Elson's three-volume history of Time Inc.

27. Charles L. Robertson, *The International Herald Tribune: The First Hundred Years* (New York, 1987), 228.

28. Eric Hawkins with Robert N. Sturdevant, *Hawkins of the Paris Herald* (New York, 1963), 257.

29. Hawkins, *Hawkins of the Paris Herald*, 257.

30. Kasper interview with Kirkpatrick, 82.

31. Hawkins, *Hawkins of the Paris Herald*, 255–56.

Chapter Eight

1. Harry C. Butcher, *My Three Years with Eisenhower: The Personal Diary of Captain Harry C. Butcher, NSNR, Naval Aide to General Eisenhower, 1942–1945* (New York, 1946), 708.

2. Tilar J. Mazzeo, *The Hotel on Place Vendôme: Life, Death, and Betrayal at the Hôtel Ritz in Paris* (New York, 2015), 99. See also, Alex Kershaw, *Avenue of Spies* (New York, 2015), 143.

3. Walter Cronkite, *A Reporter's Life* (New York, 1996), 100.

4. Andy Rooney, *My War* (New York, 2000), 184.

5. A. J. Liebling, "The A.P. Surrenders," in *Reporting World War II, Part Two: American Journalism, 1944–1946*, ed. Samuel Hynes (New York, 1995), 737–38.

6. Butcher, *My Three Years with Eisenhower*, 651.

7. R. Ernest Dupuy papers, 1943–1945, Wisconsin Historical Society Archives, Madison, Wisconsin. The papers include letters to his wife, journals, official papers,

and the typescript of an unpublished book titled *Behind the Elephants: SHAEF Public Relations from the Pentagon to Berlin*. Hereafter cited as Dupuy papers.

8. Stanley Cloud and Lynne Olsen, *The Murrow Boys: Pioneers on the Front Lines of Broadcast Journalism* (New York, 1996), 217.

9. John MacVane, *On the Air in World War II* (New York, 1979), 294–95.

10. "Suspended 30 Days in Paris Radio Breach," *New York Times*, September 17, 1944, 16.

11. Collie Small, "How to Put Salt on a German General's Tail," *Saturday Evening Post*, November 11, 1944, 22ff.

12. Small, "How to Put Salt on a German General's Tail," 22ff.

13. Small, "How to Put Salt on a German General's Tail," 22ff.

14. Dupuy papers.

15. "We Took 20,000 Germans," *Life*, October 2, 1944, 17ff.

16. Harold Acton, *Memoirs of an Aesthete, 1939–1969* (New York, 1971), 151.

17. Dupuy papers.

18. Quoted in Dupuy papers.

19. Dupuy papers.

20. Barney Oldfield, *Never a Shot in Anger* (Santa Barbara, CA, 1989), 139.

21. Butcher, *My Three Years with Eisenhower*, 688.

22. Dupuy papers.

23. "Honk's Cleanup," *Time*, November 6, 1944, 61.

24. Oldfield, *Never a Shot in Anger*, 139.

25. Henry Miller, *Tropic of Cancer* (New York, 1961), 48. See also, Clyde H. Farnsworth, "11 Rue Scribe Remains a Familiar U.S. Address," *New York Times*, August 9, 1970, 16.

26. Dupuy papers.

27. Butcher, *My Three Years with Eisenhower*, 715.

28. Oldfield, *Never a Shot in Anger*, 139.

29. Oldfield, *Never a Shot in Anger*, 139.

30. Julia Kennedy Cochran, ed., *Ed Kennedy's War: V-E Day, Censorship, and the Associated Press* (Baton Rouge, LA, 2012), 143.

31. Cochran, *Ed Kennedy's War*, 143.

32. Cochran, *Ed Kennedy's War*, 131–32.

33. Butcher, *My Three Years with Eisenhower*, 659.

34. Dupuy papers.

35. "Reporters Score SHAEF Censorship," *New York Times*, December 20, 1944, 3.

36. Butcher, *My Three Years with Eisenhower*, 727.

37. Dupuy papers.

38. "Investigate 2 Stories Put Out by Time and U.P.," *Chicago Tribune*, January 6, 1945, 3.

39. Quoted in Butcher, *My Three Years with Eisenhower*, 730.

40. Larry Rue, "Supreme HDQ. Beaten on Own News, Rue Says," *Chicago Tribune*, January 11, 1945, 4.

41. Gladwin Hill, "SHAEF a Headache to War Reporters," *Editor & Publisher*, January 13, 1945, 13ff.

42. Hill, "SHAEF a Headache to War Reporters," 13ff.

43. Butcher, *My Three Years with Eisenhower*, 741.

44. John H. Grider, "Early Will Advise SHAEF on Publicity," *New York Times*, January 14, 1945, 15.

45. Butcher, *My Three Years with Eisenhower*, 762.

46. Linda Lotridge Levin, *The Making of FDR: The Story of Stephen T. Early, America's First Modern Press Secretary* (Amherst, NY, 2008), 411–16.

47. Quirk papers.

48. Butcher, *My Three Years with Eisenhower*, 776.

Chapter Nine

1. Quoted in Harry C. Butcher, *My Three Years with Eisenhower: The Personal Diary of Captain Harry C. Butcher, NSNR, Naval Aide to General Eisenhower, 1942–1945* (New York, 1946), 744–46.

2. This point is made in Stanley Cloud and Lynne Olson, *The Murrow Boys: Pioneers on the Front Lines of Broadcast Journalism* (New York, 1996), 224.

3. Quoted in Cloud and Olson, *The Murrow Boys*, 224.

4. Quoted in Cloud and Olson, *The Murrow Boys*, 224–25.

5. Dupuy papers.

6. Barney Oldfield, *Never a Shot in Anger* (Santa Barbara, CA, 1989), 116.

7. Oldfield, *Never a Shot in Anger*, 116.

8. Dwight Bentel, "War News Tied Up, So Newsmen Make Some," *Editor & Publisher*, September 9, 1944, 9.

9. Quoted in Bentel, "War News Tied Up," 9, 68.

10. Bentel, "War News Tied Up," 68.

11. Dupuy papers.

12. Tania Long, "It's Still the Same Glowing Paris," *New York Times Magazine*, September 10, 1944, 8–10.

13. Iris Carpenter, "Parisiennes Still Chic Despite War Shortages," *Boston Globe*, September 4, 1944, 2.

14. Robert Cromie, "It's Old Paris: Pretty Girls, Sidewalk Cafe," *Chicago Tribune*, August 28, 1944, 1.

15. Butcher, *My Three Years with Eisenhower*, 699.

16. Alan Riding, "A Farewell to the Franc: Little Sorrow in France," *New York Times*, December 27, 2001, 8.

17. Butcher, *My Three Years with Eisenhower*, 671.

18. Simone de Beauvoir, *Force of Circumstance*, trans. Richard Howard (New York, 1964), 19.

19. Polly Loxton to author, October 19, 2016.

20. David E. Scherman, foreword to *Lee Miller's War: Photographer and Correspondent with the Allies in Europe, 1944–1945*, ed. Antony Penrose (New York, 2005), 11.

21. Ned Calmer, *The Strange Land* (New York, 1950), 8–9.

22. Dupuy papers.

23. Butcher, *My Three Years with Eisenhower*, 660.

24. Dupuy papers.

25. The alteration of the Scribe is largely drawn from the Dupuy papers.

26. Censorship procedure is drawn from *A History of Field Press Censorship in SHAEF, World War II*, a government report compiled by unnamed army field censors. The report includes a diagram of rooms used by censors.

27. Briefing procedure is primarily drawn from the Dupuy papers.

28. Harold Acton, *Memoirs of an Aesthete, 1939–1969* (New York, 1971), 151–52.

29. Acton, *Memoirs of an Aesthete*, 151–52

30. H. V. Kaltenborn, *Fifty Fabulous Years, 1900–1950* (New York, 1950), 151.

31. Dupuy papers.

32. Oldfield, *Never a Shot in Anger*, 116.

33. Oldfield, *Never a Shot in Anger*, 140.

34. Oldfield, *Never a Shot in Anger*, 139.

35. Cochran, *Ed Kennedy's War*, 142.

36. Cochran, *Ed Kennedy's War*, 142.

37. Dupuy papers. For more on the Brazilian correspondent, see Oldfield, *Never a Shot in Anger*, 158–59.

38. Dupuy papers.

39. Smith papers.

Chapter Ten

1. Walter Cronkite, *A Reporter's Life* (New York, 1996), 110.

2. Cronkite, *A Reporter's Life*, 110.

3. Quoted in Cronkite, *A Reporter's Life*, 111.

4. Stanley Woodward, *Paper Tiger* (New York, 1964), 200.

5. Cronkite, *A Reporter's Life*, 112.

6. Barney Oldfield, *Never a Shot in Anger* (Santa Barbara, CA, 1989), 157.

7. Lewis Gannett, "It's Smoother Going in the Newsreels," reprinted in Jack Stenbuck, ed., *Typewriter Battalion: Dramatic Front-Line Dispatches from World War II* (New York, 1995), 294–98.

8. Michael Moynihan, *War Correspondent* (London, 1994), 104–5.

9. Moynihan, *War Correspondent*, 127.

10. George Orwell, "France's Interest in the War Dwindles: Back to Normal Is the Aim," *Observer*, May 6, 1945. Reprinted in Peter Davison, ed., *The Complete Works of George Orwell*, vol. 17 (London, 1997), 136.

11. Michael Shelden, *Orwell: The Authorized Biography* (New York, 1991), 375–76. Shelden implies the meeting took place in Hemingway's room at the Scribe, but it must have been in the Ritz, if anywhere. Beevor and Cooper state that the two met at the Scribe, *Paris after the Liberation, 1944–49* (New York, 2004), 73. For a different version of the meeting, with Hemingway as source, see Gordon Bower, *Inside George Orwell* (New York, 2003), 324–25. See also John Rodden and John Rossi, "The Mysterious (Un)meeting of George Orwell and Ernest Hemingway," *Kenyon Review* 31, no. 4 (2009), 56–84.

12. Bernard Crick, *George Orwell: A Life* (Boston, 1980), 325.

13. Beevor and Cooper, *Paris after the Liberation*, 74.

14. Davison, *The Complete Works of George Orwell*, 17:139.

15. Quoted in Julie Goldsmith Gilbert, *Ferber: A Biography* (Garden City, NY, 1978), 259.

16. Gilbert, *Ferber*, 261.

17. Quoted in Antoinette May, *Witness to War: A Biography of Marguerite Higgins* (New York, 1983), 66.

18. Nancy Caldwell Sorel, *The Women Who Wrote the War* (New York, 1999), 321–22.

19. Quoted in May, *Witness to War*, 74.

20. Marguerite Higgins, *News Is a Singular Thing* (Garden City, NY, 1955), 41.

21. Higgins, *News Is a Singular Thing*, 43.

22. Higgins, *News Is a Singular Thing*, 55.

23. Higgins, *News Is a Singular Thing*, 59.

24. May, *Witness to War*, 101.

25. Quoted in May, *Witness to War*, 102.

26. Quoted in May, *Witness to War*, 103.

27. Quoted in Higgins, *New Is a Singular Thing*, 72.

Chapter Eleven

1. Dupuy papers.

2. Quirk papers.

3. Boyd DeWolf Lewis, *Not Always a Spectator: A Newsman's Story* (Vienna, VA, 1981), 132–33.

4. Lewis, *Not Always a Spectator*, 142, 146.

5. Lewis, *Not Always a Spectator*, 139.

6. Lewis, *Not Always a Spectator*, 165–66.

7. One jerry can, however, held a mixture of looted wines and liqueurs. See photo caption in Antony Penrose, ed., *Lee Miller's War: Photographer and Correspondent with the Allies in Europe, 1944–1945* (New York, 2005), 103.

8. Scherman, foreword to Penrose, *Lee Miller's War*, 11.

9. Carolyn Burke, *Lee Miller: A Life* (New York, 2005), 241.

10. Biographical information about Miller is drawn from Burke, *Lee Miller*; Antony Penrose, *The Lives of Lee Miller* (New York, 1985); and Penrose, *Lee Miller's War*.

11. Quoted in Burke, *Lee Miller*, 228.

12. John Morris, *Get the Picture: A Personal History of Photojournalism* (Chicago, 2002), 89.

13. Howard K. Smith, *Events Leading Up to My Death: The Life of a Twentieth-Century Reporter* (New York, 1996), 142–43.

14. Smith, *Events Leading Up to My Death*, 150.

15. Quoted in Stanley Cloud and Lynne Olsen, *The Murrow Boys: Pioneers on the Front Lines of Broadcast Journalism* (New York, 1996), 224.

16. Smith, *Events Leading Up to My Death*, 150.

17. Lewis, *Not Always a Spectator*, 114–15.

18. Barney Oldfield, *Never a Shot in Anger* (Santa Barbara, CA, 1989), 205.

19. Oldfield, *Never a Shot in Anger*, 208.

Chapter Twelve

1. Dupuy papers.

2. Biographical information about Davis is drawn from his obituary, *New York Times*, October 27, 1966, 47.

3. Quoted in William Murray, *Janet, My Mother, and Me: A Memoir of Growing Up with Janet Flanner and Natalia Danesi Murray* (New York, 2000), 75.

4. Quoted in Brenda Wineapple, *Genêt, A Biography of Janet Flanner* (New York, 1989), 186.

5. Janet Flanner, *Darlinghissima: Letters to a Friend*, ed. Natalia Danesi Murray (New York, 1985), 46–47.

6. Quoted in Wineapple, *Genêt*, 189.

7. For the CBS resistance to recordings, see Stanley Cloud and Lynne Olson, *The Murrow Boys: Pioneers on the Front Lines of Broadcast Journalism* (New York, 1996), 60. The authors add that the network eased the policy after D-Day.

8. Quoted in Julia Kennedy Cochran, ed., *Ed Kennedy's War: V-E Day, Censorship, and the Associated Press* (Baton Rouge, LA, 2012), 181.

9. Malcolm Muggeridge, "Importance of Being Ernest," *Observer*, August 10, 1969, 24.

10. Carlos Baker, *Ernest Hemingway: A Life Story* (New York, 1969), 442. In a note, Baker attributes the story to Barnes—and adds that it is possible that Saroyan left the George V before the brawl. Mary V. Dearborn, who repeats the story in *Ernest Hemingway: A Biography* (New York, 2017), 474, has both meetings with Saroyan taking place in the Scribe.

11. A. J. Liebling, *World War II Writings* (New York, 2008), 313.

12. Liebling, *World War II Writings*, 430.

13. Liebling, "Day of Victory," in *World War II Writings*, 528–40. A second pseudo-story by Liebling in *Mollie and Other War Pieces*, "Run, Run, Run, Run," treats Allardyce Meecham's time in Britain before D-Day.

14. Quoted in Richard Whelan, *Robert Capa: A Biography* (New York, 1985), 226.
15. Robert Capa, *Slightly Out of Focus* (New York, 1947), 189.
16. Quoted in Whelan, *Robert Capa*, 225.
17. Capa, *Slightly Out of Focus*, 205.
18. "Editor's Note," *Dateline* 23 (1979): 3.

Chapter Thirteen

1. J. C. Oestreicher, *The World Is Their Beat* (New York, 1945), 226–27. See also Nancy Caldwell Sorel, *The Women Who Wrote the War* (New York, 1999), 365–66.
2. Andrew Tully, "Three Yanks Storm Berlin," *Boston Traveler*, May 8, 1945. Reprinted in Jack Stenbuck, ed., *Typewriter Battalion: Dramatic Front-Line Dispatches from World War II* (New York, 1995), 306–14. See also Andrew Tully, *Berlin: Story of a Battle* (New York, 1963), ix.
3. Quoted in Anne R. Kenney, "'She Got to Berlin': Virginia Irwin, *St. Louis Post-Dispatch* War Correspondent," *Missouri Historical Review*, July 1985, 470–71. For information about Irwin, I draw on this article as well as Irwin's reporting of her Berlin journey.
4. Tully, "Three Yanks Storm Berlin," reprinted in Stenbuck, *Typewriter Battalion*, 311.
5. Kenney, "'She Got to Berlin,'" 474.
6. Quoted in Kenney, "'She Got to Berlin,'" 467.
7. Quoted in Kenney, "'She Got to Berlin,'" 470.
8. Barney Oldfield, *Never a Shot in Anger* (Santa Barbara, CA, 1989), 239.
9. Seymour Freidin, "'Americanski!' Is Cry as 9th's Meets the Reds," *New York Herald Tribune*, May 1, 1945, 8.
10. John Groth, *Studio: Europe* (New York, 1945), 277.
11. Groth, *Studio: Europe*, 275–83.
12. Kenney, "'She Got to Berlin,'" 474.
13. Eric Hawkins, with Robert N. Sturdevant, *Hawkins of the Paris Herald* (New York, 1963), 258–59. See also Robert W. Desmond, *Tides of War: World News Reporting, 1931–1945* (Iowa City, IA, 1984), 398–99.
14. Gladwin Hill, "SHAEF Showdown on Press Is Likely," *New York Times*, May 14, 1945, 5.
15. "Army Sends 2 Home for Trip to Berlin," *New York Times*, May 11, 1945, 6.

Chapter Fourteen

1. Harry C. Butcher, *My Three Years with Eisenhower: The Personal Diary of Captain Harry C. Butcher, NSNR, Naval Aide to General Eisenhower, 1942–1945* (New York, 1946), 822.
2. Quoted in A. M. Sperber, *Murrow: His Life and Times* (New York, 1986), 254.
3. Gladwin Hill, "Press at SHAEF Has Tense Wait," *New York Times*, May 9, 1945, 3.

4. Osmar White, *Conquerors' Road: An Eyewitness Report of Germany 1945* (Cambridge, UK, 2003; orig. pub. 1996), 110.

5. Julia Kennedy Cochran, ed., *Ed Kennedy's War: V-E Day, Censorship, and the Associated Press* (Baton Rouge, LA, 2012), 114.

6. Boyd DeWolf Lewis, *Not Always a Spectator: A Newsman's Story* (Vienna, VA, 1981), 136.

7. Barney Oldfield, *Never a Shot in Anger* (Santa Barbara, CA, 1989), 256.

8. Dupuy papers.

9. Quoted in Nancy Caldwell Sorel, *The Women Who Wrote the War* (New York, 1999), 371.

10. Gerald Clark, *No Mud on the Back Seat: Memoirs of a Reporter* (Montreal, 1995), 13.

11. White, *Conquerors' Road*, 110.

12. For the experience of the seventeen at Reims, I draw primarily on Gerald Clark, *No Mud on the Back Seat*; Osmar White, *Conquerors' Road*; and Lewis, *Not Always a Spectator*.

13. Cochran, *Ed Kennedy's War*, 157.

14. Butcher, *My Three Years with Eisenhower*, 834.

15. Lewis, *Not Always a Spectator*, 182.

16. Clark, *No Mud on the Back Seat*, 97–98.

17. White, *Conquerors' Road*, 115.

18. Quoted in Oldfield, *Never a Shot in Anger*, 249.

19. Charles Wertenbaker, "Surrender at Reims," *Life*, May 21, 1945, 27–28. Lael Wertenbaker later reported that her husband spoke with Eisenhower during his wait in Reims. See Sorel, *The Women Who Wrote the War*, 370–71. Barney Oldfield reported that Charles Wertenbaker got inside the technical school and as far as Eisenhower's outer office before being ushered from the building. Oldfield, *Never a Shot in Anger*, 243.

20. Clark, *No Mud on the Back Seat*, 97.

21. Cochran, *Ed Kennedy's War*, 160.

22. Cochran, *Ed Kennedy's War*, 161.

23. Cochran, *Ed Kennedy's War*, 110–11.

24. Cochran, *Ed Kennedy's War*, 112. For Butcher's account of Kennedy meeting Eisenhower, see *My Three Years with Eisenhower*, 403.

25. Quoted in Martin Gilbert, *The Day the War Ended: May 8, 1945* (New York, 1995), 137.

26. Cochran, *Ed Kennedy's War*, 160.

27. Cochran, *Ed Kennedy's War*, 164–65.

28. Quoted in Cochran, *Ed Kennedy's War*, 164.

29. Cochran, *Ed Kennedy's War*, 165.

30. Oldfield, *Never a Shot in Anger*, 250.

31. Quoted in Cochran, *Ed Kennedy's War*, 167.

32. "Writers' Letter to SHAEF," *New York Times*, May 9, 1945, 15.

33. Dupuy papers.

34. Butcher, *My Three Years with Eisenhower*, 849.

35. A. J. Liebling, "The A.P. Surrender," in *Reporting World War II, Part Two: American Journalism, 1944–1946*, ed. Samuel Hynes (New York, 1995), 737–38.

36. "The Army's Guests," *Time*, May 21, 1945, 56–57.

37. Quoted in Tom Curley and John Maxwell Hamilton, introduction to Cochran, *Ed Kennedy's War*, xviii–xix.

Chapter Fifteen

1. "French Politicians Return to France," in *The Complete Works of George Orwell*, ed. Peter Davison, vol. 17 (London, 1997), 140.

2. Janet Flanner, *Paris Journal, 1944–1965* (New York, 1965), 26. The letter, with a May 11 dateline, appeared in the *New Yorker* on May 19, 1945.

3. Simone de Beauvoir, *Force of Circumstance* (New York, 1964), 30.

4. Quirk papers.

5. John B. Romeiser, ed., *"Beachhead Don": Reporting the War from the European Theater, 1942–1945* (New York, 2004), 357.

6. Dupuy papers.

7. Harry C. Butcher, *My Three Years with Eisenhower: The Personal Diary of Captain Harry C. Butcher, NSNR, Naval Aide to General Eisenhower, 1942–1945* (New York, 1946), 836.

8. Geoffrey Parsons Jr., "Military Censorship Retains Curbs on News from Europe," *Paris Herald Tribune*, May 9, 1945, 1–2. The edited version of the story in the *New York Herald Tribune* on May 10 was headlined "Allied Censors in Europe Will Remain on the Job."

9. Butcher, *My Three Years with Eisenhower*, 852.

10. Butcher, *My Three Years with Eisenhower*, 852.

11. Butcher, *My Three Years with Eisenhower*, 852,

12. Boyd DeWolf Lewis, *Not Always a Spectator: A Newsman's Story* (Vienna, VA, 1981), 180.

13. Julia Kennedy Cochran, ed., *Ed Kennedy's War: V-E Day, Censorship, and the Associated Press* (Baton Rouge, LA, 2012), 169.

14. Howard K. Smith, *Events Leading Up to My Death: The Life of a Twentieth-Century Reporter* (New York, 1996), 169.

15. Butcher, *My Three Years with Eisenhower*, 835.

16. Dupuy papers. The papers include a five-page typed account called "Notes on Berlin Surrender."

17. "'Ike' Reaches Reich to Close SHAEF, Bid His Aides Adieu," *Washington Post*, July 13, 1945, 1.

18. Harold Acton, *Memoirs of an Aesthete: 1939–1969* (New York, 1971), 185.

19. Virginia Spencer Carr, *Dos Passos: A Life* (Evanston, IL, 1984), 439–40.

20. John O'Reilly, "Hotel Scribe Ends War Career," *New York Herald Tribune*, December 2, 1945, A6.

21. "Compromise Voted by Paris Reporters," *New York Times*, July 6, 1945, 6.

22. The photo appears in Carolyn Burke, *Lee Miller: A Life* (New York, 2005), 263.

23. Burke, *Lee Miller*, 267ff.

24. Quoted in Burke, *Lee Miller*, 271.

25. John Phillips, *Free Spirit in a Troubled World* (New York, 1996), 401.

26. Quoted in Burke, *Lee Miller*, 287.

27. Burke, *Lee Miller*, 288.

28. Quoted in Burke, *Lee Miller*, 289.

Chapter Sixteen

1. Edward Kennedy, "I'd Do It Again," *Atlantic Monthly*, August 1948, 41.

2. Kennedy, "I'd Do It Again," 39.

3. Julia Kennedy Cochran, *Ed Kennedy's War: V-E Day, Censorship, and the Associated Press* (Baton Rouge, LA, 2012), 171–72.

4. Cochran, *Ed Kennedy's War*, 164.

5. Smith gives no source for either quotation.

Epilogue

1. W. A. Swanberg, *Luce and His Empire* (New York, 1972), 255.

2. Swanberg, *Luce and His Empire*, 256.

3. Merle Miller, *That Winter* (New York, 1948), 172–74.

4. Ned Calmer, *The Strange Land* (New York, 1950), 3–4.

5. Calmer, *The Strange Land*, 183.

6. Calmer, *The Strange Land*, 263.

7. Calmer, *The Strange Land*, 322.

8. Meg Waite Clayton, *The Race for Paris* (New York, 2015), xiii.

9. Clayton, *The Race for Paris*, 219.

10. Gerald Clark, "Liberation Day at the Hotel Scribe," *Canadian Reader's Digest*, November 1984, 191–92. The story is retold in Gerald Clark, *No Mud on the Back Seat: Memoirs of a Reporter* (Montreal, 1995), 81–82.

Sources

Newspaper reports and archival materials cited in the notes are not included below.

Acton, Harold. *Memoirs of an Aesthete, 1939–1969*. New York, 1971.

Baker, Carlos. *Ernest Hemingway: A Life Story*. New York, 1969.

———, ed. *Ernest Hemingway, Selected Letters, 1917–1961*. New York, 1981.

Balzar, Timothy. *The Information Front: The Canadian Army and News Management during the Second World War*. Vancouver, BC, 2011.

Beauvoir, Simone de. *Force of Circumstance*. New York, 1964.

Beevor, Antony. *The Second World War*. New York, 2012.

Beevor, Antony, and Artemis Cooper. *Paris after the Liberation, 1944–49*. New York, 2004

Bentel, Dwight. "Six Newsmen Suspended in Paris by Army Censors." *Editor & Publisher*, September 2, 1944, 7.

———. "War News Tied Up, So Newsman Make Some." *Editor & Publisher*, September 9, 1944, 9.

Bower, Gordon. *Inside George Orwell*. New York, 2003.

Burke, Carolyn. *Lee Miller: A Life*. New York, 2005.

Butcher, Harry C. *My Three Years with Eisenhower: The Personal Diary of Captain Harry C. Butcher, NSNR, Naval Aide to General Eisenhower, 1942–1945*. New York, 1946.

Calmer, Ned. *The Strange Land*. New York, 1950.

Capa, Robert. *Slightly Out of Focus*. New York, 1947.

Carpenter, Iris. *No Woman's World*. Boston, 1946.

Carr, Virginia Spencer. *Dos Passos: A Life*. Evanston, IL, 1984.

Casey, Steven. *The War Beat, Europe: The American Media War against Nazi Germany.* New York, 2017.

Clark, Gerald. *No Mud on the Back Seat: Memoirs of a Reporter.* Montreal, 1995.

Clayton, Meg Waite. *The Race for Paris.* New York, 2015.

Cloud, Stanley, and Lynne Olson. *The Murrow Boys: Pioneers on the Front Lines of Broadcast Journalism.* New York, 1996.

Cobb, Matthew. *Eleven Days in August: The Liberation of Paris in 1944.* London, 2013.

Cochran, Julia Kennedy, ed. *Ed Kennedy's War: V-E Day, Censorship, and the Associated Press.* Baton Rouge, LA, 2012.

Coté, William E. "Correspondent or Warrior? Hemingway's Murky World War II 'Combat' Experience." *Hemingway Review* 22, no. 1 (2002): 88–104.

Crang, Jeremy A. "General De Gaulle under Sniper Fire in Notre Dame Cathedral, 26 August 1944: Robert Reid's BBC Commentary." *Historical Journal of Film, Radio and Television* 27, no. 3 (2007): 391–406.

Crick, Bernard. *George Orwell: A Life.* Boston, 1980.

Cronkite, Walter. *A Reporter's Life.* New York, 1996.

Cronkite, Walter IV, and Maurice Isserman. *Cronkite's War: His World War II Letters Home.* Washington, DC, 2013.

Davison, Peter, ed. *The Complete Works of George Orwell.* Vol. 17. London, 1997.

Dearborn, Mary V. *Ernest Hemingway: A Biography.* New York, 2017.

Desmond, Robert W. *Tides of War: World News Reporting, 1931–1945.* Iowa City, IA, 1984.

Drake, David. *Paris at War: 1939–1944.* Cambridge, MA, 2016.

Edel, Leon. *The Visitable Past: A Wartime Memoir.* Honolulu, 2001.

Flanner, Janet. *Darlinghissima: Letters to a Friend,* ed. Natalia Danesi Murray. New York, 1985.

———. *Paris Journal, 1944–1965.* New York, 1965.

Fuller, Robert. "Hemingway at Rambouillet." *Hemingway Review* 33, no. 2 (2014): 66–78.

Gammack, Gordon, and Andrea Clardy. *Gordon Gammack: Columns from Three Wars.* Ames, IA, 1979.

Gay, Timothy M. *Assignment to Hell: The War against Germany with Correspondents Walter Cronkite, Andy Rooney, A. J. Liebling, Homer Bigart, and Hal Boyle.* New York, 2012.

Gellhorn, Martha. *The Face of War.* New York, 1956.

———. "The Wounds of Paris." *Collier's,* November 4, 1944, 72–74.

Gilbert, Julie Goldsmith. *Ferber: A Biography.* Garden City, NY, 1978.

Gilbert, Martin. *The Day the War Ended: May 8, 1945.* New York, 1995.

Groth, John. *Studio: Europe.* New York, 1945.

Halton, David. *Dispatches from the Front: Matthew Halton, Canada's Voice at War.* New York, 2014.

Hastings, Max. *Inferno: The World at War, 1939–1945.* New York, 2011.

Hawkins, Eric, with Robert N. Sturdevant. *Hawkins of the Paris Herald*. New York, 1963.

Hélène, Pierre-Andre. *A Legend in the Heart of Paris*. Paris, n.d.

Hemingway, Mary Welsh. *How It Was*. New York, 1976.

Higgins, Marguerite. *News Is a Singular Thing*. Garden City, NY, 1955.

Hynes, Samuel, eds. *Reporting World War II, Part Two: American Journalism, 1944–1946*. New York, 1995.

Kaltenborn, H. V. *Fifty Fabulous Years*. New York, 1950.

Kasper, Anne S. Washington Press Club Foundation interview with Helen Kirkpatrick Milbank. April 1990: 73–75.

Kennedy, Edward. "I'd Do It Again." *Atlantic Monthly*, August 1948, 36–41.

Kenney, Anne R. "'She Got to Berlin': Virgin Irwin, *St. Louis Post-Dispatch* War Correspondent." *Missouri Historical Review* 79, no. 4 (1985): 456–79.

Kershaw, Alex. *Avenue of Spies: A True Story of Terror, Espionage, and One American Family's Heroic Resistance in Nazi-Occupied Paris*. New York, 2015.

———. *Blood and Champagne: The Life and Times of Robert Capa*. New York, 2004.

Knightley, Phillip. *The First Casualty: From the Crimea to Vietnam; The War Correspondent as Hero, Propagandist, and Myth Maker*. New York, 1975.

Lankford, Nelson Douglas, ed. *OSS against the Reich: The World War II Diaries of Colonel David K. E. Bruce*. Kent, OH, 1991.

Leggett, John. *A Daring Young Man: A Biography of William Saroyan*. New York, 2002.

Levin, Linda Lotridge. *The Making of FDR: The Story of Stephen T. Early, America's First Modern Press Secretary*. Amherst, NY, 2008.

Lewis, Boyd DeWolf. *Not Always a Spectator: A Newsman's Story*. Vienna, VA, 1981.

Liebling, A. J. *World War II Writings*. New York, 2008.

Lochner, Lewis. "Germans Marched into a Dead Paris." *Life*, July 8, 1940, 22ff.

Longerich, Peter. *Goebbels: A Biography*. New York, 2015.

MacVane, John. *On the Air in World War II*. New York, 1979.

Malone, Richard S. *A World in Flames, 1944–1945: A Portrait of War, Part Two*. Toronto, 1984.

———. *Missing from the Record*. Toronto, 1946.

Marshall, S. L. A. "How Papa Liberated Paris." *American Heritage* 13, no. 3 (1962): 12ff.

———. *Bringing Up the Rear*. San Rafael, CA, 1979.

May, Antoinette. *Witness to War: A Biography of Marguerite Higgins*. New York, 1983.

Mazzeo, Tilar J. *The Hotel on Place Vendôme: Life, Death, and Betrayal at the Hôtel Ritz in Paris*. New York, 2015.

Meyers, Jeffrey. *Hemingway: A Biography*. New York, 1985.

Miller, Henry. *Tropic of Cancer*. New York, 1961.

Miller, Lee G. *The Story of Ernie Pyle*. New York, 1950.

Miller, Merle. *That Winter*. New York, 1948.

Monks, Noel. *Eyewitness*. London, 1956.

Moorehead, Alan. *Eclipse*. New York, 1945.

Moorhead, Caroline. *Gellhorn: A Twentieth-Century Life.* New York, 2003.

Morris, John. *Get the Picture: A Personal History of Photojournalism.* Chicago, 2002.

Mortimer-Moore, William. *Paris '44: The City of Light Redeemed.* Oxford, UK, 2015

Moss, Marilyn Ann. *Giant George Stevens, A Life on Film.* Madison, WI, 2004.

Moynihan, Michael. *War Correspondent.* London, 1994.

Muggeridge, Malcolm. *Chronicles of Wasted Time: Chronicle 2.* New York, 1982.

Murray, William. *Janet, My Mother, and Me: A Memoir of Growing Up with Janet Flanner and Natalia Danesi Murray.* New York, 2000.

Nichols, David. *Ernie's War: The Best of Ernie Pyle's World War II Dispatches.* New York, 1986.

Occhino, Filippo, Kim Oosterlinck, and Eugene N. White. "How Much Can a Victor Force the Vanquished to Pay? France under the Nazi Boot." *Journal of Economic History* 68, no. 1 (2008): 1–45.

Oestreicher, J. C. *The World Is Their Beat.* New York, 1945.

Oldfield, Barney. *Never a Shot in Anger.* Santa Barbara, CA, 1989.

Penrose, Antony, ed. *Lee Miller's War: Photographer and Correspondent with the Allies in Europe, 1944–1945.* New York, 2005.

———. *The Lives of Lee Miller.* New York, 1985.

Phillips, John. *Free Spirit in a Troubled World.* New York, 1996.

Pogue, Forrest C. *Pogue's War: Diaries of a WWII Combat Historian.* Lexington, KY, 2001.

———. *United States Army in World War II: The European Theater of Operations, the Supreme Command.* Washington, DC, 1996.

Pudney, John. "A Paris Diary." *New Statesman and Nation,* September 23, 194, 197.

Quirk, Rory. *War and Peace: The Memoirs of an American Family.* Novato, CA, 1999.

Reynolds, Michael. *Hemingway: The Final Years.* New York, 1999.

Robertson, Charles L. *The International Herald Tribune: The First Hundred Years.* New York, 1987.

Rodden, John, and John Rossi. "The Mysterious (Un)meeting of George Orwell and Ernest Hemingway." *Kenyon Review* 31, no. 4 (2009): 56–84.

Romeiser, John B., ed. *"Beachhead Don": Reporting the War from the European Theater, 1942–1945.* New York, 2004.

Rooney, Andy. *My War.* New York, 2000.

Rosbottom, Ronald C. *When Paris Went Dark: The City of Light under German Occupation, 1940–1944.* New York, 2014.

Shaw, Irwin. "Morts pour la Patrie." *New Yorker,* August 25, 1945, 36–44.

Shaw, Irwin, and Ronald Searle. *Paris! Paris!* New York, 1977.

Shelden, Michael. *Orwell: The Authorized Biography.* New York, 1991.

Shnayerson, Michael. *Irwin Shaw: A Biography.* New York, 1989.

Small, Collie. "How to Put Salt on a German General's Tail." *Saturday Evening Post,* November 11, 1944, 22ff.

Smith, Howard K. *Events Leading Up to My Death: The Life of a Twentieth-Century Reporter.* New York, 1996.

Sokolov, Raymond A. *Wayward Reporter: The Life of A. J. Liebling*. New York, 1980.

Sorel, Nancy Caldwell. *The Women Who Wrote the War*. New York, 1999.

Sperber, A. M. *Murrow: His Life and Times*. New York, 1986.

Stenbuck, Jack, ed. *Typewriter Battalion: Dramatic Front-Line Dispatches from World War II*. New York, 1995.

Sterne, Joseph R. L. *Combat Correspondents: The Baltimore Sun in World War II*. Baltimore, 2009.

Stoneback, H. R. "Hemingway's Happiest Summer." *Hemingway Review* 64, no. 3 (1997): 184–220.

Swanberg, W. A. *Luce and His Empire*. New York, 1972.

Sweet, Matthew. *The West End Front: The Wartime Secrets of London's Grand Hotels*. London, 2011.

Thornton, Willis. *The Liberation of Paris*. New York, 1962.

Tully, Andrew. *Berlin: Story of a Battle*. New York, 1963.

Vaill, Amanda. *Hotel Florida: Truth, Love, and Death in the Spanish Civil War*. New York, 2014.

Voss, Frederick S. *Reporting the War: The Journalistic Coverage of World War II*. Washington, DC, 1994.

Weber, Ronald. *News of Paris: American Journalists in the City of Light between the Wars*. Chicago, 2006.

Welsh, Mary. "GI Crime in France." *Life*, March 12, 1945, 17–18.

Wertenbaker, Charles. *Invasion!* New York, 1944.

———. "Paris Is Free!" *Time*, September 4, 1944, 34–36.

———. "Surrender at Reims." *Life*, May 21, 1945, 27–28.

Whelan, Richard. *Robert Capa: A Biography*. New York, 1985.

White, Osmar. *Conquerors' Road: An Eyewitness Report of Germany 1945*. Cambridge, UK, 2003.

White, William, ed. *By-Line: Ernest Hemingway*. New York, 1967.

Wineapple, Brenda. *Genêt, A Biography of Janet Flanner*. New York, 1989.

Woodward, Stanley. *Paper Tiger*. New York, 1964.

Index